A CELEBRATION OF CHRISTMAS

Edited by
GILLIAN COOKE

Designed by David Fordham

G. P. PUTNAM'S SONS
NEW YORK

First published in the United States in 1980 by
G. P. Putnam's Sons
200 Madison Avenue
New York, New York 10016

Library of Congress Catalog Card Number 80-81374
ISBN 0 399 12525 6

Printed in Hong Kong

Typeset in Binny Old Style by Pierson LeVesley Ltd, Oxshott
and Facet Filmsetting Ltd, Southend.
Illustrations originated by Gilchrist Bros. Ltd, Leeds.
Printed and bound by Dai Nippon, Hong Kong.

Edited, designed and produced by
Harrow House Editions Limited,
7a Langley Street, Covent Garden, London WC2H 9JA

General Editor	Gillian Cooke
Writer and Contributing Editor	Stella Bingham
Editor	Liz Wilhide
Design	David Fordham
Design Assistants	Nigel Partridge
	Jonathan Gill-Skelton
Picture Researcher	Celia Dearing
Art Director	Nicholas Eddison
Production Manager	Kenneth Cowan
Production Editor	Fred Gill
Craft Consultant	Maureen Walker
Cookery Editor	Dinah Morrison
Carol Arrangements	Derek Walters

CONTENTS

INTRODUCTION
TO CHRISTMAS

F COURSE, it always snowed at Christmas, and children built snowmen and went tobogganing and skating on the lake. A log fire blazed in the hearth and candles flickered on the Christmas tree, laden with sweets and presents and topped by a silver star. Holly and ivy, mistletoe and laurel hung from every beam and corner, and cards hid the mantelpiece. There was turkey with stuffing and a ham and a blazing Christmas pudding full of silver coins that chipped your teeth, and nuts and fruit and pies and cakes. Everyone sang carols round the piano. The children's faces were flushed with excitement, and awe and reverence blended with fun and laughter. There were charades and forfeits, silly hats and ghost stories, beaming uncles and twinkling aunts. Red stockings bulged intriguingly with gifts, and friends and family overflowed with goodwill and high spirits. And all in celebration of the birth of Jesus Christ.

Christmas is the most widely celebrated festival in the world, but the image of the Victorian Christmas is so vivid that it has threatened to swamp the traditions of other countries and the customs of older times. Unique expressions of Christmas by different peoples throughout the world have been lost, or diverted by commercial interests and stripped of their true meaning. Many of the practices and rituals of the Christmas season are so old that their true significance can only be guessed at. Their origins date from long before the birth of Jesus, to the dark days when demons and devils threatened and gods demanded sacrifice. Early Christians, finding

The Holy Family in the stable at Bethlehem, an engraving after Gustav Doré.

that the pagans were more ready to accept a new God than new customs, adopted many heathen practices and adapted them to the new religion. Evergreens and fire, feasting and presents were given a new Christian meaning. So little is known of the Nativity that the story could usefully be embroidered to please the converts. The year and date of Christ's birth are uncertain, and even the place is open to dispute.

Jesus left no writings of His own and the only contemporary account of His life is found in the reports of the Roman Governor Pontius Pilate and concerns His death. Of the Gospels, only those of Matthew and Luke mention Jesus's birth. Both set it in Bethlehem, but this may have been the result of a wish to fulfil the Old Testament prophecy that the Messiah would be a descendant of David: Bethlehem was the home town of the Davidic family. Matthew implies that Mary and Joseph lived in Bethlehem, but settled in Nazareth after their flight to Egypt following Herod's decrees when danger still threatened the Child. According to Luke, the family lived in Nazareth and came to Bethlehem only to register in the census. Neither Luke nor Matthew gives many details of the birth. The manger, the shepherds and the angels are reported by Luke. Matthew describes the star and the Wise Men, the Magi, bringing gifts of gold, frankincense and myrrh. With so little to go on, it was inevitable that others would add to the story. Soon the ox and the ass were introduced, and the Magi acquired names and descriptions – old Melchior, young Caspar and black Balthazar.

The method of reckoning time 'by the year of our Lord' was introduced by Dionysius Exiguus in the sixth century. Unfortunately his calculations carelessly omitted the four years of the reign of the Emperor Augustus. A birth date of 4 or 5 BC is confirmed by St Matthew's report that Jesus was born 'in the days of Herod the King' – Herod the Great died in March, 4 BC. This is reinforced by references in contemporary accounts to John the Baptist's evangelizing in 'the fifteenth year of Tiberius', AD 28-29, which would tie in with Christ's baptism by John in the

Christmas in India – reading a letter from home. From The Graphic, *1881.*

River Jordan. Recent astronomical research suggests that the Star of Bethlehem was either a nova or flaring star, recorded by the Chinese in 5 BC and by the Koreans in 4 BC, or conjunctions of the planets Saturn and Jupiter, which occurred three times in 7 BC.

There is no evidence at all of the exact time of year of the Nativity and almost every month has been selected by one scholar or another. Early Christians had little interest in the birth of Christ, some holding that He was not born divine but attained divinity on His baptism, others that His spiritual and physical birth occurred on the same day, 6 January, the feast of the Epiphany or manifestation of Christ's glory. The feast commemorates three manifestations: the baptism by John the Baptist, the Adoration of the Magi and the first miracle, the transformation of water into wine. 25 December was finally selected in the fourth century AD by Pope Julius I after an appeal by St Cyril of Jerusalem to settle the matter once and for all.

The dispute did not end there, though. Over the centuries the Julian calendar dropped behind the true date. In 1582, Pope Gregory corrected what had grown into an eleven-day lag and Britain finally caught up in 1752, when by an Act of Parliament 2 September was followed by 14 September. The change was deeply resented by many people, who continued to celebrate Old Christmas on 6 January. Russia and most of Eastern Europe further complicated matters by not adopting the Gregorian calendar until 1918.

The 25 December was a sensible choice and a symbolic one. At the time of the winter solstice, when other religions were celebrating the rebirth of the sun, Christians had no festival of their own. Now they could celebrate the birth of their own sun, the Son of God, the Messiah. The date fell neatly between two popular Roman festivals – Saturnalia and the January Kalends – and on the same day that another new religion, Mithraism, the worship of Mithras, the Iranian god of the sun, celebrated *Dies Solis Invicta Nati* – the rebirth of the unconquered sun. In northern Europe the great agricultural and solar festival of Yuletide lasted from mid-November to mid-January. Elements of all these pagan celebrations were grafted on to Christmas.

Saturnalia, in honour of the gods of seeds and sowing, began on 17 December with religious rites and lasted for seven days. The festival was marked by drinking, feasting and gambling. No one was allowed to work except cooks and bakers. Slaves were freed for the period and rules of behaviour turned upside down. A mock king was selected to preside over the revelry, and presents – usually wax candles and small clay dolls – were exchanged. The Romans scarcely had time to recover when the January Kalends were upon them. Three days of feasting, merriment and laxity celebrated both the new year and the induction of new consuls into office. Houses were decorated with lights and greenery, masters and slaves mixed freely, men dressed up in animal skins and women's clothing and

everyone exchanged presents. 'The impulse to spend seizes everyone', the Greek Libanius wrote.

The less sophisticated northern Europeans began their winter festival with a feast following the slaughter of livestock which could not be kept through the winter. At the winter solstice, when daylight had all but disappeared in the long northern winter, huge bonfires were lit to drive away the devils of darkness and to symbolize warmth and the return of the sun, the everlasting light. Evergreens were cut to represent survival through the dead, dark days of winter, special food was prepared and gifts and greetings exchanged. The Vikings celebrated the winter solstice as Yuletide, named in honour of Jolnir (or Odin), the father of the gods. The Yuletide sacrificial feast incorporated fertility rites to ensure a good harvest and was held in honour of the dead, of whom Odin was god. Ghosts were said to come back at the winter solstice to haunt the living and had to be placated with food and drink. In spite of these lurking shadows, Yule was chiefly a time of merriment and good cheer.

Most of the elements of a good old-fashioned Christmas are to be found amid these pagan practices. The Church, after firing off a few broadsides against, in particular, the evils of gluttony and of dressing up in 'counterfeit forms and monstrous faces', wisely decided to adopt the customs as their own and put a Christian face on them. In Germany the eighth-century missionary St Boniface dedicated the fir tree to the Holy Child in place of the sacred oak of Odin, which he chopped down. In AD 601, Pope Gregory the Great's sensible instructions to St Augustine on how to deal with the Anglo-Saxons included the following advice: 'Nor let them now sacrifice animals to the Devil, but to the praise of God kill animals for their own eating, and render thanks to the Giver of all for their abundance'.

Gradually the pagan threads were woven into the Christmas tapestry. Everything about light and fire was considered sacred, symbolizing the triumph over darkness and cold, and commemorating the return of the sun's power after the winter solstice. The Jews celebrated Hanukkah, the Feast of the Lights, at the end of December. To the Church, candles symbolized the Light of the World, Jesus. At Christ's presentation in the Temple, Simeon called Him 'the light to lighten the Gentiles, and to be the glory of thy people Israel'. Evergreens, particularly those that bore berries, were highly prized as symbols of fertility and continuing life. Romans decked their homes with green boughs and northern Europeans brought branches indoors as refuges for wood spirits. Christians attached their own meaning to these heathen practices; for instance, holly came to represent Christ's crown of thorns. Present-giving was already well established among the Romans, the presents usually being small symbols of good luck. Christians gave gifts in memory of God's great gift to man, just as the Magi had brought gold, frankincense and myrrh to the manger in Bethlehem. The Roman custom of masters giving gifts to servants and tradesmen continued in the practice of Christmas boxes. Corn and straw had always played a large part in pagan winter fertility rites; they were brought into the house to encourage the good influences of the corn spirit on the forthcoming harvest. To Christians, straw was a reminder of the humble stable where Christ was born.

In rural farming communities midwinter is always the time when there is least work to do, and most time for merrymaking. By the Middle Ages the Church had strengthened its hold over the whole winter solstice period by establishing a series of saints' days and other holidays stretching from Advent (from the Latin 'adventus', meaning coming – the time to prepare for the coming of Christ) to Plough Monday – the first after Epiphany. The festival was celebrated with pomp, pageantry, feasting and merrymaking. Kings exchanged lavish gifts and gave vast banquets. Lords hospitably threw open their halls to tenants and strangers. The Lord of Misrule, a revival of the Saturnalian mock king, presided with his courtiers over the revels at court and in the great houses and colleges for the twelve days of Christmas, ridiculing authority and throwing over the usual rules of behaviour. The Church joined in with the Feast of the Fools – disorderly revels in which the lower clergy dressed as animals and women, burlesqued senior churchmen and mocked sacred rites. The lower clergy were mostly from the peasant classes and poorly educated. Their Feast was so scandalously reminiscent of pagan customs that it was frequently denounced and banned. Other priestly revels were presided over by the Boy Bishop, the equivalent of the 'lord' of the Feast of the Fools, chosen from among the choir boys on 5 December, the Eve of St Nicholas. The Boy Bishop, elected by the boys themselves, was invested in cope, mitre and staff and expected to undertake a variety of priestly duties. His reign ended on 28 December, Holy Innocents' Day. The Church chose to regard the Boy as a symbol of the lowly taking authority, as Christ had done. Christmas mummers and dancers toured villages and houses with the themes of death and revival at the centre of their performances – symbolic, perhaps, of the resurrection of the year.

An extraordinary range of superstitions, pagan survivals and revivals, as well as Christian

'Our Christmas Dream' by Phiz, captures all the elements of a Victorian Christmas, 1845.

celebrations were concentrated round the twelve days of the medieval Christmas. On Christmas Eve, the night of the Vigil of the Nativity and as such the most hallowed of the season, the pagan Yule log was borne into the house with singing and dancing. It was lit with a brand from last year's log to symbolize the triumph of light over darkness – both that of the sun over the long hours of the winter night and that of Christ over sin. The light from the log was supposed to be sacramental and people brought their pewter and silver within its glow. At midnight on Christmas Eve animals were said to gain the power of speech. In the oldest Christian calendars Christmas Eve was known as Adam and Eve day to celebrate the belief that Christ had by His sacrifice wiped out the burden of their sin.

26 December, St Stephen's Day, was devoted to horses, hunting and shooting, with all the undertones of sacrifice. Much noise would be made, too, to frighten away the evil spirits. St Stephen's Day commemorates two saints of that name. It is the second St Stephen, a ninth-century missionary in Sweden, who is the patron saint of horses and a number of practices connected with those beasts were associated with his day. Horses were bled for luck, or ridden into church and blessed by the priest or fed consecrated salt and bread or corn. A bizarre little ritual called 'hunting the wren' also took place: the corpse of a wren, which was believed to be a sacred bird, was carried from door to door and money solicited. At some point the robin seems to have been confused with the

wren, and so developed its traditional association with Christmas – probably helped by the fact that its red breast could be yet another symbol of fire. 26 December was also called Boxing Day, because that was when servants and tradesmen called for their annual tips which were put into little earthenware boxes that had to be broken to release the money.

Holy Innocents' Day or Childermas (28 December) commemorates Herod's massacre of the infants and was considered to be so unlucky that at one time no one would risk starting a new business or getting married on that day. Some areas practised a little ritual whipping of children in memory of Herod's action – possibly a survival of a pagan custom intended to drive out evil spirits.

Most New Year customs were associated with a determination to start the year as one meant to go on. Evil spirits were particularly prevalent at the New Year and had to be driven away with loud noises – church bells were found to be suitable. Whatever happened on New Year's Day was held to set the pattern for the rest of the year. If you ate well then, and had money in your pocket, you would be rich and well fed for the next twelve months. The first visitor on New Year's Day influenced the fortunes of the household for the year, so great importance was attached to the age, sex and even the colouring of the 'First Footer'.

The season ended at Epiphany or Twelfth Night with another great party. A King and Queen were selected for the revels by crowning the pair who found the pea and the bean in the Twelfth Night cake. The sovereign could order games and charades and forfeits, just like the Saturnalian king, though he was probably also intended to represent the three Magi, or Kings. Most people took down their decorations after Epiphany, though in some parts they stayed up till Plough Monday, when the men went back to work, or even until Candlemas, 2 February, the Feast of the Purification of the Virgin, when the candles to be used in the coming year were blessed in church.

Everyone ate and drank as much as they could throughout the twelve days of Christmas. Carol singers, going from door to door, would dip their cups into the 'wassail bowl' of hot spiced beer with toasted apples and drink the health of those whose homes they visited. Toasting was an important part of the Christmas good cheer. Wild boar, in ancient times a sacrificial animal, or the more domesticated pig, was the traditional centrepiece of the groaning board. Today we have Christmas hams or sausages instead. Christmas cakes and biscuits in a variety of significant shapes formed an important part of the seasonal spread.

Until the end of the thirteenth century the observances and rituals of Christmas were almost entirely pagan as far as they concerned ordinary people. The religious and spiritual aspects of the festival were confined largely to the aloof intellectualism of the monasteries. The move to democratize Christianity, to bring its true meaning home to the people, was led by St Francis and the Franciscans. St Francis selected the Nativity as the most human and moving aspect of the life of Christ, and in 1223 in the church at Greccio he built a life-size reproduction of the stable, manger and the Holy Family, the ox and the ass. Another Franciscan, Jacopone Da Todi, was the 'father' of Christmas carols – simple, heartfelt, even robust songs in praise of Christ's birth, sung in the common language, in contrast to the austere Latin hymns of Christmas. The same mood of democracy led to the mystery or miracle plays. These started life in church as an elaboration of the church ritual, a piece of ceremonial performed by the clergy. As they developed into more elaborate drama they moved out of the church into the churchyard and, then becoming increasingly secular, into the streets and market places. The plays, the carols and the touching picture of the crèche helped to make Christmas into a popular festival in the religious as well as the pagan sense.

Most early Protestants continued to celebrate Christmas – indeed, Martin Luther was credited with inventing the Christmas tree – but to the Puritans of the seventeenth century Christmas was anathema. Puritan settlers in America tried to substitute Thanksgiving Day, when thanks were given for the blessings of the past year, for Christmas and the Puritans of Massachusetts went so far as to forbid people *not* to work on Christmas Day. When the Puritans came to power in Britain under Oliver Cromwell they banned Christmas and all other festivals. Most people strongly resented being deprived of their fun and some defied the ban and rioted. Christmas gradually returned, but the Puritans turned out to have been oddly successful in the long run. The medieval Christmas with its open-hearted generosity and good fellowship, sumptuous feasts and tournaments, gambling, drinking and playing the fool was never revived. Christmas returned in more sober mood and retreated largely into the home. But the commentators who feared that Christmas was dying underestimated its rural vigour. The neo-pagan practices which had been ruthlessly stamped out in the towns continued to thrive in the more remote country districts, waiting only to be rediscovered in the nineteenth century.

Christmas had everything a good Victorian could desire. It had sentimentality and romance,

'Christmas in Australia: Pudding Time' from a drawing by W. Ralston.

strong family feeling and piety, colour, light and warmth, simple and boisterous fun, feasting, drinking and almsgiving, singing and dancing. In 1843, Charles Dickens commemorated the new style of Christmas in *A Christmas Carol*, a story that so moved the author that he alternately wept and laughed as he wrote it. This famous tale included ghosts and sizzling plum puddings, steaming bowls of punch and barrels of oysters, holly and ivy and blazing log fires; it had a miser reformed and poverty relieved, and it so touched the heart of one American factory owner that he decided to give his workers Christmas Day off. Others followed. The Victorians revived old customs and adopted new ones. The Christmas tree, already popular in Germany, spread through Europe and beyond. St Nicholas, Bishop of Myra, long revered as the patron saint of children, was metamorphosed by the Americans into Santa Claus, a stout jolly man who travelled the world on his reindeer sleigh delivering gifts to good children. The pantomime, crackers, Christmas cards and board games were all invented or popularized in the nineteenth century. Factories were set up to produce these novelties. The new industrial society, sensing profit, enthusiastically encouraged the renaissance of Christmas and business boomed.

The British Christmas, now rejuvenated and as fit as a fiddle, spread throughout the world. Traders exported it to the Far East and Christmas trees sprouted in Shanghai. Emigrants carried the customs with them to the heat of South Africa and Australia and the snowy wastes of Canada. Missionaries sang carols to uninterested African villagers. Queen Victoria's sons and daughters, marrying into most of the royal households of Europe, sought to recreate in foreign courts the Windsor Castle Christmases of their childhood. The British Christmas was as all-conquering as once had been the Viking Yule.

As the decades passed, the sentimental, innocent, good-humoured nineteenth-century festival seemed doomed. Mass-produced baubles replaced candles and gilt-wrapped bonbons on the tree. Paper chains instead of evergreens decked people's homes. Christmas cards, once expressions of peace and goodwill, often seemed no more than business calling cards. Local customs which could not be reproduced in factories were in danger of being swamped by a commercialized version of the Victorian Christmas. But rural traditions are strong, and family celebrations precious and perpetuated lovingly from one generation to the next. Polish children still eagerly search the sky on Christmas Eve for the first star, which signals the start of the festivals. In Sweden churchyards flicker with candles lit in centuries-old remembrance of the dead. Candles on windowsills in rural Ireland still guide the Holy Family to shelter on Christmas Eve. The ancient practices and true meaning of the season have not really disappeared. They have merely gone underground, as they did in the time of the Puritans. They are still there, treasured, heartfelt and true, diverse and moving. If we unravel the string and peel off the wrappings, we can find the gift of Christmas within.

DATES TO CELEBRATE

30 NOVEMBER – ST ANDREW'S DAY
One of the twelve Apostles, brother of Simon Peter, 'Andrew' means 'manly' in Greek. He is the patron saint of Scotland. In Germany St Andrew's Eve was an important time for looking into the future, particularly for girls who wanted to know who they would marry. In Romania vampires were said to rise from their graves on St Andrew's Eve and haunt the houses where they used to live.

FIRST SUNDAY IN ADVENT
Sunday nearest to St Andrew's Day and the fourth Sunday before Christmas. Advent is the period of preparation for Christ's coming.

6 DECEMBER – ST NICHOLAS'S DAY
First of the Christmas season's gift-giving days, particularly celebrated now in Holland and Belgium. Good children are rewarded with presents and bad ones, traditionally, are punished. St Nicholas was a fourth-century bishop of Myra and is the patron saint of children, unmarried girls, scholars, merchants, sailors and Russia and is one of the ancestors of Santa Claus.

12 DECEMBER – FIESTA OF OUR LADY OF GUADALUPE
Mexico's most important religious festival which commemorates the appearance in 1531 of the Virgin Mary to an Indian boy. It is marked by religious ceremonies and pilgrimages, processions, fireworks and dances.

13 DECEMBER – ST LUCIA'S DAY
Fourth-century Sicilian girl martyr. Her name day is celebrated in Sweden and Finland with candles and processions.

16 DECEMBER – POSADAS DAYS
The start of the posadas in Mexico and other South American countries when processions set out to re-enact Mary and Joseph's search for shelter. ('Posada' means 'inn'.)

21 DECEMBER – ST THOMAS'S DAY
Feast of St Thomas the Apostle and a day associated with a wide range of unrelated customs and beliefs. In England poor people used to go round Thomasing, or begging for food for Christmas. In several countries it was a day for schoolboy pranks against their masters. St Thomas's Eve was supposed to be one of the uncanniest nights of the year and was an important time for divination. Tyrolean peasants eat 'zelten', a pie of dried fruit bearing the sign of the cross and sprinkled with holy water. In Finland a window or door decoration made of two strips of wood stuck together and pared so that the shavings curl inward is called the Cross of St Thomas.

21/22 DECEMBER – WINTER SOLSTICE
The shortest, darkest day of the year and thus associated with many pagan customs connected with death, rebirth and the survival of the sun.

23 DECEMBER – JOHN CANOE DAY
The start of a month-long Jamaican fiesta. John Canoe was a leader of black traders active in Guinea in 1720. The Jamaican Jonkunnu dancers may be named after him.

END DECEMBER – HANUKKAH
Eight-day Jewish festival of lights which commemorates the rededication of the Temple.

24 DECEMBER – CHRISTMAS EVE
Eve of Christ's Nativity, celebrated with reverence and fasting, or family parties and feasting. The final preparations for Christmas are made, the Yule log lit, decorations put up and the tree is trimmed. Gift bringers visit during the evening or night. The holiest night of the year.

25 DECEMBER – CHRISTMAS DAY
Feast of the Nativity of Our Lord. Commonly a holiday celebrated at home and in church. A family occasion marked by feasting and gifts.

26 DECEMBER – ST STEPHEN'S DAY
Commemorates two saints of that name, one the first Christian martyr and the other the patron saint of horses. Often a holiday celebrated with games and sports – particularly those connected with horses. Also called Boxing Day.

27 DECEMBER – FEAST OF ST JOHN
One of the Apostles, 'the Beloved' of Jesus. Where celebrated, it is a day devoted to visiting friends. In parts of Germany and Austria, wine to be drunk at home used to be brought into church to be blessed by the priest.

28 DECEMBER – HOLY INNOCENTS' DAY OR CHILDERMAS
Commemorates Herod's massacre of the children. It is noted as a particularly unlucky day on which to marry or to embark on any new venture. In the Eastern churches the massacre is commemorated on 29 December.

31 DECEMBER – NEW YEAR'S EVE AND ST SYLVESTER'S DAY
St Sylvester was a third century pope and his day is observed in many parts of Europe with ceremonies connected with the New Year. New Year's Eve (Hogmanay in Scotland) is celebrated with noise, masking, merrymaking and parties and is associated with a number of superstitions all to do with turning your back on the past and starting afresh in the coming year.

1 JANUARY – NEW YEAR'S DAY, THE FEAST OF THE CIRCUMCISION OF JESUS CHRIST AND ST BASIL'S DAY
Commonly a public holiday. What happens on this day is held to set the pattern for the rest of the year. Day of celebration of Christ's submission to the Jewish law. The feast of St Basil, fourth century Bishop of Caesarea, is celebrated in Greece and traditionally Basil cakes are eaten. The Mummers' Day Parade takes place in Philadelphia and the Tournament of the Roses has been held annually in Pasadena on 1 January since 1886.

5 JANUARY – EPIPHANY EVE OR TWELFTH NIGHT
Celebrated with parties featuring the Twelfth Night cake and presided over by a King and Queen. The last of the season's gift bringers, the Three Magi and Befana, visit during the night.

6 JANUARY – EPIPHANY
Commemorates the arrival of the Three Magi at the Bethlehem stable, Christ's baptism and the first miracle when, at His mother's request, Jesus turned water into wine at the wedding feast at Cana. In Ireland the day is called Women's Christmas and it is believed that all water becomes wine between sunset on 5 January and sunrise on 6 January. The day marks the end of the Christmas season and decorations are taken down.

13 JANUARY – ST KNUT'S DAY
End of the Christmas season in Sweden, so-called because Canute (Knut) the Great forbade fasting from Christmas to the Octave of Epiphany – January 13.

2 FEBRUARY – CANDLEMAS
Commemorates Christ's presentation in the Temple and the Purification of the Virgin. Candles are blessed in church for the coming year. The final farewells are said to Christmas.

ADVENT

HE FOUR weeks of Advent were said to symbolize the four comings of the Son of God: in the flesh, in the hearts of believers through the Holy Spirit; at the death of every man; and at the Day of Judgement. The fourth week is never completed, just as the glory of His coming will never end. Advent is the period of preparation for Christ's coming. In the Western Church it starts on the Sunday nearest to 30 November, St Andrew's Day, and includes the four Sundays before Christmas. Advent is a season of awe, joy and longing which used to be kept as a solemn fast – and still is by Eastern churches, where it lasts for six weeks.

In Rome the Nativity used to be heralded by the Piferari, who came down from the mountains ten days before Christmas and played wild and plaintive music on their bagpipes before shrines to the Madonna. Today in Italy the period of preparation is characterized by the Christmas Novena – a series of nine nightly church services with carols. In Colombia the Christmas Novena, which starts on 16 December and officially opens the Christmas season, is a combination of evening devotions, carols and prayers, followed by parties and dancing. Every day from 16 December to Christmas Eve, Puerto Ricans attend the Mass of the Carols at five-thirty in the morning – and carry on singing the familiar songs as they go to work. Christmas begins in Spain on 8 December, the Feast of the Immaculate Conception and Mothers' Day. Irish children customarily amass as many pre-Christmas Paters and Aves as they can in spiritual readiness for the birth of Christ. The period of Advent has become increasingly important and popular in Sweden since the First World War as the excitement mounts for the preparation for Christmas, and today there are often larger congregations in church for the first Sunday of Advent than at Christmas.

The season is also marked by a number of less holy practices. Although Advent officially starts in Finland on the first Sunday in Advent, when church congregations sing the Hosiana hymn, Little Christmas parties are enjoyed by adults as early as October. In the rural east of Holland the ancient Yuletide custom of Midwinter Horn Blowing survives. At dusk on the first Sunday of Advent and then daily until Christmas Eve,

'Christmas in Arcadia', a topical engraving from 1859 commenting of social inequalities.

farmers blow on long, slightly crooked horns made from hollowed branches of elder trees. The horns are held over wells for amplification and the weird sound is repeated from farm to farm to announce the coming of Christ.

The countdown to Christmas is brought home in other visual ways. The topmost of the twenty-four sections of the Advent candle is lit on 1 December, and on the same day children open the first window of the Advent calendar to reveal a Christmas scene or these days even a chocolate. Sometimes hooks are substituted for the windows and a tiny present hung from each. On the first Sunday in Advent the first of four candles on the evergreen Advent wreath is lit, to be joined by the second on the second Sunday, and so on. The candle and calendar are quite recent developments in Scandinavia and Germany, but like the wreath are now popular worldwide. In Sweden, electrically-lit paper Advent stars hang in windows, as glowing reminders of the Bethlehem star.

Drama has ancient links with Christmas, and during Advent all sorts of Christmas performances get under way. In England every village used to be visited by a band of mummers – masked and blackened players whose name probably derives from German or Greek words meaning 'mask' and whose origins lie in ancient pagan rites connected with the triumph of life over death. Although the plots and characters vary widely, generally one character is killed, just as the crops are by the winter cold, later to be revived by a doctor figure to symbolize new life in spring. Stock characters include St George, the Turkish Knight and the Bold Slasher – all led by Father Christmas.

Traditional mummers performing in a country house. An engraving by Seymour, 1836.

Sketches performed by fearsome Jamaican Jonkunnu dancers, which get under way in December, also involve combat, death and resuscitation. Each character has a different name and costume. Jonkunnu dancers first performed at the start of the eighteenth century and may be named after a leader of black traders in Guinea called John Canoe, or the name may derive from the French 'gens inconnu'.

The Nativity Players of Hungary set out on their rounds early in December. In Poland the szopka, a tiny puppet theatre, begins its seasonal performances of nativity plays. The nine days before Christmas in Mexico and other South American countries are marked by posadas, processions which accompany figures of Mary and Joseph from house to house in a dramatic re-creation of their search for shelter, which tradition says lasted for nine days. Each evening

A Turkey-Shooting Match in the United States. An engraving from Christmas 1852.

the procession ends with dancing, singing and a party. Elsewhere, especially in Europe, star singers set out carolling and acting Christmas scenes. In Holland, Belgium and Switzerland St Nicholas processions get under way and everywhere small children compete for the roles of angels and shepherds in nativity plays.

Advent is the time to make practical as well as religious preparations for Christmas. Traditionally, houses were swept, barns whitewashed and everything was mended and polished. The last Sunday before Christmas is still called Dirty Sunday in Norway. Presents and cards are bought and sent amid mounting excitement and public announcements about last posting dates to the four corners of the earth. Holly, mistletoe and the Christmas tree are brought in ready to decorate the house, crib figures are unwrapped and tree baubles and lights are unpacked and checked. To avoid last-minute panic and unseasonal bad temper, as much as possible is bought, made or at least planned, in advance. But the greatest amount of planning is connected with the Christmas food.

Christmas markets selling all the ingredients for the feast proliferate. On the Saturday before Christmas Irish families 'bring home the Christmas': geese, turkeys, fresh farm produce, currant loaves, sweets and biscuits, fruit, whiskey, wine and beer, from the local market. On the same day Jamaicans make a family outing to the Grand Market, which starts at five in the morning. German towns hold Christmas markets throughout December. Probably the best known is the Christkindlesmarkt at Nuremburg, over 300 years old, which displays the work of local

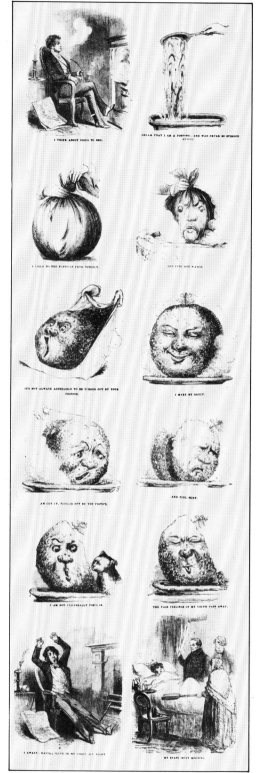

'Plum Puddings: A Dream of Christmas'. Designed and drawn by Watts Phillips, 1852.

craftsmen as well as the produce of speciality cooks. In Mexico, for days before Christmas, booths in the marketplace sell handicrafts, food and toys brought down from the mountains by Indians. In markets in Italy, Spain and southern France special stalls sell figures for the crib.

Seasonal biscuits and breads that will keep are baked as early as possible to leave time for last-minute cooking. In England the Christmas pudding, which improves with keeping, is traditionally made no later than Stir-Up Sunday – the last Sunday before Advent, so called because the collect for the day begins, 'Stir up, we beseech Thee, O Lord, the wills of thy faithful people.' Hungarians used to enjoy a December pig-killing feast, when the preparation of the pig was accompanied by a lot of traditional fun.

Equally careful planning and thought is necessary for that most vital of Christmas ingredients, consideration for others. Christmas is a time for sharing and for giving. Charities organizing seasonal benefits such as toys for children's homes or a Christmas dinner for the homeless need to know as early as possible what they can expect in donations and help. At a time when the emphasis on family can seem exclusive, even the most fiercely independent person might

'Auctioning Christmas Poultry', by J. Morgan, from Illustrated London News, December, 1878.

appreciate a tactful – and early – invitation to join the household for a meal. House guests for the Christmas period should also be invited early so that they can make their plans in advance, and feel genuinely wanted. Most prefer to be included in the family bustle of preparations as well as the actual celebrations and would enjoy being given jobs to do.

Perhaps your house, already bursting with guests, can stretch even further to take in someone who really needs a good old-fashioned family Christmas. Many hospitals and homes for children and the elderly, the handicapped and the sick, try to arrange for their residents to get

Crowds shopping for poultry in Leadenhall Market on Christmas Eve.

away for a few days. Charities and social services departments should be able to advise. Once again, careful planning is essential, so don't let your heart rule your head. Bear in mind the physical limitations of your house, the needs of your guests and the sort of company you are asking them to share. It would not be fair to ask a lively young child to join a house-party that is made up of middle-aged bridge players, or to suggest that an elderly lady should sleep on the sitting-room sofa. If you invite a severely handicapped visitor everything could go wrong disastrously soon if your front door is too narrow for the wheelchair or if you don't have a downstairs lavatory. Issue your invitation early and learn about any special needs or problems well in advance so that when Christmas comes you can make your guest feel quite at home. And remember to tell everyone else so that they can include him or her in their Christmas shopping.

On the other side of the coin, if you are going to be alone at Christmas, instead of waiting for an invitation, why not find out where your help is needed. Many charities provide short-term shelter and food for the homeless over the Christmas period and need voluntary help. Permanent hospitals and homes usually like to do something special for their residents and welcome outside assistance and your presence could release full time staff to spend a few hours with their families. A lot of hard work and careful planning goes into giving everyone a happy Christmas, but it is well worth the effort and can even be fun.

Christmas
JOHN BETJEMAN

The bells of waiting Advent ring,
The Tortoise stove is lit again
And lamp-oil light across the night
Has caught the streaks of winter rain
In many a stained-glass window sheen
From Crimson Lake to Hooker's Green

The holly in the windy hedge
And round the Manor House the yew
Will soon be stripped to deck the ledge,
The altar, font and arch and pew,
So that the villagers can say
'The church looks nice' on Christmas Day.

Provincial public houses blaze
And Corporation tramcars clang,
On lighted tenements I gaze
Where paper decorations hang,
And bunting in the red Town Hall
Says 'Merry Christmas to you all.'

And London shops on Christmas Eve
Are strung with silver balls and flowers
As hurrying clerks the City leave
To pigeon-haunted classic towers,
And marbled clouds go scudding by
The many-steepled London sky.

And girls in slacks remember Dad,
And oafish louts remember Mum,
And sleepless children's hearts are glad,
And Christmas-morning bells say 'Come!'
Even to shining ones who dwell
Safe in the Dorchester Hotel.

And is it true? And is it true,
This most tremendous tale of all,
Seen in a stained-glass window's hue,
A Baby in an ox's stall?
The Maker of the stars and sea
Become a Child on earth for me?

And is it true? For if it is,
No loving fingers tying strings
Around those tissued fripperies,
The sweet and silly Christmas things,
Bath salts and inexpensive scent
And hideous tie so kindly meant,

No love that in a family dwells,
No carolling in frosty air,
Nor all the steeple-shaking bells
Can with this single Truth compare –
That God was Man in Palestine
And lives to-day in Bread and Wine.

The Twelve Days of Christmas

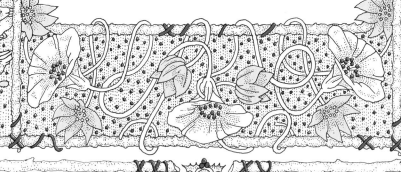

On the first day of Christmas my true love sent to me
A partridge in a pear tree.
On the second day of Christmas my true love sent to me
Two turtle doves and a partridge in a pear tree.
On the third day of Christmas my true love sent to me
Three french hens, etc . . .
On the fourth day of Christmas my true love sent to me
Four calling birds, etc . . .
On the fifth day of Christmas my true love sent to me
Five gold rings, etc . . .
On the sixth day of Christmas my true love sent to me
Six geese a-laying, etc . . .
On the seventh day of Christmas my true love sent to me
Seven swans a-swimming, etc . . .
On the eighth day of Christmas my true love sent to me
Eight maids a-milking, etc . . .
On the ninth day of Christmas my true love sent to me
Nine pipers piping, etc . . .
On the tenth day of Christmas my true love sent to me
Ten drummers drumming, etc . . .
On the eleventh day of Christmas my true love sent to me
'leven lords a-leaping, etc . . .
On the twelfth day of Christmas my true love sent to me
Twelve ladies dancing, etc . . .

ST LUCIA

In Sweden Christmas starts on the morning of 13 December, Lucia Day, when the daughter of the house, clad in a white robe and wearing a crown of candles, wakes the rest of the family with food, drink and a traditional song. Later in the day there are Lucia processions and the beautiful blond girl elected to preside over the Stockholm parade is crowned at the city hall by the winner of the Nobel Prize for Literature.

Quite why St Lucia, a young Sicilian girl martyred in AD 304 for her Christian beliefs, should have become so closely linked with Sweden and Swedish-speaking Finland is unclear. There is a legend that during a famine she provided the country with food, her head circled in light. More probably the connection developed from the coincidence that under the old calendar her name day fell on the shortest day of the year, which was celebrated with candles and lights to drive away dark winter and welcome back the sun. Her name also suggests the Latin *lux*, meaning light, and possibly the monks who converted Sweden to Christianity used lights to celebrate her day. The Swedish custom spread to North America with Scandinavian immigrants, and Canadian and American fathers of flaxen-haired girls are at risk of being woken horribly early by a Lucia-crowned daughter offering such Scandinavian specialities as lussekatter, a saffron-coloured bread, pepparkakor, spicy gingerbread biscuits, and coffee.

Originally Lucia Day was marked throughout Scandinavia with processions. Only last century did the domestic practices develop. 13 December was called Little Yule and the girl who woke the family at first cock crow was named Lussi or Lussibruden – Lucia bride. After her visit everyone dressed and ate by brilliant candlelight. Animals, rarely overlooked in Scandinavian celebrations, received special food. In some parts Lussi toured the villages led by torchbearers and in one village Lussi was a cow wearing a crown of candles.

Celebrations took quite different forms in other countries. In Denmark the Lucia Eve was a time for girls to foresee their husbands. At midnight young Austrian men looked for the Luzieschein, a strange light which might form shapes indicative of the future. Witchcraft was a great threat and had to be averted by prayer and incense. Girls were afraid to spin in case they found their threads knotted and broken in the morning. In some regions of central Europe Lucia played the role of gift-bringer – either as a horned monster giving good children fruit and threatening bad ones, or as the female counterpart of St Nicholas, bringing presents for the girls.

The Eve of Lucia Day in Sicily, her birthplace, was marked by an extraordinary procession. Men and children carrying lighted bundles of straw rushed, shrieking wildly, through the villages to the piazza, where they threw their torches on to a huge straw bonfire. Bringing up the end of the parade was a statue of St Lucia carrying a tray on which lay her eyes – she is said to have torn them out because they were so beautiful they drove a prince to try to seduce her away from her convent.

Luca Day in Hungary is the day of the harvest blessing. Traditionally children carrying bundles of straw go in pairs from house to house, where they spread the straw on the floor, kneel on it and give good wishes. In some areas adults wrapped up in sheets rap on doors with wooden spoons. When they are let in they use the spoon to scoop out a nest for the best layer in the hen house – villagers used to believe that an abundance of eggs signified prosperity.

Like many other saints, this young Sicilian martyr attracted many and varied customs to her name, none of which have much relevance to her own short life. Today she is best known for the crown of lighted candles which, because of their ancient association with midwinter and the Church, are at least very much in the spirit of Christmas.

Shepherds, Shake Off Your Drowsy Sleep

ELEANOR FARJEON

People, look East. The time is near
Of the crowning of the year.
Make your house fair as you are able,
Trim the hearth and set the table
People, look East, and sing today:
Love the Guest is on the way.

Furrows, be glad. Though earth is bare.
One more seed is planted there:
Give up your strength the seed to nourish,
That in course the flower may flourish.
People, look East, and sing today:
Love the Rose is on the way.

Birds, though ye long have ceased to build.
Guard the nest that must be filled.
Even the hour when wings are frozen
He for fledging-time has chosen.
People, look East, and sing today:
Love the Bird is on the way.

Stars, keep the watch. When night is dim
One more light the bowl shall brim.
Shining beyond the frosty weather.
Bright as sun and moon together.
People look East, and sing today:
Love the Star is on the way.

Angels, announce to man and beast
Him who cometh from the East.
Set every peak and valley humming
With the word, the Lord is coming.
People look East, and sing today:
Love the Lord is on the way.

CHRISTMAS CARDS & CRACKERS

Two of the jolliest and most popular latecomers to the Christmas festivities developed as a direct result of Victorian enterprise and Victorian technology. Christmas crackers were the invention of one man inspired by a good idea; Christmas cards the logical outcome of improved printing techniques and the penny post.

Humorous Christmas card theme featuring children exploring the Christmas hamper.

director of the Victoria and Albert Museum, and Royal Academician John Calcott Horsley. A card was designed by Horsley in 1843 at the suggestion of his friend Cole and in 1846 a thousand copies were sold at a shilling each from the offices of Felix Summerly's Home Treasury in Old Bond Street. The card depicts a family merrily sipping wine and the two side panels show acts of charity. It bore the message, 'A Merry Christmas and A Happy New Year To You'.

Robins were an early feature on Christmas cards, their red breasts giving a seasonal touch.

Postmen, called Robins after the colour of their uniforms, were a popular card motif.

Although it is such a recent addition to the season, controversy surrounds the date of the first Christmas card and the name of its creator. There was an earlier custom of schoolboys writing 'Christmas pieces' – specimens of calligraphy on specially decorated sheets of paper to take home with them at Christmas to show their parents. New Year cards were already available in Europe, and in England people commonly exchanged written Christmas greetings. Advances in printing and the institution of the penny post in 1840 made the development of the Christmas card inevitable. The credit is generally given to Mr (later Sir) Henry Cole, the first

Rival contenders for the title of inventor of the first Christmas card include the Reverend Edward Bradley and the painter W. Dobson. In 1844 Mr Dobson sent out hand-painted Christmas cards to his friends instead of writing his usual letters. In the same year, Mr Bradley, a Newcastle vicar who wrote such best-selling

Victorian Father Christmas delivering presents on a Penny-Farthing bicycle.

novels as *Cuthbert Bede*, had his cards lithographed and circulated to his friends. In neither case was the card for sale. The third contestant, William Maw Egley, may have a more serious claim. His card, of similar design to Horsley's, is dated, but the final number printed is not clear and the date may read either 1842 or 1849. If the earlier date is accepted Egley must have had a precocious talent as he would have been only sixteen at the time. For the moment the Horsley–Cole card is generally accepted as having been the first.

Christmas cards did not become generally popular until the growth of cheaper printing techniques and the introduction of a halfpenny stamp for cards in 1870, but they then caught on so fast that by 1880 the Post Office was asking everyone to post early for Christmas. Early designs were more Dickensian than religious and commonly featured stagecoaches and snowbound villages, Christmas puddings and Yule

Christmas greed epitomized with pigs sorrowfully bearing in the boar's head.

logs, and the ever popular robin with his fiery red breast, who became doubly connected with the season as early postmen were called Robins after the colour of their uniform. Cards became more and more exotic and sported silk fringes, gilding, and satin and plush insets. They appeared in the shape of fans, stars, scrolls and other novelty cut-outs. 'Art' Christmas cards, trick Christmas cards, even 'sick' Christmas cards joined the flood, but on the whole, sentiment and religion in pictures and message conquered all.

Religious themes featured in later Victorian Christmas cards, here framed in embossed lace.

The first Christmas cards reached America in the 1850s, but only became popular with the work of Louis Prang, a German-born printer living in Roxbury, Massachusetts, who printed his first cards in 1875. They were of the highest quality and at first were mainly floral designs, though later he moved on to such seasonal themes as the Madonna and Child and Santa Claus. He helped to popularize Christmas cards by organizing nationwide competitions for the best designs and awarding prizes. But Prang could not compete with the influx of cheaper cards from Europe in the 1890s and eventually gave up that side of his business.

There is no dispute about who invented the Christmas cracker. Tom Smith was a confectioner's apprentice before setting up on his own making wedding cake decorations. In 1847, on

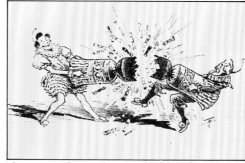

'Clowns and Crackers', an engraving from Strand *magazine, 1891.*

a visit to Paris in search of new ideas, he spotted in a shop window sugared almonds wrapped in twists of coloured tissue paper. He dashed back home and introduced the British public to these fascinating 'bon-bons'. They were quite popular, but demand fell off sharply after Christmas, so Smith decided to exploit the seasonal angle. First love messages or 'kiss mottoes', then toys, charms, jokes and jewellery joined the almond inside the wrapping, but still something was missing. One winter evening Tom Smith sat at home listening to the comforting crackle of the log fire when a sensational idea struck him – he would put a bang into his bon-bons. In 1860, after two years of experiment, he hit upon the saltpetre friction strip. Crackers became immensely popular and over the years practically everything went into the cardboard cracker tube. Arctic expeditions were commemorated with miniature bears and bear masks, 'press' crackers contained tiny magazines and grotesque headdresses. There were mottoes for cricketers, crackers for bachelors, even puns for suffragettes, but the most consistent theme was love, with sentimental trinkets, verses and mottoes predicting future husbands.

Today thousands of crackers are sold and millions of cards posted, but sadly many people feel cheated by both. Even an expensive cracker can go off with a phut, not a bang, and burst to reveal one paper hat, one tired motto and a piece of plastic jewellery. The cost of cards and postage, their common use as a piece of business public relations, and the competitiveness involved in size and date of posting have only been partially offset by the increasing sale of cards in aid of charities. But still no Christmas table

'Nothing in it' illustration of child with newly fashionable crackers. The Graphic *magazine.*

setting would be complete without the cheerful paper-covered tubes, and few can resist rushing to see what the postman has brought as Christmas gets near. Those two late arrivals on the Christmas scene are now an integral part of the festivities and with a little ingenuity and the minimum of manual skill they can be reinvested with the seasonal spirit. Making your own crackers is one sure and easy way of getting value for money and pleasing everyone. Bearing in mind the length of most people's Christmas card list, handmade cards for all would be out of the question, unless the design was particularly simple, but they are well worth the time and effort spent for a few special friends, rarely seen but warmly remembered at Christmas.

Making Christmas Cards

The design and technique you choose for making your own Christmas cards will depend largely on whether you are making one or two extra special cards or are hoping to save money by mass producing your own. The easiest, and cheapest, way of producing cards is by the simplest of all printing

must be done with a thick straight-ended brush and is most effective if the design is reasonably simple (fig 2). Cut-outs on the front of cards can also be very effective, particularly if the inside of the card is decorated, perhaps with a metallic or patterned paper. The cut-out must be done with a very

fig 4

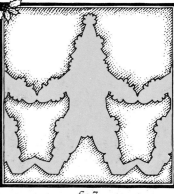
fig 6

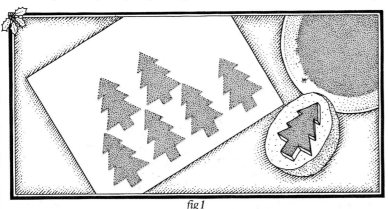
fig 1

techniques, the potato-cut. Just cut a potato in half and carve until the design stands out in relief (fig 1). Dip this into a saucer of thickly mixed poster paint and print onto the ready folded cards. Stencilling or spray painting is also very easy. You could try spraying gold paint over a small lace doily against a white or dark toned paper background. This will give you a pretty snowflake pattern and as a by-product provide a pile of gold mats for the Christmas table. Stencilling by stippling paint through a cut-out shape

sharp craft knife and again professional looking results are easiest to achieve if the shape is simple (fig 3).

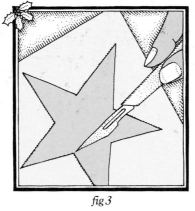
fig 3

Coloured self-adhesive peel-off shapes can be bought at most good stationers and can be used to make attractive stylized modern cards (fig 4). Victorian scrap-book cut-outs can also look very pretty and decorative stuck onto a simple card. Glitter frost can be used to make festive looking cards (fig 5). Use a good glue and paintbrush and either paint a design onto the card,

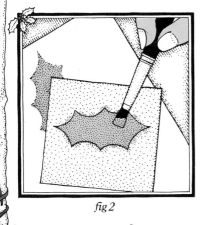
fig 2

or cover the whole card with glue leaving the design free. Sprinkle glitter over the card, press down with a sheet of paper and shake off the surplus.

fig 5

Old Christmas cards can be reused successfully if properly mounted and given a contrasting frame, either with different coloured paper or with lines drawn round the picture in coloured inks. Tissue paper cut-outs can be made by drawing half a pattern on a pile of folded tissues. Cut out the design and unfold the sheets to reveal the complete picture. The cut-outs can then be stuck onto your folded cards with glue. Alternatively you can fold a long narrow strip of tissue concertina style and either cut out a whole figure taking care to leave linkage at the folds, (fig 6) or fold in half again for a more complicated figure. These hand-in-hand shapes can be cut in groups to

fig 7

stick around the outside or inside of cards (fig 7). If you are deft at folding you can make interesting three dimensional cards with origami shapes to stick on the front of your cards. You can find books of instructions and origami paper at many good craft or toyshops.

Sending cards with an up-to-date photograph of the family is a nice idea for relatives or friends you haven't seen for some time. An interesting way to do this is with an opening door on the front of the card (fig 8)—you can add your house number to personalize it further. The doors can be drawn, printed with a potato cut or you might cut them from magazine pictures and stick them on the card. Cut round three sides of the door with a sharp craft knife so that it will open and add a paperclip doorknob. Inside the card glue a family photograph.

fig 8

fig 12

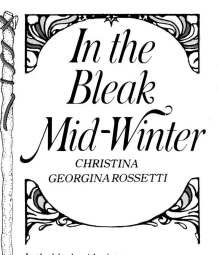
With some forward planning you could press a collection of spring and summer flowers to use on your Christmas cards. Press the flowers, if possible with leaves and at all stages of blooming, between sheets of blotting paper. Put between layers of newspaper and leave under a heavy pile of books, or better still under the carpet. When Christmas comes, arrange the flowers on a suitable coloured card and cover with transparent adhesive film. Glue to the front of your folded card leaving room to write underneath the name of the flower and where you found it (fig 9).

fig 9

Children like moving, jointed cards, showing their favourite characters or animals. From coloured card cut body, arms, legs, head, ears, tail, tongue, sack of toys etc. depending on the figure. Keep the various sections simple and joint together with paperclips (fig 10) so that the figure can move freely. The greeting can be written on one of the Christmas parcels or on a label round an animal's neck.

Stand up cards are a little more complicated but they can be very original and make a good decoration for the mantelpiece. The two simplest

fig 10

methods of making stand up cards are the tab and slot, or two slot systems. The tree (fig 11) can be cut out of green

fig 11

card and decorated with gold or coloured adhesive shapes. The slots must be cut accurately so that the card stands securely at all four points. If attempting the slot and tab method make sure that the width at the bottom of the card is sufficient to give a stable base in proportion to the height of the card, so experiment first with stapled newspaper cut-outs until you reach the right shape (fig 12).

There are several different ways of using collage to make special cards. For a Bethlehem stable, cut out the fabrics and glue onto card. Sequins can be glued to cards to make attractive

fig 13

sparkling designs (fig 13). Time consuming but beautiful is a card with beads and rhinestones sewn or stuck onto a strong backing which is then cut and folded round card as though covering a book. The greeting is written on paper pasted inside.

In the bleak mid-winter
Frosty wind made moan,
Earth stood hard as iron,
Water like a stone;
Snow had fallen, snow on snow,
Snow on snow,
In the bleak mid-winter
Long ago.

Our God, Heaven cannot hold Him,
Nor earth sustain;
Heaven and earth shall flee away
When He comes to reign:
In the bleak mid-winter
A stable-place sufficed
The Lord God Almighty
Jesus Christ.

Enough for Him, whom cherubim
Worship night and day,
A breastful of milk
And a mangerful of hay;
Enough for Him, whom angels
Fall down before,
The ox and ass and camel
Which adore.

Angels and archangels
May have gathered there,
Cherubim and seraphim
Thronged the air;
But only His mother
In her maiden bliss
Worshipped the Beloved
With a kiss.

What can I give Him,
Poor as I am?
If I were a shepherd
I would bring a lamb;
If I were a wise man
I would do my part;
Yet what I can I give Him,
Give my heart.

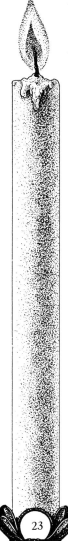

23

Making Crackers

Making crackers may seem a daunting task, but is actually very straightforward and can be fun. Decorating with sequins, feathers, bows and other trimmings gives scope for artistic fantasy. Snaps for home-made crackers are not always easy to find but some craft shops do have them, or you can write to enquire from regular cracker manufacturers who will sometimes supply materials or can suggest firms or novelty shops who could help you with snaps, mottoes and small gifts.

Take three cardboard tubes – the ones inside toilet rolls are perfect for this purpose. Place the rolls end to end and trim the outer rolls if you wish the two cracker ends to be shorter than the middle section (fig 1).

Roll the tubes up in double thickness tissue paper cut to ½-inch (1cm) longer than the combined length of the tubes and ½-inch (1cm) wider than their

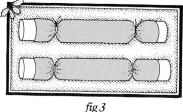

fig 1

circumference. When rolled fix in place with glue.

Roll on the outer paper which can be crêpe, fancy wrapping paper, or almost any attractive paper which is not

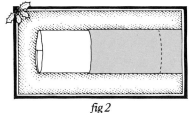

fig 2

too thick. The outer paper can be the same width as the tissue, or shorter if you want contrasting tissue to show. Fold in edge of length for neatness then stick with glue (fig 2).

fig 3

Place motto, snap and gift in cracker. Wind strong button thread two or three times round the cracker where the tubes meet. Pull the thread tightly and knot until the cracker has been pressed into shape, then remove thread (fig 3). Decorate the ends of the crackers with pinking shears or cut fringes (fig 4).

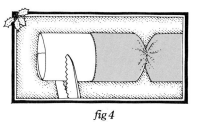

fig 4

Decorate the crackers as you wish using sequins, feathers, pieces of fancy paper doilies or cut-outs (fig 5). Take out the cardboard tube at either end if you wish.

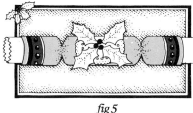

fig 5

Making Advent Cards

For most children the time spent waiting for Christmas seems interminable. The daily excitement of opening the doors in an Advent card, makes time pass more quickly. You can make a glittering Christmas tree card quite easily. Cut two tree shapes, one in dark green card, the other to exactly the same outline in mirror paper. Glue the mirror tree onto a backing of strong card. On the green card tree

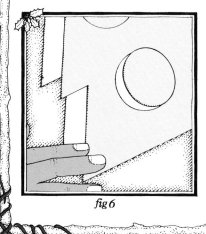

fig 6

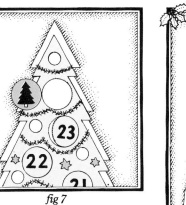

fig 7

draw 24 circles. Number the circles 1-24 in gold ink and cut round each with a sharp craft knife, leaving a small section of the circle intact to act as a hinge. On the back of each circular door paste a cut out Christmas picture or motif. Glue the green card tree over the mirror tree, taking care not to glue the doors or they will not open. Position the card tree just slightly below the mirror tree (fig 6) so that

fig 8

the mirror outline shows. Decorate the tree with tinsel, adhesive decorations or sequins if you wish. When each door is opened the picture inside will reflect in the mirror (fig 7).

If you want to make an Advent card which would be an attractive wall decoration for a child's room when all the excitement is over, cut out a figure, such as a snowman, in thick felt. The rest of the design will depend on how you plan to arrange 24 small pockets on the figure. On a snowman they could be hidden in his black top hat, in the bowl of the pipe, in the muffler, or in place of buttons down the front (fig 8). Stitch on the accessories, add a felt mouth, black button eyes and a sprig of holly in the hat. When the figure is finished paste it onto strong card and fix a ring on the back to suspend it. Write numbers 1-24 twice on 48 adhesive gold stars and pair them together sandwiching narrow red ribbon between. At the other end of the ribbon tie a small present or sweet and pop into the pockets.

PRESENT GIVING

Piles of gaily wrapped presents under the tree, intriguing in shape and full of secret promise, belong to the Victorian Christmas revival, but midwinter gift-giving has a long ancestry. At the January Kalends Romans exchanged small gifts and made seasonal offerings to the Emperor – in the reign of Caligula this was by order. These presents were called 'strenae' and were initially branches from the grove of the goddess Strenia. As time went by they became more costly symbols of good wishes for the coming year: 'honeyed things' for sweetness, lamps for light, and gold, silver and copper for wealth. The custom survives in the French word for New Year gifts, 'étrennes'. On 1 January Parisian bachelors traditionally give sweets to friends who have entertained them during the year – a relic of the

Victorian doll with a trunkful of clothes.

Roman 'honeyed things'. While the Romans were pressing gifts on each other, the Norse god Odin was riding across the midwinter night sky scattering punishments to the wicked and presents to the good.

The Church, having failed to suppress these harmless but pagan customs, substituted the Magi and St Nicholas as gift-bringers and decreed that presents were to be given in the name of Jesus, God's gift to man. Medieval kings exchanged lavish gifts of carefully calculated value, but on the whole present-giving was a one-way operation. Good children received 'surprise' presents of nuts and sweets and small toys, clerics and institutions gave charitable gifts to the needy. Employers presented servants with something useful – usually clothing. Tradesmen

pressed small tokens on customers, peasants gave presents to landlords, in gratitude for past patronage and in the hope of future favour. Apprentices and servants called for their Christmas boxes and waits and mummers performed in exchange for money, food and drink to fill their Christmas larders.

Today gift-bringers secretly give presents to children on a number of days from the Eve of St Nicholas on 5 December to the Eve of Epiphany, 5 January, when Befana and the Three Kings pass by, and there is often a separate day when adults exchange presents among family and friends. The giving of Christmas presents on a large scale is a comparatively recent development and for many people has come to typify the commercialism of the modern Christmas, but in some countries the custom is lifted above the level of mere greed by the traditional ways in which the gifts are given.

In Holland Sinterklaas' (St Nicholas') gifts are imaginatively wrapped to disguise their contents and are accompanied by a witty, pertinent verse designed to embarrass or amuse the recipient. Giver and versifier are anonymous. After supper on Sinterklaas Eve the basket of presents and verses is passed round, the gifts opened and the poems read amid blushes and laughter. In Sweden Christmas presents are called 'julklappur' from the ancient custom of giving joke presents anonymously. 'Klappa' means to wrap or knock and the donor would knock on the door, throw the presents into the house and dash away to avoid recognition. The gifts themselves were cunningly wrapped to disguise their contents. In another old custom, gifts were delivered by two masked figures, an old man ringing a bell and an old woman carrying a basket of presents. Surprise is also an important element in Denmark. If, for example, a girl is to be given a watch, her family might make a screen which she stands behind, arm stretched out through a hole to receive the gift.

Even in countries where these customs are not indigenous, thought and care are as important as the gift itself. Nothing is so disappointing or so clearly lacking in effort as a book token, nothing so heart-warming as a carefully chosen gift that comes as a surprise and is exactly right. You do not have to keep buying someone soap or socks just because you always have done in the past. Playing safe is just another excuse for laziness. If you know someone well enough to give them a present, you must know something about their tastes and interests – and if you do not, ask

someone who does. Not everyone wants to shop or plan for Christmas all year round, but people quite unconsciously drop hints all the time and it is easy enough to make a note that one friend intends to treat herself to a hanging basket for the terrace or another has a secret yearning for a red satin cummerbund. Then all that is needed is a tactful check near to Christmas that these dreams remain unfulfilled. It is still possible to buy local craftwork on holiday that is not on sale in every high street store – though it would be wise to check that your neighbour or maiden aunt actually likes tooled leather or exquisite lace. Shopping early may seem the counsel of perfection, but it is the only sensible course for the conscientious gift-giver. The most carefully

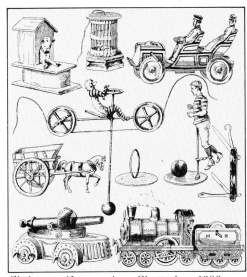

Christmas gift suggestions, Chatterbox, *1908.*

prepared list is quite useless if the shops have sold out of everything or prices have gone beyond your reach in the pre-Christmas rush.

If you really do not know what to buy your teenage nephew or bed-ridden aunt, ask someone who does. Remember some people really do prefer garden fertilizer or a casserole dish to brandy and cigars, silk scarves and scent. Finally, extend more time and thought to wrapping the gifts. Even the perfect present looks less than lovely in crumpled wrapping paper with ancient sticky tape still adhering to it. Choosing and giving the ideal present is as much fun for the donor as the recipient and the pleasure of giving and receiving still remains one of the greatest lessons of the Christmas season.

Wrapping Christmas Parcels

A present which is carefully and imaginatively wrapped is twice as exciting to receive than one which is badly put together, no matter how expensive the trimmings. Think ahead what your packing requirements will be and allow yourself time to make a good job of it. Decide if you wish to keep to a particular colour scheme and find paper, tissue and ribbon which will carry it through, or perhaps choose two or three different papers in the same colour theme so that you can switch them around interestingly. Make sure you have everything you need for your wrapping-up session, give yourself plenty of time and clear a table-top to work on. Remember that it is far better to have lots of cheap paper, than to buy a few sheets of very expensive paper and have to skimp. Keep your parcels neat, especially at the corners and folds. Many people rely heavily on long strips of adhesive tape to hold their parcels together, but if the paper is wrapped and folded properly only a small neat tab of tape is needed. Cut several small tabs of adhesive tape and have them ready when you need them. Wrapping paper can be prohibitively expensive.

One way to have interesting Christmas wrapping at a reasonable price is to make your own paper. A roll of shelving or lining paper can be decorated by lightly spattering paint over it, spray painting shapes or printing with a potato-cut design as described on

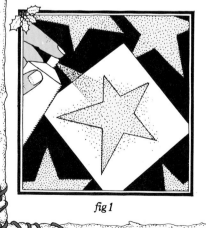

fig 1

page 22. Apply the potato-cut all over the paper or pack the parcel first and then apply the design at specific points to create a particular design. Simple tissue paper can be effective provided you use enough sheets, so buy it from a paper shop that sells in bulk, not a few sheets at a time in an expensive polythene package. The tissue can be decorated by spray painting through a stencil shape (fig 1) or wrap the parcel and spray-paint on your message. You could try using several layers of plain white tissue paper, tying the parcel with generous bows of haberdashery ribbon and decorating with Victorian scrapbook cut-outs. Leave the ends of the ribbons long enough to curl by pulling them firmly and very quickly over the blade of a knife or scissors (fig 2). Write your message on

fig 2

the paper in your best script before you wrap the parcel – it is always difficult to write neatly on a package with uneven or soft surfaces.

Some interesting effects can be achieved by using simple wrapping paper but being more adventurous with the tying of the package. Try tying the ribbon around the corners of a box as a change from the usual criss-cross method, or position the tie off centre and spray a bunch of dried flower heads or seed pods gold to tie into the bow, or use a pretty pastel paper and team it with softly coloured dried flowers and tiny silver baubles. You could wire a small arrangement

fig 3

of evergreen, holly, fir, bay, add some artificial holly berries and attach to broad ribbon on the top of a simply boxed parcel (fig 3).

Any child would enjoy receiving a parcel packaged like their favourite animal. Wrap the present neatly in a shape to suggest the body of the animal and cut head, ears, tongue and tail from coloured card, joint with paper-clips and attach to the parcel (fig 4).

You can make personal parcels by using plain paper and making an original decoration for the top. Try a

fig 4

pale pastel or even white paper and paint with wild flowers, glue on some pressed flowers (fig 5) or use self-adhesive flower decorations and write your greeting onto the parcel in an appropriately coloured ink. Other ways to decorate plainly wrapped parcels are to paint pictures on the top, or stick on a coloured card cut-out and decorate with beads, sequins or self-adhesive shapes.

HAPPY CHRISTMAS

fig 5

Christmas presents have a habit of coming in almost unwrappable shapes. Often the only way out is to put them in a box or container and wrap the box. Large posters can be rolled inside a long cardboard tube which can then be decorated with

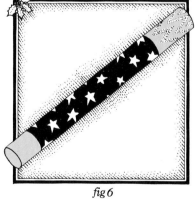

fig 6

black and white paper, silver adhesive stars and a pattern in glue and glitter to look like a conjuror's wand (fig 6).

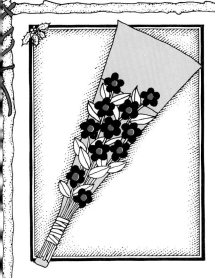

fig 7

In some instances the present itself will indicate a shape which you can use to make an original wrapping. A tennis racquet could suggest a bouquet

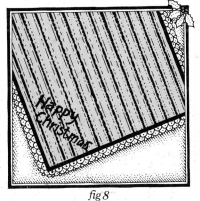

fig 8

of flowers and be wrapped accordingly with paper flowers arranged on the package to emphasize the theme (fig 7).

With a little care a soft item like a shawl or sweater can be placed between two sheets of paper with the edges turned in. Using double-sided adhesive tape you can join the two sides together, sandwiching ribbon or lace between to resemble a pretty pillow. Your greeting can be added with glue and glitter. If you find a paper of gingham or ticking print the pillow will look more convincing (fig 8).

Gift boxes are usually even more expensive than paper but they are an exciting way to give or receive a present. If you plan ahead you can make many of your own containers by collecting cardboard boxes or tins and either painting them with small tins of lacquer paint, aerosol spray paint, or you could cover them with wrapping paper or even pieces of pretty wallpaper. If you are covering a box in paper do one side at a time. Smooth the paper on gently to remove any air bubbles or excess glue and leave to dry before starting on the next side.

You can also make your own gift boxes following the shape shown for a basic cube box (fig 9). Cut out in strong card and score where indicated by dotted lines. Apply glue to shaded area and stick A behind B, fold in six tabs C, fold in ends D and tuck in as indicated. Once you have mastered the box-making technique you can vary the shape as you wish, but it is safest to keep to a simple cube at the beginning. You can also make pretty ribbon threaded carrier bags to pop presents in using brightly coloured papers. Take apart a suitably sized carrier bag and use that as a pattern to cut from, modifying the shape and size as you wish.

fig 9

The Christmas Hamper

A homely pleasure – to receive
A hamper upon Christmas Eve;
To know that someone kindly thinks
Of Norwood, and Professor Jinks.

Who sent it? – not my brother Jim –
I'm not on speaking terms with him.
My sister Caroline – ah, no!
I quarrelled with her long ago.

It might have been my cousin Kate,
Only we've not been friends of late;
Aunt Harrison or Uncle Clem,
But then I've had a row with them.

Let's cut the string! No card or name –
Will it be turkey, goose, or game?...
An unfledged chick – of straggling limb!
It *must* be from that scoundrel Jim.

A CHRISTMAS MEMORY
Truman Capote

IMAGINE A MORNING IN late November. A coming of winter morning more than twenty years ago. Consider the kitchen of a spreading old house in a country town. A great black stove is its main feature; but there is also a big round table and a fireplace with two rocking chairs placed in front of it. Just today the fireplace commenced its seasonal roar.

A woman with shorn white hair is standing at the kitchen window. She is wearing tennis shoes and a shapeless gray sweater over a summery calico dress. She is small and sprightly, like a bantam hen; but, due to a long youthful illness, her shoulders are pitifully hunched. Her face is remarkable – not unlike Lincoln's, craggy like that, and tinted by sun and wind; but it is delicate too, finely boned. and her eyes are sherry-colored and timid. 'Oh my,' she exclaims, her breath smoking the windowpane, 'it's fruitcake weather!'

The person to whom she is speaking is myself. I am seven; she is sixty-something. We are cousins, very distant ones, and we have lived together – well, as long as I can remember. Other people inhabit the house, relatives; and though they have power over us, and frequently make us cry, we are not, on the whole, too much aware of them. We are each other's best friend. She calls me Buddy, in memory of a boy who was formerly her best friend. The other Buddy died in the 1880s, when she was still a child. She is still a child.

'I knew it before I got out of bed,' she says, turning away from the window with a purposeful excitement in her eyes. 'The courthouse bell sounded so cold and clear. And there were no birds singing; they've gone to warmer country, yes indeed. Oh, Buddy, stop stuffing biscuit and fetch our buggy. Help me find my hat. We've thirty cakes to bake.'

It's always the same: a morning arrives in November, and my friend, as though officially inaugurating the Christmas time of year that exhilarates her imagination and fuels the blaze of her heart, announces: 'It's fruitcake weather! Fetch our buggy, Help me find my hat.'

The hat is found, a straw cartwheel corsaged with velvet roses out-of-doors has faded: it once belonged to a more fashionable relative. Together, we guide our buggy, a dilapidated baby carriage, out to the garden and into a grove of pecan trees. The buggy is mine; that is, it was bought for me when I was born. It is made of wicker, rather unraveled, and the wheels wobble like a drunkard's legs. But it is a faithful object; springtimes, we take it to the woods and fill it with flowers, herbs, wild fern for our porch pots; in the summer, we pile it with picnic paraphernalia and sugar-cane fishing poles and roll it down to the edge of a creek; it has its winter uses, too: as a truck for hauling firewood from the yard to the kitchen, as a warm bed for Queenie, our tough little orange and white rat terrier who has survived distemper and two rattlesnake bites. Queenie is trotting beside it now.

Three hours later we are back in the kitchen hulling a heaping buggyload of windfall pecans. Our backs hurt from gathering them: how hard they were to find (the main crop having been shaken off the trees and sold by the orchard's owners, who are not us) among the concealing leaves, the frosted, deceiving grass. Caarackle! A cheery crunch, scraps of miniature thunder sound as the shells collapse and the golden mound of sweet oily ivory meat mounts in the milk-glass bowl. Queenie begs to taste, and now and again my friend sneaks her a mite, though insisting we deprive ourselves. 'We mustn't, Buddy. If we start, we won't stop. And there's scarcely enough as there is. For thirty cakes.' The kitchen is growing dark. Dusk turns the window into a mirror: our reflections mingle with the rising moon as we work by the fireside in the firelight. At last, when the moon is quite high, we toss the final hull into the fire and, with joined sighs, watch it catch flame. The buggy is empty, the bowl is brimful.

We eat our supper (cold biscuits, bacon, blackberry jam) and discuss tomorrow. Tomorrow the kind of work I like best begins: buying. Cherries and citron, ginger and vanilla and canned Hawaiian pineapple, rinds and raisins and walnuts and whiskey and oh, so much flour, butter, so many eggs, spices, flavourings: why, we'll need a pony to pull the buggy home.

But before these purchases can be made, there is the question of money. Neither of us has any. Except for skinflint sums persons in the house occasionally provide (a dime is considered very big money); or what we earn ourselves from various activities: holding rummage sales, selling buckets of hand-picked blackberries, jars of homemade jam and apple jelly and peach preserves, rounding up flowers for funerals and weddings. Once we won seventy-ninth prize, five dollars, in a national football contest. Not that we know a fool thing about football. It's just that we enter any contest we hear about: at the moment our hopes are centered on the fifty-thousand-dollar Grand Prize being offered to name a new brand of coffee (we suggested 'A.M.';

and, after some hesitation, for my friend thought it perhaps sacrilegious, the slogan 'A.M.! Amen!'). To tell the truth, our only *really* profitable enterprise was the Fun and Freak Museum we conducted in a back-yard woodshed two summers ago. The Fun was a stereopticon with slide views of Washington and New York lent us by a relative who had been to those places (she was furious when she discovered why we'd borrowed it); the Freak was a three-legged biddy chicken hatched by one of our own hens. Everybody hereabouts wanted to see that biddy: we charged grownups a nickel, kids two cents. And took in a good twenty dollars before the museum shut down due to the decease of the main attraction.

But one way and another we do each year accumulate Christmas savings, a Fruitcake Fund. These moneys we keep hidden in an ancient bead purse under a loose board under the floor under a chamber pot under my friend's bed. The purse is seldom removed from this safe location except to make a deposit, or, as happens every Saturday, a withdrawal; for on Saturdays I am allowed ten cents to go to the picture show. My friend has never been to a picture show, nor does she intend to: 'I'd rather hear you tell the story, Buddy. That way I can imagine it more. Besides, a person my age shouldn't squander their eyes. When the Lord comes, let me see Him clear.' In addition to never having seen a movie, she has never: eaten in a restaurant, traveled more than five miles from home, received or sent a telegram, read anything except funny papers and the Bible, worn cosmetics, cursed, wished someone harm, told a lie on purpose, let a hungry dog go hungry. Here are a few things she has done, does do: killed with a hoe the biggest rattlesnake ever seen in this county (sixteen rattles), dip snuff (secretly), tame hummingbirds (just try it) till they balance on her finger, tell ghost stories (we both believe in ghosts) so tingling they chill you in July, talk to herself, take walks in the rain, grow the prettiest japonicas in town, know the recipe for every sort of old-time Indian cure, including a magical wart-remover.

Now, with supper finished, we retire to the room in a faraway part of the house where my friend sleeps in a scrap-quilt-covered iron bed painted rose pink, her favorite color. Silently, wallowing in the pleasures of conspiracy, we take the bead purse from its secret place and spill its contents on the scrap quilt. Dollar bills, tightly rolled and green as May buds. Somber fifty-cent pieces, heavy enough to weight a dead man's eyes. Lovely dimes, the liveliest coin, the one that really jingles. Nickels and quarters, worn smooth as creek pebbles. But mostly a hateful heap of bitter-odored pennies. Last summer others in the house contracted to pay us a penny for every twenty-five flies we killed. Oh, the carnage of August: the flies that flew to heaven! Yet it was not work in which we took pride. And, as we sit counting pennies, it is as though we were back tabulating dead flies. Neither of us has a head for figures; we count slowly, lose track, start again. According to her calculations, we have $12.73. According to mine, exactly $13. 'I do hope you're wrong, Buddy. We can't mess around with thirteen. The cakes will fall. Or put somebody in the cemetery. Why, I wouldn't dream of getting out of bed on the thirteenth.' This is true: she always spends thirteenths in bed. So, to be on the safe side, we subtract a penny and toss it out the window.

Of the ingredients that go into our fruitcakes, whiskey is the most expensive, as well as the hardest to obtain: State laws forbid its sale. But everybody knows you can buy a bottle from Mr. Haha Jones. And the next day, having completed our more prosaic shopping, we set out for Mr. Haha's business address, a 'sinful' (to quote public opinion) fish-fry and dancing café down by the river. We've been there before, and on the same errand; but in previous years our dealings have been with Haha's wife, an iodine-dark Indian woman with brassy peroxided hair and a dead-tired disposition. Actually, we've never laid eyes on her husband, though we've heard that he's an Indian too. A giant with razor scars across his cheeks. They call him Haha because he's so gloomy, a man who never laughs. As we approach his café (a large log cabin festooned inside and out with chains of garish-gay naked light bulbs and standing by the river's muddy edge under the shade of river trees where moss drifts through the branches like gray mist) our steps slow down. Even Queenie stops prancing and sticks close by. People have been murdered in Haha's café. Cut to pieces. Hit on the head. There's a case coming up in court next month. Naturally these goings-on happen at night when the colored lights cast crazy patterns and the victrola wails. In the daytime Haha's is shabby and deserted. I knock at the door, Queenie barks, my friend calls: 'Mrs. Haha, ma'am? Anyone to home?'

Footsteps. The door opens. Our hearts overturn. It's Mr. Haha Jones himself! And he *is* a giant; he *does* have scars; he *doesn't* smile. No, he glowers at us through Satan-tilted eyes and demands to know: 'What you want with Haha?'

For a moment we are too paralyzed to tell. Presently my friend half-finds her voice, a whispery voice at best: 'If you please, Mr. Haha, we'd like a quart of your finest whiskey.'

His eyes tilt more. Would you believe it? Haha is smiling! Laughing too. 'Which one of you is a drinkin' man?'

'It's for making fruitcakes, Mr. Haha. Cooking.'

This sobers him. He frowns. 'That's no way to waste good whiskey.' Nevertheless, he retreats into the shadowed café and seconds later appears carrying a bottle of daisy-yellow unlabeled liquor. He demonstrates its sparkle in the sunlight and says: 'Two dollars.'

We pay him with nickels and dimes and pennies. Suddenly, as he jangles the coins in his hand like a fistful of dice, his face softens. 'Tell you what,' he proposes, pouring the money back into our bead purse, 'just send me one of them fruitcakes instead.'

'Well,' my friend remarks on our way home, 'there's a lovely man. We'll put an extra cup of raisins in *his* cake.'

The black stove, stoked with coal and firewood, glows like a lighted pumpkin. Eggbeaters whirl, spoons spin round in bowls of butter and sugar, vanilla sweetens the air, ginger spices it; melting, nose-tingling odors saturate the kitchen, suffuse the house, drift out to the world on puffs of chimney smoke. In four days our work is done. Thirty-one cakes, dampened with whiskey, bask on window sills and shelves.

Who are they for?

Friends. Not necessarily neighbor friends: indeed, the larger share is intended for persons we've met maybe once, perhaps not at all. People who've struck our fancy. Like President Roosevelt. Like the Reverend and Mrs. J.C. Lucey, Baptist missionaries to Borneo who lectured here last winter. Or the little knife grinder who comes through town twice a year. Or Abner Packer, the driver of the six o'clock bus from Mobile, who exchanges waves with us every day as he passes in a dust-cloud whoosh. Or the young Wistons, a California couple whose car one afternoon broke down outside the house and who spent a pleasant hour chatting with us on the porch (young Mr. Wiston snapped our picture, the only one we've ever had taken). Is it because my friend is shy with everyone *except* strangers that these strangers, and merest acquaintances, seem to us our truest friends? I think yes. Also, the scrapbooks we keep of thank-you's on White House stationery, time-to-time communications from California and Borneo, the knife grinder's penny post cards, make us feel connected to eventful worlds beyond the kitchen with its view of a sky that stops.

Now a nude December fig branch grates against the window. The kitchen is empty, the cakes are gone; yesterday we carted the last of them to the post office, where the cost of stamps turned our purse inside out. We're broke. That rather depresses me, but my friend insists on celebrating – with two inches of whiskey left in Haha's bottle. Queenie has a spoonful in a bowl of coffee (she likes her coffee chicory-flavored and strong). The rest we divide between a pair of jelly glasses. We're both quite awed at the prospect of drinking straight whiskey; the taste of it brings screwed-up expressions and sour shudders. But by and by we begin to sing, the two of us singing different songs simultaneously. I don't know the words to mine, just: *Come on along, come on along, to the dark-town strutters' ball.* But I can dance: that's what I mean to be, a tap-dancer in the movies. My dancing shadow rollicks on the walls; our voices rock the chinaware; we giggle: as if unseen hands were tickling us. Queenie rolls on her back, her paws plow the air, something like a grin stretches her black lips. Inside myself, I feel warm and sparky as those crumbling logs, carefree as the wind in the chimney. My friend waltzes round the stove, the hem of her poor calico skirt pinched between her fingers as though it were a party dress: *Show me the way to go home,* she sings, her tennis shoes squeaking on the floor. *Show me the way to go home.*

Enter: two relatives. Very angry. Potent with eyes that scold, tongues that scald. Listen to what they have to say, the words tumbling together into a wrathful tune: 'A child of seven! whiskey on his breath! are you out of your mind? feeding a child of seven! must be loony! road to ruination! remember Cousin Kate? Uncle Charlie? Uncle Charlie's brother-in-law? shame! scandal! humiliation! kneel, pray, beg the Lord!'

Queenie sneaks under the stove. My friend gazes at her shoes, her chin quivers, she lifts her skirt and blows her nose and runs to her room. Long after the town has gone to sleep and the house is silent except for the chimings of clocks and the sputter of fading fires, she is weeping into a pillow already as wet as a widow's handkerchief.

'Don't cry,' I say, sitting at the bottom of her bed and shivering despite my flannel nightgown that smells of last winter's cough syrup, 'don't cry,' I beg, teasing her toes, tickling her feet, 'you're too old for that.'

'It's because,' she hiccups, 'I *am* too old. Old and funny.'

'Not funny. Fun. More fun than anybody. Listen. If you don't stop crying you'll be so tired tomorrow we can't go cut a tree.'

She straightens up. Queenie jumps on the bed (where Queenie is not allowed) to lick her cheeks. 'I know where we'll find real pretty trees, Buddy. And holly, too. With berries big as your eyes. It's way off in the woods. Farther than we've ever been. Papa used to bring us Christmas trees from there: carry them on his shoulder. That's fifty years ago. Well, now: I can't wait for morning.'

Morning. Frozen rime lusters the grass; the sun, round as an orange and orange as hot-weather moons, balances on the horizon, burnishes the silvered winter woods. A wild turkey calls. A renegade hog grunts in the undergrowth. Soon, by the edge of knee-deep, rapid-running water, we have to abandon the buggy. Queenie wades the stream first, paddles across barking complaints at the swiftness of the current, the pneumonia-making coldness of it. We follow, holding our shoes and equipment (a hatchet, a burlap sack) above our heads. A mile more: of chastising thorns, burs and briers that catch at our clothes; of rusty pine needles brilliant with gaudy fungus and molten feathers. Here, there, a flash, a flutter, an ecstasy of shrillings reminding us that not all the birds have flown south. Always, the path unwinds through lemony sun pools and pitch-black vine tunnels. Another creek to cross: a disturbed armada of speckled trout froths the water round us, and frogs the size of plates practice belly flops; beaver workmen are building a dam. On the farther shore, Queenie shakes herself and trembles. My friend shivers, too: not with cold but enthusiasm. One of her hat's ragged roses sheds a petal as she lifts her head and inhales the pine-heavy air. 'We're almost there; can you smell it, Buddy?' she says, as though we were approaching an ocean.

And, indeed, it is a kind of ocean. Scented acres of holiday trees, prickly-leafed holly. Red berries shiny as Chinese bells: black crows swoop upon them screaming. Having stuffed our burlap sacks with enough greenery and crimson to garland a dozen windows, we set about choosing a tree. 'It should be,' muses my friend, 'twice as tall as a boy. So a boy can't steal the star.' The one we pick is twice as tall as me. A brave handsome brute that survives thirty hatchet strokes before it keels with a creaking rending cry. Lugging it like a kill, we commence the long trek out. Every few yards we abandon the struggle, sit down and pant. But we have the strength of triumphant huntsmen; that and the tree's virile, icy perfume revive us, goad us on. Many compliments accompany our sunset return along the red clay road to town; but my friend is sly and noncommittal when passers-by praise the treasure perched in our buggy: what a fine tree and where did it come from? 'Yonderways,' she murmurs vaguely. Once a car stops and the rich mill owner's lazy wife leans out and whines: 'Giveya two-bits cash for that ol tree.' Ordinarily my friend is afraid of saying no; but on this occasion she promptly shakes her head: 'We wouldn't take a dollar.' The mill owner's wife persists. 'A dollar, my foot! Fifty cents. That's my last offer. Goodness, woman, you can get another one.' In answer, my friend gently reflects: 'I doubt it. There's never two of anything.'

Home: Queenie slumps by the fire and sleeps till tomorrow, snoring loud as a human.

A trunk in the attic contains: a shoebox of ermine tails (off the opera cape of a curious lady who once rented a room in the house), coils of frazzled tinsel gone gold with age, one silver star, a brief rope of dilapidated, undoubtedly dangerous candy-like light bulbs. Excellent decorations, as far as they go, which isn't far enough: my friend wants our tree to blaze 'like a Baptist window,' droop with weighty snows of ornament. But we can't afford the made-in-Japan splendors at the five-and-dime. So we do what we've always done: sit for days at the kitchen table with scissors and crayons and stacks of colored paper. I make sketches and my friend cuts them out: lots of cats, fish too (because they're easy to draw), some apples, some watermelons, a few winged angels devised from saved-up sheets of Hershey-bar tin foil. We use safety pins to attach these creations to the tree; as a final touch, we sprinkle the branches with shredded cotton (picked in August for this purpose). My friend, surveying the effect, clasps her hands together. 'Now honest, Buddy. Doesn't it look good enough to eat?' Queenie tries to eat an angel.

After weaving and ribboning holly wreaths for all the front windows, our next project is the fashioning of family gifts. Tie-die scarves for the ladies, for the men a home-brewed lemon and licorice and aspirin syrup to be taken 'at the first Symptoms of a Cold and after Hunting.' But when it comes time for making each other's gift, my friend and I separate to work secretly. I would like to buy her a pearl-handled knife, a radio, a whole pound of chocolate-covered cherries (we tasted some once, and she always swears: 'I could live on them, Buddy, Lord yes I could – and that's not taking His name in vain'). Instead, I am building her a kite. She would like to give me a bicycle (she's said so on several million occasions: 'If only I could, Buddy. It's bad enough in life to do without something *you* want; but confound it, what gets my goat is not being able to give somebody something you want *them* to have. Only one of these days I will, Buddy. Locate you a bike. Don't ask how. Steal it, maybe'). Instead, I'm fairly certain that she is building me a kite – the same as last year, and the year before: the year before that we exchanged slingshots. All of which is fine by me. For we are champion kite-fliers who study the wind like sailors; my friend, more accomplished than I, can get a kite aloft when there isn't enough breeze to carry clouds.

Christmas Eve afternoon we scrape together a nickel and go to the butcher's to buy Queenie's traditional gift, a good gnawable beef bone. The bone, wrapped in funny paper, is placed high in the tree near the silver star. Queenie knows it's there. She squats at the foot of the tree staring up in a trance of greed: when bedtime arrives she refuses to budge. Her excitement is equaled by my own. I kick the covers and turn my pillow as though it were a scorching summer's night. Somewhere a rooster crows: falsely, for the sun is still on the other side of the world.

'Buddy, are you awake?' It is my friend, calling from her room which is next to mine; and an instant later she is sitting on my bed holding a candle. 'Well, I can't sleep a hoot,' she declares. 'My mind's jumping like a jack rabbit. Buddy, do you think Mrs. Roosevelt will serve our cake at dinner?' We huddle in the bed, and she squeezes my hand I-love-you. 'Seems like your hand used to be so much smaller. I guess I hate to see you grow up. When you're grown up, will we still be friends?' I say always. 'But I feel so bad, Buddy. I wanted so bad to give you a bike. I tried to sell my cameo Papa gave me, Buddy' – she hesitates, as though embarrassed – 'I made you another kite.' Then I confess that I made her one, too; and we laugh. The candle burns too short to hold. Out it goes, exposing the starlight, the stars spinning at the window like a visible caroling that slowly, slowly daybreak silences. Possibly we doze; but the beginnings of dawn splash us like cold water: we're up, wide-eyed and wandering while we wait for others to waken. Quite deliberately my friend drops a kettle on the kitchen floor. I tap-dance in front of closed doors. One by one the household emerges, looking as though they'd like to kill us both; but it's Christmas, so they can't. First, a gorgeous breakfast: just everything you can imagine – from flapjacks and fried squirrel to hominy grits and honey-in-the-comb. Which puts everyone in a good humor except my friend and me. Frankly, we're so impatient to get at the presents we can't eat a mouthful.

Well, I'm disappointed. Who wouldn't be? With socks, a Sunday school shirt, some handkerchiefs, a hand-me-down sweater and a year's subscription to a religious magazine for children. *The Little Shepherd.* It makes me boil. It really does.

My friend has a better haul. A sack of Satsumas, that's her best present. She is proudest, however, of a white wool shawl knitted by her married sister. But she *says* her favorite gift is the kite I built her. And it *is* very beautiful; though not as beautiful as the one she made me, which is blue and scattered with gold and green Good Conduct stars; moreover, my name is painted on it, 'Buddy.'

'Buddy, the wind is blowing.'

The wind is blowing, and nothing will do till we've run to a pasture below the house where Queenie has scooted to bury her bone (and where, a winter hence, Queenie will be buried, too). There, plunging through the healthy waist-high grass, we unreel our kites, feel them twitching at the string like sky fish as they swim into the wind. Satisfied, sun-warmed, we sprawl in the grass and peel Satsumas and watch our kites cavort. Soon I forget the socks and hand-me-down sweater. I'm as happy as if we'd already won the fifty-thousand-dollar Grand Prize in that coffee-naming contest.

'My, how foolish I am!' my friend cries, suddenly alert, like a woman remembering too late she has biscuits in the oven. 'You know what I've always thought?' she asks in a tone of discovery, and not smiling at me but a point beyond. 'I've always thought a body would have to be sick and dying before they saw the Lord. And I imagined that when He came it would be like looking at the Baptist window: pretty as colored glass with the sun pouring through, such a shine you don't know it's getting dark. And it's been a comfort: to think of that shine taking away all the spooky feeling. But I'll wager it never happens. I'll wager at the very end a body realizes the Lord has already shown Himself. That things as they are' – her hand circles in a gesture that gathers clouds and kites and grass and Queenie pawing earth over her bone – 'just what they've always seen, was seeing Him. As for me, I could leave the world with today in my eyes.'

This is our last Christmas together.

Life separates us. Those who Know Best decide that I belong in a military school. And so follows a miserable succession of bugle-blowing prisons, grim reveille-ridden summer camps. I have a new home too. But it doesn't count. Home is where my friend is, and there I never go.

And there she remains, puttering around the kitchen. Alone with Queenie. Then alone. ('Buddy dear,' she writes in her wild hard-to-read script, 'yesterday Jim Macy's horse kicked Queenie bad. Be thankful she didn't feel much. I wrapped her in a Fine Linen sheet and rode her in the buggy down to Simpson's pasture where she can be with all her Bones...'). For a few Novembers she continues to bake her fruitcakes single-handed; not as many, but some: and, of course, she always sends me 'the best of the batch.' Also, in every letter she encloses a dime wadded in toilet paper: 'See a picture show and write me the story.' But gradually in her letters she tends to confuse me with her other friend, the Buddy who died in the 1880s; more and more thirteenths are not the only days she stays in bed: a morning arrives in November, a leafless, birdless coming of winter morning, when she cannot rouse herself to exclaim: 'Oh my, it's fruitcake weather!'

And when that happens, I know it. A message saying so merely confirms a piece of news some secret vein had already received, severing from me an irreplaceable part of myself, letting it loose like a kite on a broken string. That is why, walking across a school campus on this particular December morning, I keep searching the sky. As if I expected to see, rather like hearts, a lost pair of kites hurrying toward heaven.

A Carol

What sweeter music can we bring
Than a carol for to sing
The birth of this our heav'nly King
Awake the voice! Awake the string:
Dark and dull night fly hence away,
And give the honour of this day,
That sees December turned to May:

If we may ask the reason, say
The why and wherefore all things here
Seem like the Springtime of the year?
Why does the chilling Winter's morn,
Smile like a field beset with corn?
We see Him come and know Him ours,
Who with His sunshine and His showers
Turns all the patient ground to flowers.

The Darling of the world is come,
And fit it is we find a room
To welcome Him. The nobler part
Of all the house here is the heart,
Which we will give him and bequeath
This holly and this ivy wreath,
To do Him honour who's our King
And Lord of all this revelling.

ROBERT HERRICK

SYMBOLS OF ANCIENT YULE

Straw plays a significant and ancient part in the Christmas celebrations of northern and central Europe, both as an ancient appeal to the spirits for a good harvest and as a reminder of the Bethlehem stable. Hay and straw are symbols of the fertility of the earth, while the manger and the Nativity are heavenly reminders of fertility.

Yule straw, preferably from the last sheaf of the harvest, which was believed to contain the corn spirit, was spread over floors, scattered on to fields and bound round trees to encourage fruitfulness. It was also believed to cure sick cattle. Grain from the same last sheaf was used in Sweden and Denmark to bake the Yule Boar, a loaf in the shape of a boar, which stood on the table throughout the Christmas season and was held to be yet another embodiment of the corn spirit. Four sheafs, one each of rye, oats, wheat and barley were placed in the corners of Polish homes. Poles, Lithuanians and Serbs spread hay under the best white tablecloth at the Christmas feast to commemorate Christ's birth. In the old days a whole sheaf was used, but now only a few blades suffice. Norwegian farmers used to hang straw crosses above doors as protection against evil spirits and today many Scandinavian families still hang out sheafs of oats for the birds, probably a relic of an ancient sacrifice to the agricultural gods.

Norwegians used to sleep on Yule straw so that the ghosts of the dead that threatened at that time of year could occupy their beds; dreams dreamt on the Yule straw were believed to come true. A grain found by someone's seat at the Christmas table presaged death in the coming year and grains from the Christmas straw also indicated the nature of the coming harvest.

To further encourage a good harvest it was usual in many areas to sprinkle corn and wine on the Yule log when it was first lit. In the Slavic areas of Eastern Europe the Polaznik – a sort of First Footer – would visit the house at dawn on Christmas Eve carrying a handful of wheat which he threw over the members of the household before wishing them a Merry Christmas. He stayed on to enjoy a pre-Christmas feast with the family, accepted their gift and left in the evening. His visit was an omen of prosperity for the year to come. In Poland on St Stephen's Day peasants used to throw grain at each other to bring a good harvest.

Straw and corn figure prominently in seasonal decorations. In Sweden the 'julbock', a straw goat, spends the Christmas season on the table, or next to the tree. Its origins are obscure. The devil is commonly represented as a goat, but the 'julbock' is probably connected with the kindlier figure of the god Thor, a friend of mankind, who was said to ride on a goat. In Scandinavia straw stars, crosses, and figures, probably derived from ancient fertility symbols, decorate every home, and straw mobiles hanging from the ceilings turn gently in the warmth from the candles.

Candles are inseparable from any midwinter festival. When there is scarcely any natural light or warmth from the sun, fires and candles become both a physical necessity and a symbol of the spring to come. Druids and Norsemen lit fires to drive away evil spirits and to welcome the rebirth of the sun. At Saturnalia Romans gave each other small candles as charms or tokens. Jews celebrate Hanukkah, the Feast of Lights, at the end of December, by lighting candles each evening to commemorate the re-dedication of the temple and to assert that the light of faith is bound to grow. Similarly, the Christian Church uses candles to represent Christ, the Light of the World.

In England a great candle often used to take the place of, or supplement, the Yule log. It had to burn throughout Christmas Day or bad luck would plague the family in the coming year. In Ireland, the Christmas Candle, large, usually red and decorated with sprigs of holly, is lit on Christmas Eve, put safely in a scooped-out tur-

'Yuletide in Norway'. Following ancient tradition a sheaf of corn is offered to the birds.

nip or vessel filled with bran and set in the main window to guide the Holy Family to shelter. Sometimes smaller candles are also lit in other windows. It has been claimed that this practice grew up in the years of religious persecution and was a sign of safe houses for fugitive priests.

Yule candles are very popular in Scandinavia and various superstitions used to be attached to them. In one region of Denmark two great candles stood for the husband and wife, and whichever burnt down first indicated which of the couple would die soonest. Throughout Scandinavia candles lit on Christmas Eve had to burn through the night; if one went out, death was presaged. Sometimes the Yule candle had to be extinguished by a particular member of the family – the oldest, perhaps, or the father. Various practices were also connected with the candle stubs. They might be used to brand a cross on the farm animals, to smear on the plough in the winter, or be fed to the hens. In Denmark the stubs were preserved and, like the Yule log elsewhere, burnt during storms to protect the house against lightning.

Today in Scandinavia and Germany real candles still burn on the Christmas tree, reproducing, according to legend, the starlit sky Martin Luther saw on Christmas Eve.

Candles and lanterns illuminate the whole of the festive period. In Sweden candles crown the daughter of the house on St Lucia Day, 13 December. On the first Sunday in Advent the first of four red candles is lit on the Advent wreath and the first of twenty-four sections on the Advent candle is burnt on 1 December. Waits used to sing carols by the soft light of lanterns. Star singers carry candlelit stars in memory of the star over Bethlehem. Today in every Filipino home hangs a huge star lantern, looking like a gigantic lighted flower, and to mark the end of the festive season, in Denmark on Twelfth Night they light three candles as a token substitute for the Christmas tree. At Candlemas, the feast of the Presentation of Christ in the Temple, on 2 February, candles are blessed in church for use in the coming year.

Lighting candles on the graves of ancestors is a fairly recent Scandinavian custom which may derive from the Viking belief that at the winter solstice the dead return to haunt the living. Candles begin and end the festive season and light up Christmas with their warm glow. They are particularly popular in dark northern Europe, but they have a part to play, religious or secular, symbolic or practical, everywhere.

Weaving with Straw

Working in straw is not easy. It takes a lot of practice to achieve satisfactory results. It is possible to make fairly simple but effective Christmas decorations if you give yourself time and prepare your materials well. In Scandinavian countries supplies of straw are available where you purchase your Christmas tree but elsewhere good craft shops or florists are the best sources. If you have been able to glean long stalks of wheat or barley from the fields after harvesting, peel off the rough outer casing to leave a smooth stalk and hang the straw head down until it is required. Usually the heads are cut off before weaving can begin and this is done by cutting as close to the head as possible with a sharp craft knife. Soak the straw for at least half an hour in warm water, or leave it soaking over night. Dry straw is very brittle and damping it thoroughly makes it more supple and manageable. Wrap the straw in a damp towel while you are working, using a little at a time. Any straw left over can be rehung to dry. Use raffia, fine thread or string to secure the decorations, dampened so that it tightens with the drying decoration. Join straws by slipping the narrow end of one into the wider end of the next and continue working.

MAKING MOBILES

To make a diamond shape frame use eight bundles of ten straws measuring 36 cms without their heads. Tie each

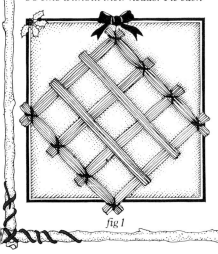

fig 1

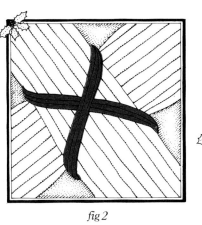

fig 2

bundle about 2 cms in from either end. Arrange four of the bunches to form a square, overlapping the corners, and bind strongly with thread in a figure of eight (fig 2). Place the remaining four bunches within this frame, laying two in each direction so that nine equal small squares are formed. Bind securely in a figure of eight at each intersection. Attach string to one corner of the frame so that it hangs as a diamond shape (fig 1). Use any small straw shapes to fill the mobile, or several different ones. Suspend each decoration by a thread from the top of one of the small diamonds so it moves freely.

The triangle frame is made with just three bunches of ten straws each, again approximately 36 cms without heads, and tied at either end. Arrange bunches to form a triangle and bind intersections in a figure of eight. To hang the decoration horizontally suspend the mobile by thread from each corner, gathering the threads to a central point at the length you require, making sure the mobile hangs evenly. Hang the decorations from each corner of the triangle and suspend one from the centre point of the hanging threads so that it comes down through the centre of the decoration. To hang the triangular mobile vertically simply suspend by a strong thread from the apex of the triangle and attaching decorations to the corner.

The following small straw shapes are all suitable for mobiles.

THE STAR

Use 24 12-cm straws and tie the bundle very tightly in the middle (fig 3). Spread out the straws and weave round going under one straw and over the next. Repeat going over the ones you went under last time and vice

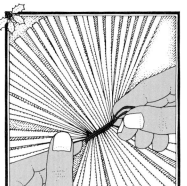

fig 3

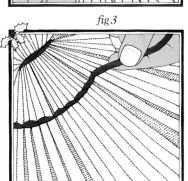

fig 4

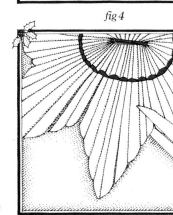

fig 5

versa until the straws are secured (fig 4) as evenly as possible. Allow to dry and trim the straws in six groups of eight until they form a six point star (fig 5).

ANGELS

To make figure approximately 18 cms high, cut 30 straws of 22 cms for the body and 20 straws of 18 cms for the wings. Tie the body bundle tightly 4 cms from one end, gently turn the bundle until it bends inside out and tie again at 4 cms to form the head (fig 6).

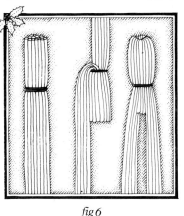

fig 6

Tie the wing bundle firmly in the centre and spread out the straws. Weave either side of the tie going under and over, then over and under as before, until the straws spread evenly (fig 7). Divide the body straws in half and slot wings through, tying body underneath to hold wings firmly

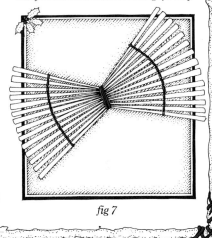

fig 7

YULETIDE STRAW

Straw decorations are a symbolic reminder of ancient tributes made to the agricultural spirits at Yule to promote the good harvest vital in rural areas. Straw plays an important part in the decorations of most Scandinavian homes at Christmas and the practice is spreading rapidly through other parts of Europe and America. Most people will content themselves with buying from the enormous selection of imported straw decorations available in the shops at Christmas but those who really enjoy making decorations for themselves may like to try their hand at this comparatively unusual, though traditional, craft.

1 Straw angels can be made large enough to grace the top of the Christmas tree, or small and light to suspend from a mobile.

2 Small traditional braided twist with the corn ears as a decorative feature.

3 The julbock or Yule goat, most popular of all straw decorations. Usually made to stand on the Christmas table or under the tree, but can be scaled down to tree decoration size.

4 Barley wreath woven in a heart shape, surprisingly simple to make and an attractive wall decoration.

5 Diamond frame mobile to hang with stars or any of the shapes shown.

6 Triangular mobile frame to hang vertically or horizontally, simplest of all shapes to make.

6, 7, 8 & 9 are all straw shapes used to decorate mobiles or to hang on the Christmas tree. These can be made in a simple three strand plait, or you can work up to a complicated five strand braid with patience and practice. Suspend them on fine thread or raffia so that they move gently in the currents of air and decorate with red ribbon bows or card cut-outs. If you find working in straw too complicated these can also be made from the woven bands of straw or raffia obtained by unpicking your discarded summer holiday hat.

4

5

6

7

8

9

35

Weaving with Straw

continued

in place. Spread out skirt straws, attach a thread to the neck tie. Smaller angels can be made for mobile or tree.

PLAITING WITH STRAW

Several attractive decorations are based on plaiting, but this is more difficult than ordinary plaiting as straw is less flexible. Tie the straws before you start and plait by bending and folding at right angles. Practice first with just three straws to make fine plaits suitable for hanging decorations, then increase to six, working two straws at a time, or nine, using groups of three until you achieve an even, flat braid (fig 8). Dry pressed

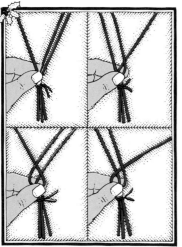

fig 8

between sheets of blotting paper under a heavy book in a warm place. Two 24 cm plaits tied or stapled in a circle (fig 9) with a red heart suspended in the centre make an attractive decoration. Two 18 cm plaits tied or stapled as shown in fig 10 form a heart shape. Use eight 10 cm plaits for a star. Make two small cuts in each about 2½ cms in from ends, securing straws immediately with a dab of glue. Tie or staple ends of four plaits together (fig 11) and repeat with a second set of four. Lay one set across the other so that slots correspond and press together. Secure with glue at the point where the plaits intersect.

fig 9

fig 10

fig 11

CORN EAR TWIST

Make a nine straw plait leaving the head on one straw in each group of three. Don't flatten plait but loop once, or twice, and tie ends with a ribbon bow leaving the three heads of wheat hanging as a feature of the decoration.

THE GOAT

This is the most popular of all straw decorations in Scandinavian homes

at Christmas. Goats can be made quite large to stand on the table or under the Christmas tree or small enough to suspend on a mobile. The method for making them is the same, only the length and amount of straw will vary. Take a nice fat bundle of straw and tie round twice to form three equal parts (fig 12). Divide the

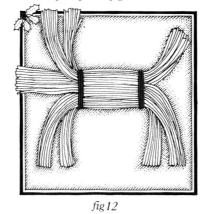

fig 12

back section into three, plaiting the top and trimming to form the tail. The lower two-thirds are tied top and bottom or braided to form legs. The front section is divided into three horizontal parts. The top section is divided into two to form two backward curving plaited horns, the centre is bent, trimmed and tied to form the head and the lower section is divided into two to form front legs. These may need supporting with a little wire or additional straw. Tie goat round gently at any point that appears to need support and trim neatly.

CORN WREATHS

To make a wreath approximately 20

cms in diameter as illustrated on page 67 you will require at least 170 ears of wheat with stalks left as long as possible and a 75 cm length of wire to hold the shape. Start with three heads of wheat in the left hand, holding the wire among the stalks. Working from left to right place three heads of wheat on top and at right angles to the first (fig 13). Bend the stalks of these three underneath the original three, up to the left of the heads and over the base to follow the line of the original stalks and hold securely (fig 14). Continue adding the ears of wheat three at a time (fig 15), spaced about 1½ cms apart until you have a length of approximately 70 cms. Overlap the two ends and bind with raffia. Dry the wreath in a perfect circle by leaving on a suitably round bowl, vase or ball. To make the heart-shaped wreath use barley and make two strips approximately 60 cms each. Tie top and bottom with raffia, bending wire to form the correct curves, and leave to dry flat. Corn wreaths can be made to smaller dimensions.

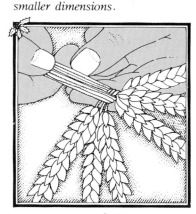

fig 14

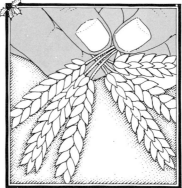

fig 13

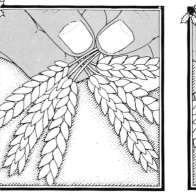

fig 15

Making Candles

Now that candlemaking has become one of the most popular of all home crafts it is usually easy to find the correct materials in any good craft shop. There are also specialist candlemaking suppliers from whom dyes, perfumes, wick tabs, special silicone spray to release the candle from the mould, and unusual moulds can be obtained. However, candlemaking can be done with a minimum of equipment. You will need some paraffin wax, either in powder or granule form, a small packet of stearin, colouring and a card of wick. You will also need a double saucepan for melting the wax, a funnel to fill small moulds, a sharp knife, a fine skewer and newspaper to cover your working surface.

You can buy moulds or gather together suitable household containers which will also do the job. Anything in glass or metal such as jelly moulds, bun or cake tins, or fancy pastry cutters can be used. There are also any number of disposable items which will make interesting candle moulds, such as unusually shaped empty bottles or jars, cardboard cups, tins, ice trays or even eggs. To break a disposable glass mould when the candle is set put it into a strong paper bag and tap lightly with a hammer.

Melt the wax, adding approximately 3 tablespoons of stearin to ½kg of paraffin wax. The stearin makes the wax more opaque so that white candles are whiter and colour appears deeper. You will need to use slightly less stearin for coloured candles. Add colour until you get the shade you require. Test by dropping a small amount of melted wax onto a white saucer or into water. The colour will be a little lighter than the finished candle. Heat wax slowly in a double saucepan, taking adequate safety precautions. Wax gets very hot and if spilled will ignite. If the wax ignites in the saucepan turn off the heat and put on a saucepan lid to suffocate the flames. If the wax spills onto the stove and catches fire again turn off the heat and throw on handfuls of baking soda. Never throw water on burning wax. If you should spill hot wax on your hand or arm put it immediately under cold water, peel off the wax and treat the burn underneath in the usual way. Never leave wax unattended.

While the wax is on the stove prepare the moulds by coating with silicone spray or wipe round with a little vegetable oil and fix the wick in place. You can use special wick tabs to do this or simply twist the wick into a small coil and set it on the bottom of the container with a blob of melted wax. Leave enough wick at the top to wind around a pencil or skewer across the top of the mould to prevent the wick from falling back into the container (fig 1). Centre the wick so that the candle burns correctly. This can also be done by threading it through a strip of adhesive tape across the top of the mould (fig 2). Another

fig 1

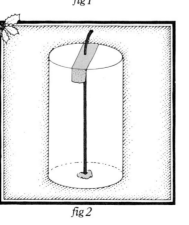

fig 2

method of inserting a wick is to add it to the finished candle. Push a fine, heated skewer through the candle and immediately insert a pre-waxed wire core wick. The pre-waxing is done by dipping the wick into melted wax and holding taut until cooled. Fill any small hole which remains around the wick by adding a little melted wax.

When the wax in the double saucepan has melted pour it carefully into the centre of the mould using a funnel if necessary. As the candle cools a scum of little bubbles or a dip may appear around the wick. Scrape away debris with a knife and top up with more melted wax. The cooling period will vary depending on the size of candle or type of mould. When the candle is thoroughly cooled remove from the mould and trim away any imperfections with a sharp knife. Give the candle a sheen by holding the free end of the wick and dipping the candle quickly into boiling water or melted wax, this time without the addition of stearin so that the candle has a translucent glaze. Trim the wick to approximately 1 cm.

SNOWBALLS, APPLES AND PUDDINGS

These candles can all be made from a basic ball-shaped mould. It might be worth investing in a proper mould from a candlemakers' supplier for these, but for one or two you could probably find a suitable mould around the house. You could use a discarded glass Christmas bauble, cracking it open to remove the candle when set; or make the ball in two halves using a small round bottomed cup or bowl. Fix the two halves together with hot melted wax when set and pare away join with a sharp knife. Add a wire core wick and dip the ball into a bath of hot wax to cover the join completely. To make the apple candle, pare down a dip around the wick with a sharp knife before putting it into the wax bath. To make the Christmas pudding candle the ball will need to be made in brown wax. When the ball is formed insert a wire

fig 3

core wick and whip up some more of the brown wax with a fork in a saucepan until it is light and fluffy. Mould this around the candle ball until a nicely textured pudding is formed (fig 3). Burn an ordinary white candle so that it drips over the top of the pudding to form cream and add a couple of fake holly leaves. Snowballs are formed in the same way by whipping up white wax with stearin and pressing the light fluffy mixture around the ball. For the snowman two of these balls are fixed together with hot melted wax, using a smaller size for the head. A wire core wick is then inserted through the two balls. Details such as eyes, mouth, pipe and buttons are moulded by hand in warm wax. The hat is made with a hollow inside to cover the wick.

FLOATING CANDLES

Keep the candles small and light, using little bun tins or fancy pastry cutters for moulds. The wick should not go right through a floating candle so insert a wire core wick while the candle is setting by holding it centred in the soft wax until it is cool enough to be secure. If you are using pastry cutter moulds stop the wax leaking out at the bottom by pressing moulds into self-hardening modelling clay wiped with oil.

When you have finished your candles leave them for at least twenty-four hours to harden completely.

CANDLE-LIGHT

Christmas is the one time of year when almost everyone buys, makes or is given candles. They provide soft, intimate lighting on a festive table, trim special evergreen wreaths or are used by themselves as amusing decorations. Most people buy their Christmas candles, and this can be expensive for anything out of the ordinary. Candlemaking is an increasingly popular home craft and many people are finding that they can make very satisfactory Christmas candles in their own kitchens.

1 A cakestand filled with simple white household candles, or soft cream coloured candles makes a glowing centrepiece for a Christmas table. The more widths and lengths of candles you use the better.

2 Floating candles in a bowl or tray of water are unusual and safer than other types of candles. Small and light, they are easy to make.

3 Star-shaped candles made with fancy pastry cutters, can also be used as floaters but look pretty arranged in clusters on the table.

4 Christmas tree candles are more difficult for the beginner and require proper moulds from candlemaker's suppliers. Practise first with simple shapes before attempting this design.

5 The Christmas pudding candle is formed by moulding whisked wax around a simple ball candle and dripping white wax on top for cream. The holly is wired on for decoration but should be removed before lighting, unless the leaves themselves are modelled in softened candle wax.

6 Snowballs are also made by moulding fluffy, whisked wax around a simple ball. The snowman is made with two snowballs and trimmed with moulded softened wax.

7 Apples can be made from specially designed moulds, or by paring down the top of a ball candle to give the apple shape before dipping the candle into its final glossy red wax finish.

1

2

3

4

5

6

7

Making Paper Decorations

Everyone likes to join in making decorations, the most talented and the most fumble fingered can all contribute their best efforts. In Poland homemade decorations take the form of intricately cut out paper shapes and complicated, light as air, mobiles of straw, paper and feathers. In Denmark they go so far as to have a special 'cut and stick' day when friends, adults and children, get together with supplies of paper, glue, scissors and paint and join forces to make their Christmas decorations, each one contributing according to their experience or expertise.

Usually the first decoration English children learn to make is the humble paper chain, often from rather dreary ready-cut and gummed packs. Using the same simple principle of looping and sticking you can achieve much prettier colour schemes by buying your own selection of coloured paper and cutting it into strips approximately 4 by 24 cm and securing the loops with a dab of glue. More decorative paper chains can be made by cutting the strips from crêpe paper and either fringing the edges before looping, painting on a pattern in glue and sprinkling with glitter, or frilling the edges of the crêpe by gently stretching the edges between thumbs and forefingers for a fluted effect.

Card, or stiff paper cut-out shapes strung on thread are another very easy decoration to make. Cut a card pattern of a star, heart, tree, snowflake, Santa Claus or angel and using this cut a pile of similar shapes. If you wish to suspend these horizontally from a thread cut the pattern with a small tab which can be folded and glued over the thread. If you prefer to hang the shapes vertically glue them together in pairs with the thread passing straight down through the centre between them. You could also thread the shapes on cotton with a darning needle and suspend them from a mobile.

Garlands look very complicated to make but are well within the ability of most people. First draw out a pattern in strong card. Four examples of suit-

fig 1

fig 2

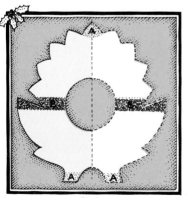

fig 3

able shapes are shown. The heart and flower garlands (figs 1 & 2) are best cut first on folded newspaper and opened out for a perfect pattern which can be transferred flat onto card. The leaf and snowflake patterns can be cut as half shapes directly onto

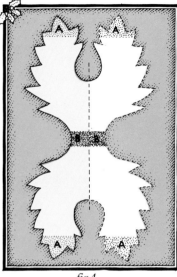

fig 4

card since they will need to be cut on folded tissue to make the more complicated cut-out shapes easier to achieve (figs 3 & 4). With the first two shapes cut a pile of tissues, hearts or flowers to the pattern. The half shapes must be cut from folded tissues with the indicated edge of the pattern lying along the fold. These half shapes are then opened out and pressed flat before assembling to make the garlands. The technique for making garlands is similar whatever the basic shape. First glue the shapes together in pairs at the points marked A. When these are dry glue together the pairs at the points marked B. Use a stick glue or one which will not soak through more than one layer of paper. To hang the decorations cut card shapes and glue at each end of the garlands, cutting out a small tab to be threaded with twine or fine string.

An eye-catching decoration for the centre or the corners of the room is a giant bunch of holly. Cut outsized holly leaves in glossy surfaced stiff dark green paper. Pair the leaves together and glue securely sandwiching a length of green gardening wire between the two to form a central rib. Taking two leaves at a time twist the ends of the wires together adding small

shiny red baubles as holly berries. When you have a pile of wired and berried holly leaves tie all the ends together in a big bunch with an enormous red ribbon bow and let the ends hang down through the leaves.

If you are energetic enough to tackle a whole ceiling, perhaps in a dark hallway or a small child's room, you could cut out a pile of fluffy white cloud shapes, gilded card stars and snowflakes and hang them on different lengths of thread from the ceiling with small tabs of adhesive tape.

The following group of decorations can all be used to decorate the Christmas tree or to hang from mobiles.

The method for making the cut-out heart and three dimensional Christmas tree is similar but both take a very steady hand. Cut out a basic heart or tree shape in stiff card. Draw the outline again twice inside the shape with 1 cm space between (fig 6). Cut round each of these with a sharp craft knife. For the cut-out heart shape

fig 5

remove the centre outline leaving outer and inner shapes (fig 5). Glue strong fine thread down the centre of each decoration leaving enough spare thread to attach other decorations for a mobile, or to form a loop to hang the decoration on the tree. When the glue is dry the central heart will move gently in its frame. To finish the tree, carefully push the three shapes out and round until they form the three dimensional shape (fig 6).

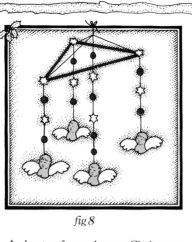

fig 6

A starry snowflake can be made from four cocktail sticks broken in half or eight matching short lengths of straw. Using self-adhesive white or gold star shapes, arrange eight ends to centre on the sticky surface of one star, adding a little more glue if necessary. Cover ends with another star. Sandwich the eight points between pairs of stars and add a loop of cotton to hang the decoration by (fig 7).

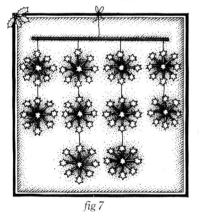

fig 7

Simple glitter stars can be made by cutting out different sized stars in card and coating them either side with glue. Press each side firmly on a paper generously sprinkled with glitter and then press the star between two sheets of paper and shake off surplus to use next time. Thread a strong cotton loop through the tip of the star with a darning needle.

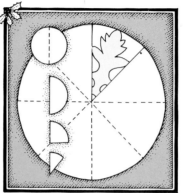

fig 8

A host of angels or Christmas cherubs can be made very simply by cutting photographs of babies out of magazines. In gold card cut two backing shapes for each photograph adding pairs of wings. Glue the two winged shapes together and stick the photograph into position. If you are using these shapes to make a mobile it may take time and patience to balance the mobile correctly as each cut-out will vary slightly in weight depending on the size of the original picture (fig 8).

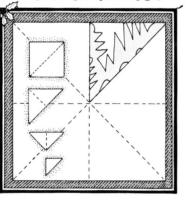

fig 9

Fine tissue paper snowflakes can be used to make delicate mobiles, to decorate Christmas cards or to make a snowstorm on the window. Snowflakes can have a square or circular form following the folding shown in the diagrams. Make a card pattern as shown (figs 9 & 10) and cut out of the folded tissue. With a little practice you will be able to cut several snowflakes at once.

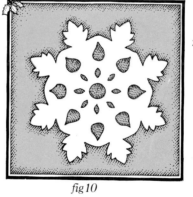

fig 10

Mobiles can be made in any number of shapes and combinations from very simple to highly complicated depending on your expertise and also your patience in achieving the correct balance. There are three very simple, basic shapes. The first is a straight bar of strong wire or a fine wooden rod from which the decorations hang (fig 7). The second is a circle of stiff card stapled or glued securely and suspended on threads attached at four equidistant points. Hang decorations at differing lengths around the frame and also from the centre point. The third mobile is a triangle formed in strong wire or fine wooden rods. The

wire is twisted or hooked together at each corner and the wooden rods secured with glue. Self-adhesive star shapes form strengthening backing on either side of the joints and strong thread is attached at each corner both to hang the decorations on and to suspend the mobile from. A string of the chosen shapes can again be hung from the central point to give the mobile added interest (fig 8).

The traditional Danish red and white woven paper hearts are easy to make with practice and can also be used to make attractive mobiles or to hang on the Christmas tree. Fold two pieces of paper in half as shown in fig 11, one red and one white. Draw a semi-circle at the open ends as shown, and cut away. Cut up to point where paper curves, once, twice, or more depending on how complicated you wish the weaving of the hearts to be. Weave the hearts together in a lattice pattern tucking the edge strips into each other to secure, as shown in fig 11. It may take some experimentation to get the pattern right both sides, but once you have mastered the technique you can

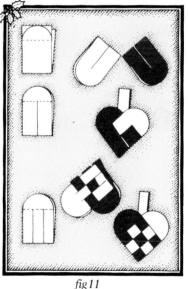

fig 11

make the hearts quickly and easily. Move on to more complicated lattice as you get more skilful but remember it is always more satisfactory to have nicely made simple decorations than elaborate designs which haven't quite worked. Thread gold cord through the top of the heart or glue on a tab loop.

PAPER DECORATIONS

An essential part of Christmas for families all over the world is home decoration. Paper garlands, chains, fringes and friezes festoon ceilings and walls and elaborate mobiles twist and turn in the warm currents of air.

1 Christmas red, *heart-shaped garland to loop around the room.*

2 An open, leafy design makes an original garland, quite complicated to cut but the result more than justifies the effort.

3 Garland with a stylized snowflake motif. Make it in soft coloured tissue, or emphasize the snowflake pattern with pure white.

4 and 5 Brilliant circus coloured garlands based on simple flower shape. The character changes completely if *cut in pastel tissue or if one colour only is used.*

6 Fragile, twisting, *heart-shaped cut-outs to hang on the Christmas tree or use to decorate a mobile.*

7 Star flakes made with fine toothpicks, centred and tipped with paired adhesive stars.

8 Three dimensional Christmas tree cut-out. Make one in stiff card, large enough for the centre of the room or cut several in smaller sizes to hang on a mobile.

9 Snowflakes to cut out in icy tissue to decorate the windows or in card to suspend from tree, mobile or ceiling.

10 Make your own choir of Christmas angels from magazine cut-outs, or colour prints of your own child, to decorate the nursery. Glue the faces to pairs of golden wings.

11 Spangled stars of card, covered in glue and dipped in glitter frost. Make dozens in different sizes as the sole decoration for your Christmas tree or hang them from a mobile.

12 Friezes of one or a multitude of shapes can be cut from coloured card. A small tab secures them to a thread to loop around the room, wind through a Christmas tree or edge the Christmas table cloth.

NEW YORK   LONDON   PARIS

ST NICHOLAS
& SANTA CLAUS

N ALMOST every country in the world, some time between 5 December and 6 January, a red-robed and white-bearded figure is to be found distributing gifts from a bottomless sack. His merry twinkle and his booming ho-ho-ho are as familiar in Times Square, New York, as in Sydney, Australia. His names are legion, his mode of transport often eccentric, his ancestry baffling. He is the latest manifestation of an age-old tradition. The turn of the year has always been a time for exchanging gifts. Romans gave each other small tokens at Saturnalia and Kalends. Woden, or Odin, was credited with scattering gifts down upon the sleeping children of the frozen north. Norsemen left out food and drink for the wild hordes of dead souls who used to sweep across the land at the winter solstice. Benevolent gnomes of the underworld used to reward good children in midwinter.

The gift-giving custom was far too popular and entrenched to be eradicated by the early Church, which sensibly decreed that gifts should be given in honour of the Infant Jesus. Different countries adopted their own gift-bringers. Spanish children received their presents at Epiphany from the Three Kings. In Italy Befana, a kind old witch on a broomstick, and in Russia a grandmotherly figure called Babouschka undertook the duty. In parts of Germany an angelic messenger from Jesus left presents. This was Christkind, who, exported to America, became Kriss Kringle. In Scandinavia the duty fell to assorted gnomes, or nisser, who were stripped of their sinister and evil aspects and imbued with the

Christmas spirit. But by far the most dominant and widespread of these beneficent people is, of course, Santa Claus.

Santa Claus's ancestry goes back on the one hand to the Norse Yule gods, on the other to St Nicholas, a fourth-century bishop of Myra about whom little is known but many stories are told. Over the years this distinguished prelate took under his wing a wide range of citizens, countries and cities, but his association with Christmas stems from his patronage of children and unmarried girls. He was given charge of children following his miraculous restoration to life of

Thomas Nast's first published Santa Claus illustration, from Christmas Poems, *1863-64.*

three boys slaughtered by a village innkeeper and preserved in a barrel of brine. St Nicholas said a prayer over the tub and then converted the innkeeper to be on the safe side. His protection of unmarried girls followed an incident where he secretly provided dowries for the three daughters of an impoverished nobleman. One of the bags of gold which he supposedly threw through the window came to rest in a stocking hung up to dry, though another version has it that he dropped the gold down the chimney and it landed in a stocking, or shoe. Either way, several Christmas traditions were born.

St Nicholas was allotted 6 December for his day – probably to coincide with one of the start-of-winter festivals. The custom developed that on St Nicholas Eve a figure dressed in full episcopal garb of red and white vestments, gold embroidered cope, mitre and staff visited small children and inquired about their behaviour. Good children were rewarded, bad ones threatened with punishment. In some districts, St Nicholas was accompanied by a terrible shaggy monster known variously as Klaubauf, Krampus (or Grampus) or Bartel, whose job it was to carry out the punishment. Sometimes St Nicholas was supported by his better self, represented by an angel, St Peter or a skin-clad figure called Knecht Ruprecht. A composite figure with some of the characteristics of St Nicholas and Klaubauf might appear instead. As Pelznickel or Fur Nicholas he travelled to America with settlers of German origin.

The St Nicholas tradition is still very much alive in Holland. In mid-November St Nicholas, clothed as a bishop, arrives by boat from Spain (perhaps a relic of the Spanish occupation of the

GIFT BRINGERS

Father Christmas in his many guises is the most popular of all gift-bringers, but St Nicholas and various angels, gnomes and old ladies still delight children in many countries.

Old Christmas wreathed in holly.

1 The Christkind angel brings gifts from the Christ Child in Germany.

2 According to legend the Magi asked directions from an old lady. Busy with housework she promised to follow later. Now, like a witch on a broomstick, the Italian Befana seeks the Infant Jesus, bringing presents to good children.

3 Scandinavian nisser are gnomes who are given porridge at Christmas.

4 The kindly Russian Baboushka derives from the same legend as Befana.

5 St Nicholas, riding a white horse, brings gifts to Dutch children.

6 The modern Father Christmas, based on the prototype Santa Claus drawn by Thomas Nast in the 1870s.

7 The Finnish Father Christmas lives at Korvantunturi. He receives letters from children everywhere.

8 The old Father Christmas wore a long, fur-trimmed coat and hood.

1

2

3

4

5

6

7

8

Netherlands, as he is actually buried in Bari, Italy). He is mounted on a white horse and accompanied by his Moorish servant Zwarte Piet, Black Pete. They visit hospitals and shops and take part in parades until St Nicholas Eve, when hopeful children put hay- or carrot-filled shoes by the fireplace in anticipation of a visit from the couple. In the morning the shoes are filled with sweets and small presents, though there is always the danger that a naughty child will find instead a rod. The rumour that St Nicholas rides across the roofs to pay his visits may derive from the story of the gift-bringing Norse goddess Freya, who drove through the air in a chariot drawn by cats.

Sint Nicolaas, colloquially Sinterklaas, travelled to America with the first Dutch settlers—the earliest church built in New York City, then New Amsterdam, was dedicated to him. When the English gained control of the city in the seventeenth century they adopted Sinterklaas and he became anglicized into Santa Claus.

After the Reformation most Protestant countries rejected St Nicholas as too Popish. Protestant Germany deliberately substituted as gift-bringer the Christkind or Christ Child, a sort of angel messenger or representative of the Infant Jesus, sometimes a boy, sometimes a white-clothed girl, sometimes only existing in the abstract. In some areas the Christkind was accompanied, like St Nicholas, by a hideous punisher of evil. The Christkind visited on Christmas Eve.

The Germans and German-speaking Swiss took the Christ Child with them to America in the eighteenth century. Their version was a boy who arrived laden with presents and mounted on a grey or white mule; the children left out straw for the mule and nuts and cookies for the Christ Child. Over the years Christkind was transformed into Kriss Kringle and changed his identity so much that by the middle of the nineteenth century he was being confused with Santa Claus or St Nicholas.

The final transformation of the saintly and just Bishop of Myra, even-handedly rewarding good and punishing evil, into the chortling and commercial Father Christmas of today was begun by Dr Clement Clarke Moore, a professor of Hebrew and Greek Literature in New York. On the night of 23 December 1822 he read to his children some verses of his own entitled 'A Visit from St Nicholas'. A lady guest so enjoyed the poem that the following year she sent a copy anonymously to the *Troy Sentinel*, which published it. Overnight the dignified and ascetic St Nicholas became a 'jolly old elf'. Under the influence of magazine illustrators, particularly Thomas Nast in *Harper's Weekly*, he developed into the full size and jovial Santa of today, the very spirit of Christmas, yet totally devoid of any

Illustration by A. Forestier for 'Santa Claus the Toyman'. Illustrated London News, *1895.*

religious significance, and purged entirely of all forces of evil, darkness and retribution. When Santa recrossed the Atlantic to England he merged with Father Christmas or Old Christmas, a thoroughly pagan character from old

mummers' plays, traditionally represented with a beard, a lump on his back, a club in his hand and wearing a crown of holly.

Moore's St Nicholas incorporated all the gift-bringer legends: the chimney, the night-time

'Christmas with the Yule Log', drawn by Alfred Crowquill for Illustrated London News, *1848.*

secrecy, the stocking, the sleigh drawn by reindeer, the drive across the rooftops and the sack of toys. Only the origins of his clothing are obscure. Nast originally drew him wearing an undignified red romper suit. In America this developed into a red flannel suit and cap with a red point and white tassel, while the British Father Christmas dons a long red robe and white fur-trimmed red hood.

Before long the spirit of Santa was being evoked to assist in the commercial success of almost every product. Children were encouraged to write to Santa with their Christmas present list and post office centres were set up to deal with the flood of mail. A town in the state of Indiana named itself Santa Claus, with both eyes on the seasonal advantages to business. So many department stores employed Santas to boost sales that a college was established to train them. It was a terrible trick to play on a bishop.

For decades many countries held out against the increasingly greedy attractions of Santa. Northern European countries clung affectionately to their gnomes. Sweden's Father Christmas figure for the past fifty years has been the Jultomte, or Christmas gnome, a tiny creature who dwelt in an outhouse. Norway nominated the Julenisse, a descendant of the old man of the mound (traditionally the first settler of a farm), a much respected and feared ghost who over the

years changed into the less fearsome hobgoblin or nisse of fairy-tales. Inevitably this tiny grey-clad, bearded fellow sporting a pointed red cap has become confused with Santa. Most Danes have their own nisse, a gruff greybeard wearing grey breeches and smock and a red cap. He too was traditionally a farm dweller, a household spirit controlling domestic fortunes. All these gnomes have uncertain tempers and used to be appeased at Christmas with bowls of porridge.

Iceland has a whole family of Christmas gnomes. Naughty children used to expect a visit from Grýla, who liked to eat humans, and her husband Leppalúôi, the ugliest monster of all. This delightful couple had thirteen gnomic sons, or 'jólasveiner', with comic names like Sausage Thief and Candle Beggar, who descended from the mountains onto the farmhouses once a day for the thirteen days before Christmas, then reversed the process during the thirteen days after.

In southern Italy children receive their presents from a broomstick-mounted witch called Befana, who appears on 5 January. According to legend the Three Kings told her of the birth of Jesus, but she delayed setting out to find Him until she had finished her work. Losing her way, she now wanders all over in search of the Holy Child, leaving presents at every home in case it houses Him. Bad children receive a lump of coal. In Spain, on the night of 5 January, the Three Kings–Los Reyes Magos–parade through every town distributing presents to all children. Spanish youngsters used to leave out straw for the Three Kings' tired camels and wake up to find it had been mysteriously replaced with presents.

Many areas of Switzerland still keep St Nicholas Eve, when 'Samichlaus' appears in Catholic regions in episcopal clothing and in Protestant districts as an old man in a Capuchin cloak. He rides in from the snowbound winter forests on a little donkey, often accompanied by a demonic figure, Schmutzli, the Black One. The appearance of St Nicholas is often the signal for noisy processions, the most spectacular of which is at Küssnacht, where a procession of men wearing enormous decorated mitres lit up inside parade through the streets to the accompaniment of shaking bells and cracking whips. Many Swiss children receive personal visits from white-robed bearded Santas, who advertise their services in the classified sections of newspapers.

St Nicholas still survives in Belgium, in some areas of France, in Hungary, where he goes by the name of Mikulas, in parts of Germany, and of course, in Holland. Germany also recognizes the Christkind still. Russian children receive their presents on New Year's Eve from Father or Grandfather Frost, who looks remarkably like Father Christmas. But almost everywhere

Most famous of all Thomas Nast's Santa Claus illustrations. Harper's Weekly, *1881.*

the older figures–the Kings, the nisser, the bishop, Befana–are fighting a losing battle with Santa Claus. Papa Noël appears in France, Babbo Natale in Italy. In Brazil Papai Noel arrives under a baking sun clad American style in red flannel suit and rubber boots with simulated snow on his whiskers. In Australia a similarly anachronistic figure arrives by sleigh, camel, water skis, even helicopter. In Germany a Santa Claus figure called Weihnachtsmann, or Christmas Man, is gradually taking precedence, while Denmark now enjoys the visitations of a similar figure called the Julemand. Everyone knows that the Finnish Father Christmas lives in Lapland on a hill called Korvantunturi. Even in Holland commercial pressures ensure that the Dutch have Santa Claus at Christmas as well as St Nicholas.

The Three Kings are more spectacular, Befana more thought-provoking, the gnomes more unpredictable and St Nicholas more spiritual than the ubiquitous forever laughing fat figure in red. Before all the old-fashioned elements of the season–justice, thoughtfulness, kindness to animals, appeasement of ghosts–are buried for ever under the straightforward commercial acquisitiveness of Santa Claus, there is still time to launch a movement to preserve gnomes, nisser and St Nicholas, and revive the true traditions, pagan and Christian, of the season.

ST NICHOLAS GINGERBREAD HOUSE

DECORATING THE GINGERBREAD HOUSE

Materials required: Icing sugar with water or lemon juice to mix. Selection of gingerbread, biscuits and sweets. Sort biscuits and sweets into shapes so that you can work rapidly on your design, applying the biscuits before the icing has time to harden. Mix a small bowlful of icing, keeping the mixture fairly thick. Have icing sugar and water at hand to thicken or soften the icing as necessary. Don't make up too much at a time or the icing will set and become unusable. A cloth wrung out in cold water placed over the bowl will slow down the drying process so you can work with larger quantities.

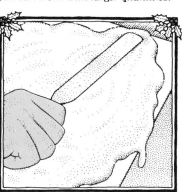

Start work on one side of the cardboard house, applying icing thickly and quite roughly with a knife or spatula.

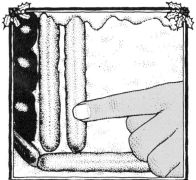

While the icing is soft the biscuits and sweets will tend to slide down, so

'Nicholas, I beg of you, drop into my little shoe,
Something sweet or sweeter. Thank you, Saint and Peter!'

In most countries Christmas Eve and Christmas Day have overtaken St Nicholas Day. However, 5 December, St Nicholas Eve, is still celebrated as a special night for children in many parts of Europe. Honey cakes are baked and spice or gingerbread biscuits are made and cut out into fanciful shapes and iced. In Germany St Nicholas 'gingerbread' houses are popular, often not made completely of gingerbread these days, but built on a cardboard base, iced and decorated with spicy biscuits. On the opposite page are diagrammatic instructions for making a cardboard model house, the result iced and decorated with biscuits you can see below.

start at the base of the wall and work upwards, pressing biscuits firmly into the icing. Finish one side before starting on the next, but leave the smaller details such as shutters, doors and chimney until last, since these may need smaller sweets and can provide an interesting contrast in the design.

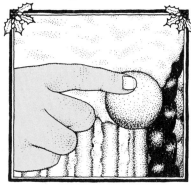

When all sides of the house are finished, repeat the process with the roof, allowing the biscuits to overlap the edge of the roof just a little.

When the walls and roof of the 'gingerbread' house are firm, decorate doors, shutters and chimney. Allow icing to harden and add icicles by dripping icing off the back of a spoon. Roughly ice around base of house to give the effect of snow. Add cotton wool smoke from the chimney, a pile of chocolate finger logs, lollipop trees or fruit gum flowers. The whole joy of making a St Nicholas cake is to work out your own individual design, something all children will love to do.

Making a Model House

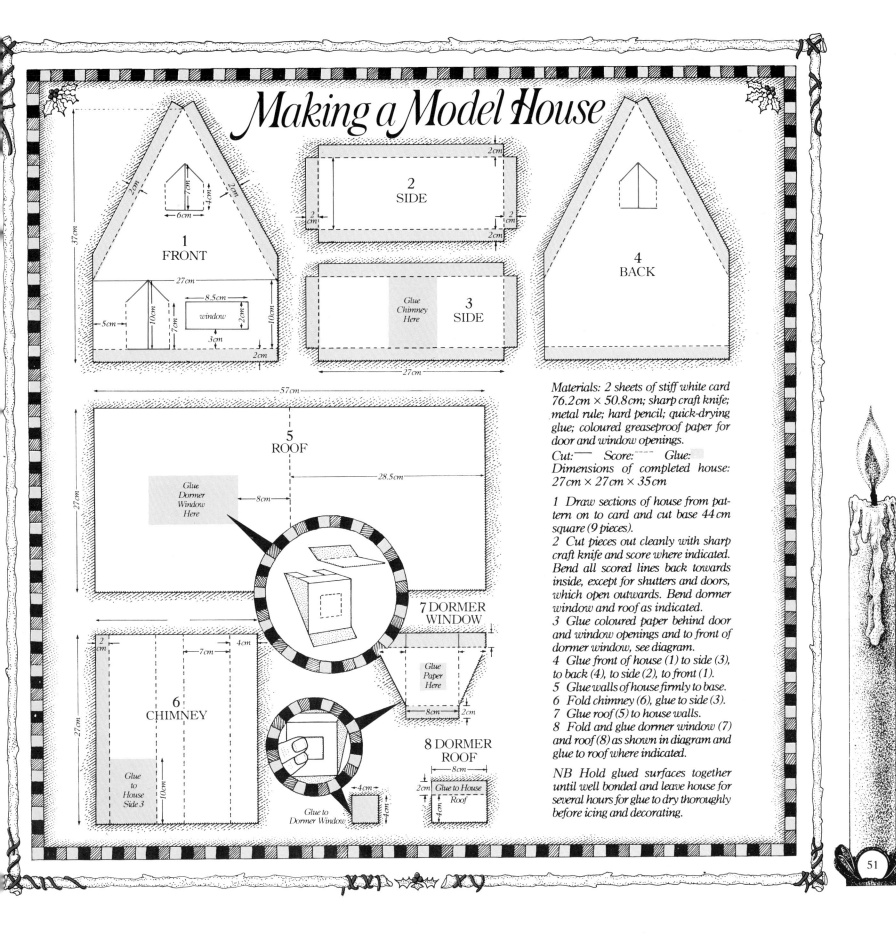

1 FRONT
37cm
2cm
2cm
6cm
4cm
27cm
5cm
10cm
7cm
8.5cm
window
2cm
3cm
10cm
2cm

2 SIDE
2cm
2 2
2cm

3 SIDE
Glue Chimney Here
27cm

4 BACK

5 ROOF
57cm
27cm
28.5cm
8cm
Glue Dormer Window Here

6 CHIMNEY
27cm
2cm
7cm
4cm
10cm
Glue to House Side 3

7 DORMER WINDOW
Glue Paper Here
8cm
2cm

8 DORMER ROOF
8cm
2cm Glue to House
Roof
4cm
4cm

Glue to Dormer Window

Materials: 2 sheets of stiff white card 76.2cm × 50.8cm; sharp craft knife; metal rule; hard pencil; quick-drying glue; coloured greaseproof paper for door and window openings.

Cut:—— Score:---- Glue:
Dimensions of completed house: 27cm × 27cm × 35cm

1 Draw sections of house from pattern on to card and cut base 44cm square (9 pieces).

2 Cut pieces out cleanly with sharp craft knife and score where indicated. Bend all scored lines back towards inside, except for shutters and doors, which open outwards. Bend dormer window and roof as indicated.

3 Glue coloured paper behind door and window openings and to front of dormer window, see diagram.

4 Glue front of house (1) to side (3), to back (4), to side (2), to front (1).

5 Glue walls of house firmly to base.

6 Fold chimney (6), glue to side (3).

7 Glue roof (5) to house walls.

8 Fold and glue dormer window (7) and roof (8) as shown in diagram and glue to roof where indicated.

NB Hold glued surfaces together until well bonded and leave house for several hours for glue to dry thoroughly before icing and decorating.

Christmas Cookie Bake

Baking gingerbread and cookies is an enjoyable part of Christmas preparation everywhere. The whole family can join in, measuring, mixing, making shapes and decorating. The cookies can be used to decorate the St Nicholas 'gingerbread' house, hang on the Christmas tree, give as presents or greetings cards or just to munch for tea around the fire. Ask friends to join in your cookie bake so that you can increase the variety of cookies you produce. The quantities given in the recipes should make a good pile of cookies, depending on the size of cutter or mould you use. Most cookies and gingerbread improve with keeping for a week or two, provided they are put in an airtight tin.

FUNNY FACES

¾ cup (170 g) butter
1⅛ cups (200 g) light brown sugar
1 large egg
1⅞ cups (280 g) all-purpose flour
½ teaspoon salt
2 oz (55 g) cooking chocolate
red food colouring

Beat butter and sugar until pale and creamy and add beaten egg. Sift flour and salt into bowl and add to creamy mixture gradually to make a soft dough. Divide dough into three, keeping one part plain, colouring the second with a few drops of red food dye: melt cooking chocolate in a bowl over a saucepan of hot water and mix with third part. Roll three different colours into balls and leave in refrigerator to cool for about 15 minutes. Roll out three colours separately on a floured board to about ¼ in thickness and cut round face shapes. Lift gently onto a greased baking sheet and use remaining odds and ends to mould hair, lips, beards, hats or moustaches and add these to faces, using currants for eyes. Use a fork to make other marks for whiskers, hair, mouths or cheeks. Bake at 350°F (180°C or Gas Mark 4) for 15 minutes.

MEXICAN SPICE COOKIES

1 cup (225 g) lard or butter
1 cup (225 g) granulated sugar
1 egg
1⅞ cups (280 g) all-purpose flour
1½ teaspoons baking powder
¼ teaspoon salt
3 teaspoons crushed anise seeds
4 tablespoons brandy or sherry
¼ cup (55 g) granulated sugar with 2 teaspoons ground cinnamon in a shaker

Cream the butter and the sugar until light and fluffy, and beat in the egg. sift the flour together with the baking powder, salt and crushed anise seeds and gradually add this to the mixture together with the brandy or sherry to form a pliable, but not too sticky, dough. Add a little more brandy or sherry if the mixture seems too stiff. Knead well and divide the dough into four pieces. Roll out one piece at a time on a floured board with a lightly floured rolling pin, to just under ¼ in thick, keeping the rest of the dough covered. Cut out into fancy shapes. For the traditional Mexican shapes cut with oblong cutter approximately 2½ in by 1¼ in and with a sharp knife cut strips down the length to within ¾ in of the bottom. Curl strips outwards to varying lengths, making different arrangements of strips and curls. Place cookies slightly apart on baking sheets and sprinkle with the sugar and cinnamon mixture. Bake in a moderate oven, 350°F (180°C or Gas Mark 4) for 10-12 minutes until a light golden brown. Cool on racks and store in an airtight tin.

DUTCH SPECULAAS

1⅔ cups (225 g) all-purpose flour
pinch of baking soda
1-2 tablespoons mixed spices: ground cinnamon, nutmeg, cloves and cardamom
pinch of salt
grated peel of 1 orange and ½ a lemon
¾ cup (170 g) butter
¾ cup (140 g) soft light brown sugar
3 drops almond extract
2 oz (55 g) flaked almonds
1½ tablespoons milk
a few whole almonds (optional)

Sift the flour, baking soda, spices and salt into a bowl. Add grated orange and lemon peel. Mix well. Chop butter into small pieces and add, together with the sugar, to the mixture. Add almond extract, flaked almonds and milk and work into a thick dough. Leave overnight in a cool place. Roll out on a floured board to a maximum of ¼ in and cut into fancy shapes or figures. (If larger figures are wanted leave paste at ⅜ in and use the whole almonds to trim clothes.) Brush off flour and put on greased baking sheet. Cook in a moderate oven 350°F (180°C or Gas Mark 4) for 20-30 minutes.

AUSTRIAN HONEY CAKES

1 cup (225 g) granulated sugar
4 tablespoons runny honey
2 tablespoons hot water
2⅝ cups (400 g) all-purpose flour
½ cup (115 g) butter
1 egg, beaten
1 teaspoon baking soda
pinch each of ground cinnamon, cloves, nutmeg and mixed spice
4 oz (115 g) ground almonds
¾ cup (115 g) chopped candied orange and lemon peel
pinch of salt

Mix honey, sugar and water together in a bowl and gradually stir in the sifted flour. Melt the butter and stir into the mixture a little at a time alternately with the beaten egg. Add the remaining ingredients and mix well. Wrap the dough in foil and rest in the refrigerator for two or three hours. Roll out on a floured board to approximately ¼ in thick and cut into fancy shapes. Place on a greased baking sheet with ¾ in between the cakes. Bake in a moderate oven, 350°F (180°C or Gas Mark 4) for 15-20 minutes, watching carefully, as they are inclined to burn.
These cookies can be iced when cold or eaten plain.

CINNAMON STARS

3 egg whites
2⅛ cups confectioners' sugar
1 tablespoon vanilla sugar, made by keeping one or two whole vanilla pods in a jar of granulated sugar
3 drops almond extract
1 teaspoon ground cinnamon
10-12 oz (180-340 g) finely ground almonds

Whisk the egg whites until very stiff, gradually beating in sifted confectioners' sugar. Put to one side two heaped tablespoons of this mixture for coating the finished cookies. Stir flavourings, spice and about half the ground almonds into the remainder. Knead enough of the remaining ground almonds in to make the dough scarcely sticky. Sprinkle pastry board generously with ground almonds or confectioners' sugar and roll dough out to ¼ in thickness and cut into star shapes. Arrange the biscuits on baking parchment or lightly oiled greaseproof paper on a baking sheet and brush tops with stiff egg white mixture put by for the purpose. If mixture is too stiff to spread evenly add a few drops of water. Bake in a low oven 325°F (170°C or Gas Mark 3) for 30-40 minutes. The cookies will be soft when taken out of the oven, but will harden.

NÜRNBERGER LEBKUCHEN
¾ cup (170g) runny honey
1¼ cups (225g) light brown sugar
1 egg, beaten
1 tablespoon rum or orange juice
1 teaspoon grated orange peel
1½ cups (225g) all-purpose flour
½ teaspoon each ground cinnamon, ground cloves, mace and ginger
½ teaspoon baking soda
½ teaspoon salt
⅜ cup (55g) chopped candied peel
2oz (55g) ground almonds
⅜ cup (55g) glacé cherries (approximately)
6oz (170g) whole blanched almonds (approximately)

Melt the honey and sugar together over a low heat and allow to cool. Beat in the orange juice, the grated peel and the egg. Sift the flour, spices, baking soda and the salt into a large bowl and stir in the honey mixture, the peel and the ground almonds. Wrap the soft dough in greased aluminium foil and keep overnight in the refrigerator. Taking a quarter of the dough at a time from the refrigerator roll out to ⅜ in thick on a well-floured board. Cut the dough into rounds with a 2½ in cutter and place well apart on a baking sheet lined with baking parchment or oiled greaseproof paper. Decorate with half a cherry and five

almonds to make a flower on the top of each one. Bake in a moderate oven, 375°F (190°C or Gas Mark 5) for 10-12 minutes. Allow to cool on the baking sheet and store in an airtight tin for a week or two.

PAIN D'EPICE
3 cups (450g) all-purpose flour
2½ teaspoons bicarbonate of soda
¼ teaspoon salt
¼ teaspoon ground aniseed (optional)
1 teaspoon ground cinnamon
1 teaspoon ground cloves
7oz (200g) pale, soft brown sugar
10oz (280g) runny honey
8fl oz (225ml) warm water
3 tablespoons rum or orange juice

Sift the flour together with the baking soda, the salt and the spices into a large bowl. Dissolve the sugar and honey in the warm water and add the rum or orange juice. Beat this gradually into the sifted flour and continue beating until the batter is free of lumps. Pour into two greased and lined tins 8in square. If you wish to use heart-, star-shaped or other tins pour the batter to

a depth of approximately ¾ in. Leave the tins of batter to stand for 15 minutes and then cook in a moderate oven 350°F (180°C or Gas Mark 4) for approximately 40 minutes. Test with a skewer and cook a further few minutes if it does not come out clean. When the gingerbread loaves are cool remove the paper and decorate with icing or confectioners' sugar and a picture for a special gift.

SWEDISH GINGER COOKIES
½ pint (275ml) whipping cream
1½ cups (280g) dark brown sugar
⅝ cup (140g) molasses
1 tablespoon baking soda
1½-2 teaspoons ground ginger
1 teaspoon ground cardamom or cinnamon
1-1½ teaspoon grated lemon peel
¼ teaspoon salt
3 cups (505g) all-purpose flour

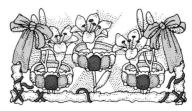

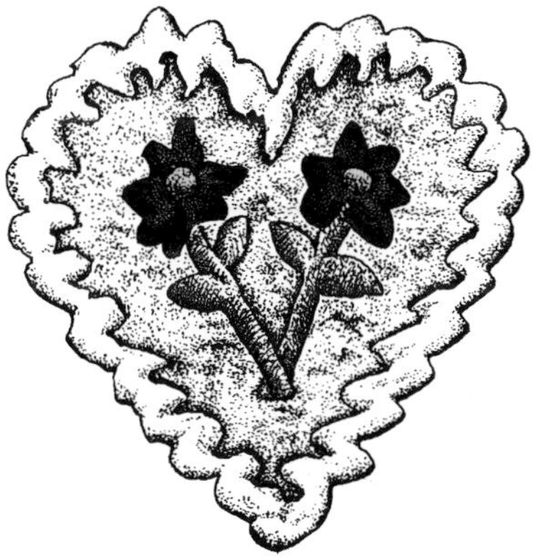

Beat the cream until soft peaks form and then gradually beat in the sugar, molasses, baking soda, spices, lemon peel and salt. Stir in the flour gradually, mixing well until dough is formed. Wrap dough in plastic and leave overnight in the refrigerator. Roll out on a lightly floured board to ¼ in thick. Cut into fancy shapes and place about ¾ in apart on a lightly greased baking sheet. Brush the cookies lightly with cold water and bake in a moderate oven 350°F (180°C or Gas Mark 4) for about 10-12 minutes until light brown. Cool on a rack. Serve plain or decorate with confectioners' sugar for cards or to hang on the Christmas tree. If the cookies are to be hung on the tree, make a hole in each one with a skewer while they are still hot.

Innocents' Song

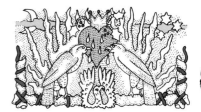

Who's that knocking on the window,
Who's that standing at the door,
What are all those presents
Lying on the kitchen floor?

Who is the smiling stranger
With hair as white as gin,
What is he doing with the children
And who could have let him in?

Why has he rubies on his fingers,
A cold, cold crown on his head,
Why, when he caws his carol,
Does the salty snow run red?

Why does he ferry my fireside
As a spider on a thread,
His fingers made of fuses
And his tongue of gingerbread?

Why does the world before him
Melt in a million suns,
Why do his yellow, yearning eyes
Burn like saffron buns?

Watch where he comes walking
Out of the Christmas flame,
Dancing, double-talking:

Herod is his name.

CHARLES CAUSLEY

DEAR FATHER CHRISTMAS

As Christmas draws near, children all over the world write to Father Christmas to explain that they have been good and ask him to bring them the presents they want. Some letters are sent to the North Pole via the chimney, but in the absence of a fireplace, the more conventional postal services have been known to work just as well. Father Christmas answers many letters, but for most children the proof that their letters have reached their destination comes on Christmas Day.

Dreaming of happy Christmases at home. 'The Holiday letter from school.' Late Victorian illustration from The Graphic *magazine.*

Chère papa noël

J'ai été très bon cette anneé. Je voudrai vraiment un poné mais maman ne veut pas parceque elle dit qu'il n'y a pas assé de place alors je veux un bébé chien et beaucoup d'autre choses.

Marie

Dear Father Christmas, I was very good this year. I would really like a pony but Mummy doesn't want me to have one because she says there isn't enough room so I want a puppy and lots of other things. Marie.

Dear Santa,
   I hope you are well, I am. Please may I have a fairy dolly and a Miffy book. I am a good girl so please come. My mummy says you come down the chimniy, why dont you come in the door?

Luv from
Mary

Dear father Christmas,
   I would like an action man with his camping things. Also I want a game of cludo and a game of hats off. Also I want a train with a station. Also I want a box of sweets.
   Love from
   Charlie.

♡ Dear Santa clause, ♡
      Please come and see me I would like a ballet dress and shoes I like ballet that is why I want these things also I would like a bicical if it is to much may I have the bricical next year that is all I want
      Love CATHY

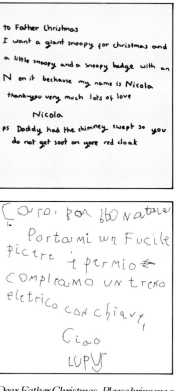

to Father Christmas
I want a giant snoopy for christmas and a little snoopy and a snoopy badge with an N on it bechause my name is Nicola thank-you very much lots of love
   Nicola
ps Daddy had the chimney swept so you do not get soot on yore red cloak

Caro Babbo Natale
   Portami un Fucile picere i permio compleamo un treno eletrico con chiave,
   Ciao
   LUPY

Dear Father Christmas, Please bring me a gun and an electric train with a key for my birthday. Bye, Lupus

chere Papa—noël
   j'espère que tes rennes vont bien. je voudrai un Nounours aussi grand que moi et beaucoup de bonbons. je te broisserai un verre d'eau.
   Pierre—Louis

Dear Father Christmas, I hope your reindeer are alright. I would like a teddy bear as big as me and lots of sweets. I will leave you a glass of water. Pierre-Louis

YES, VIRGINIA

THERE IS A SANTA CLAUS

FIRST PRINTED IN THE NEW YORK SUN, *SEPTEMBER 21, 1897*
We take pleasure in answering at once and thus prominently the communication below, expressing at the same time our great gratification that its faithful author is numbered among the friends of *The Sun*:

Dear Editor:
I am 8 years old.
Some of my little friends say there is no Santa Claus. Papa says, 'If you see it in *The Sun* it's so.' Please tell me the truth, is there a Santa Claus?
Virginia O'Hanlon, 115 West 95th Street

Virginia, your little friends are wrong. They have been affected by the skepticism of a skeptical age. They do not believe except they see. They think that nothing can be which is not comprehensible by their little minds. All minds, Virginia, whether they be men's or children's, are little. In this great universe of ours man is a mere insect, an ant, in his intellect, as compared with the boundless world about him, as measured by the intelligence capable of grasping the whole of truth and knowledge.

Yes, Virginia, there is a Santa Claus. He exists as certainly as love and generosity and devotion exist, and you know that they abound and give to your life its highest beauty and joy. Alas! how dreary would be the world if there were no Santa Claus! It would be as dreary as if there were no Virginias. There would be no childlike faith then, no poetry, no romance to make tolerable this existence. We should have no enjoyment, except in sense and sight. The eternal light with which childhood fills the world would be extinguished.

Not believe in Santa Claus! You might as well not believe in fairies! You might get your papa to hire men to watch in all the chimneys on Christmas Eve to catch Santa Claus, but even if they did not see Santa Claus coming down, what would that prove? Nobody sees Santa Claus, but that is no sign that there is no Santa Claus. The most real things in the world are those that neither children nor men can see. Did you ever see fairies dancing on the lawn? Of course not, but that's no proof that they are not there. Nobody can conceive or imagine all the wonders there are unseen and unseeable in the world.

You tear apart the baby's rattle and see what makes the noise inside, but there is a veil covering the unseen world which not the strongest man, nor even the united strength of all the strongest men that ever lived, could tear apart. Only faith, fancy, poetry, love, romance, can push aside that curtain and view and picture the supernal beauty and glory beyond. Is it all real? Ah, Virginia, in all this world there is nothing else real and abiding. No Santa Claus! Thank God he lives, and he lives forever. A thousand years from now, Virginia, nay 10 times 10 thousand years from now, he will continue to make glad the heart of childhood.

THE FIR TREE
Hans Christian Andersen

UT IN the forest stood a pretty little Fir Tree. It had a good place; it could have sunlight, air there was in plenty, and all around grew many larger comrades – pines as well as firs. But the little Fir Tree wished ardently to become greater. It did not care for the warm sun and the fresh air; it took no notice of the peasant children, who went about talking together, when they had come out to look for strawberries and raspberries. Often they came with a whole pot-full, or had strung berries on a straw; then they would sit down by the little Fir Tree and say, 'How pretty and small that one is!' and the Tree did not like to hear that at all.

Next year he had grown a great joint, and the following year he was longer still, for in fir trees one can always tell by the number of rings they have how many years they have been growing.

'Oh, if I were only as great a tree as the others!' sighed the little Fir, 'then I would spread my branches far around, and look out from my crown into the wide world. The birds would then build nests in my boughs, and when the wind blew I could nod just as grandly as the others yonder.'

He took no pleasure in the sunshine, in the birds, and in the red clouds that went sailing over him morning and evening.

When it was winter, and the snow lay all around, white and sparkling, a hare would often come jumping along, and spring right over the little Fir Tree. Oh! this made him so angry. But two winters went by, and when the third came the little Tree had grown so tall that the hare was obliged to run around it.

'Oh! to grow, to grow, and become old; that's the only fine thing in the world,' thought the Tree.

In the autumn woodcutters always came and felled a few of the largest trees; that was done this year too, and the little Fir Tree, that was now quite well grown, shuddered with fear, for the great stately trees fell to the ground with a crash, and their branches were cut off, so that the trees looked quite naked, long, and slender – they could hardly be recognized. But then they were laid upon waggons, and horses dragged them away out of the wood. Where were they going? What destiny awaited them?

In the spring, when the swallows and the Stork came, the Tree asked them 'Do you know where they were taken? Did you not meet them?'

The swallows knew nothing about it, but the Stork looked thoughtful, nodded his head, and said,

'Yes, I think so. I met many new ships when I flew out of Egypt; on the ships were stately masts; I fancy that these were the trees. They smelt like fir. I can assure you they're stately – very stately.'

'Oh that I were only big enough to go over the sea! What kind of thing is this sea, and how does it look?'

'It would take too long to explain all that,' said the Stork, and he went away.

'Rejoice in thy youth,' said the Sunbeams; 'rejoice in thy fresh growth, and in the young life that is within thee.'

And the wind kissed the Tree, and the dew wept tears upon it; but the Fir Tree did not understand that.

When Christmas-time approached, quite young trees were felled, sometimes trees which were neither so old nor so large as this Fir Tree, that never rested but always wanted to go away. These young trees, which were always the most beautiful, kept all their branches; they were put upon waggons, and horses dragged them away out of the wood.

'Where are they all going?' asked the Fir Tree. 'They are not greater than I – indeed, one of them was much smaller. Why do they keep all their branches? Whither are they taken?'

'We know that! We know that!' chirped the Sparrows. 'Yonder in the town we looked in at the windows. We know where they go. Oh! they are dressed up in the greatest pomp and splendor that can be imagined. We have looked in at the windows, and have perceived that they are planted in the middle of the warm room, and adorned with the most beautiful things – gilt apples, honey-cakes, playthings, and many hundreds of candles.'

'And then?' asked the Fir Tree, and trembled through all its branches. 'And then? What happens then?'

'Why, we have not seen anything more. But it was incomparable.'

'Perhaps I may be destined to tread this glorious path one day!' cried the Fir Tree rejoicingly. 'That is even better than travelling across the sea. How painfully I long for it! If it were only Christmas now! Now I am great and grown up, like the rest who were led away last year. Oh, if I were only on the carriage! If I were only in the warm room, among all the pomp and splendor! And then? Yes, then something even better will come, something far more charming, or else why should they adorn me so? There must be something grander, something greater still to come; but what? Oh, I'm suffering, I'm longing! I don't know myself what is the matter with me!'

'Rejoice in us,' said Air and Sunshine. 'Rejoice in thy fresh youth here in the woodland.'

But the Fir Tree did not rejoice at all, but it grew and grew; winter and summer it stood there, green, dark green. The people who saw it said, 'That's a handsome tree!' and at Christmastime it was felled before any one of the others. The axe cut deep into its marrow, and the tree fell to the ground with a sigh: it felt a pain, a sensation of faintness, and could not think at all of happiness, for it was sad at parting from its home, from the place where it had grown up: it knew that it should never again see the dear old companions, the little bushes and flowers all around – perhaps not even the birds. The parting was not at all agreeable.

The Tree only came to itself when it was unloaded in a yard, with other trees, and heard a man say,

'This one is famous; we only want this one!'

Now two servants came in gay liveries, and carried the Fir Tree into a large beautiful salon. All around the walls hung pictures, and by the great stove stood large Chinese vases with lions on the covers; there were rocking-chairs, silken sofas, great tables covered with picture-books, and toys worth a hundred times a hundred kroner, at least the children said so. And the Fir Tree was put into a great tub filled with sand; but no one could see that it was a tub, for it was hung round with green cloth, and stood on a large many-colored carpet. Oh, how the Tree trembled! What was to happen now? The servants, and the young ladies also, decked it out. On one branch they hung little nets, cut out of colored paper; every net was filled with sweetmeats; golden apples and walnuts hung down as if they grew there, and more than a hundred little candles, red, white, and blue, were fastened to the different boughs. Dolls that looked exactly like real people – the Tree had never seen such before – swung among the foliage, and high on the summit of the Tree was fixed a tinsel star. It was splendid, particularly splendid.

'This evening,' said all, 'this evening it will shine.'

'Oh,' thought the Tree, 'that it were evening already! Oh that the lights may be soon lit up! When may that be done? I wonder if trees will come out of the forest to look at me? Will the sparrows fly against the panes? Shall I grow fast here, and stand adorned in summer and winter?'

Yes, he did not guess badly. But he had a complete backache from mere longing, and the backache is just as bad for a Tree as the headache for a person.

At last the candles were lighted. What a brilliance, what splendor! The Tree trembled so in all its branches that one of the candles set fire to a green twig, and it was scorched.

'Heaven preserve us!' cried the young ladies; and they hastily put the fire out.

Now the Tree might not even tremble. Oh, that was terrible! It was so afraid of setting fire to some of its ornaments, and it was quite bewildered with all the brilliance. And now the folding doors were thrown open, and a number of children rushed in as if they would have overturned the whole Tree; the older people followed more deliberately. The little ones stood quite silent, but only for a minute; then they shouted till the room rang: they danced gleefully round the Tree, and one present after another was plucked from it.

'What are they about?' laughed the Tree. 'What's going to be done?'

And the candles burned down to the twigs, and as they burned down they were extinguished, and then the children received permission to plunder the Tree. Oh! they rushed in upon it, so that every branch cracked again: if it had not been fastened by the top and by the golden star to the ceiling, it would have fallen down.

The children danced about with their pretty toys. No one looked at the Tree except one old man, who came up and peeped among the branches, but only to see if a fig or an apple had not been forgotten.

'A story! a story!' shouted the children: and they drew a little fat man towards the Tree; and he sat down just beneath it, – 'for then we shall be in the green wood,' said he, 'and the tree may have the advantage of listening to my tale. But I can only tell one. Will you hear the story of Ivede-Avede, or of Klumpey-Dumpey, who fell down stairs, and still was raised up to honor and married the Princess?'

'Ivede-Avede!' cried some, 'Klumpey-Dumpey!' cried others, and there was a great crying and shouting. Only the Fir Tree was quite silent, and thought, 'Shall I not be in it? Shall I have nothing to do in it?' But he had been in the evening's amusement, and had done what was required of him.

And the fat man told about Klumpey-Dumpey, who fell down stairs, and yet was raised to honor and married the Princess. And the children clapped their hands, and cried, 'Tell another! tell another!' for they wanted to hear about Ivede-Avede; but they only got the story of Klumpey-Dumpey. The Fir Tree stood quite silent and thoughtful; never had the birds in the wood told such a story as that. Klumpey-Dumpey fell down stairs, and yet came to honor and married the Princess!

'Yes, so it happens in the world!' thought the Fir Tree, and believed it must be true, because that was such a nice man who told it. 'Well, who can know? Perhaps I shall fall down stairs too, and marry a Princess!' And it looked forward with pleasure to being adorned again, the next evening, with candles and toys, gold and fruit. 'To-morrow I shall not tremble,' it thought. 'I will rejoice in all my splendor. To-morrow I shall hear the story of Klumpey-Dumpey again, and, perhaps, that of Ivede-Avede too.'

And the Tree stood all night quiet and thoughtful.

In the morning the servants and the chambermaid came in.

'Now my splendor will begin afresh,' thought the Tree. But they dragged him out of the room, and up stairs to the garret, and here they put him in a dark corner where no daylight shone.

'What's the meaning of this?' thought the Tree. 'What am I to do here? What is to happen?'

And he leaned against the wall, and thought, and thought. And he had time enough, for days and nights went by, and nobody came up; and when at length someone came, it was only to put some great boxes in a corner. Now the Tree stood quite hidden away, and the supposition was that it was quite forgotten.

'Now it's winter outside,' thought the Tree. 'The earth is hard and covered with snow, and people cannot plant me; therefore I suppose I'm to be sheltered here until spring comes. How considerate that is! How good people are! If it were only not so dark here, and so terribly solitary! – not even a little hare! That was pretty out there in the wood, when the snow lay thick and the hare sprang past; yes, even when he jumped over me; but then I did not like it. It is terribly lonely up here!'

'Piep! piep!' said a little Mouse, and crept forward, and then came another little one. They smelt at the Fir Tree, and then slipped among the branches.

'It's horribly cold,' said the two little Mice, 'or else it would be comfortable here. Don't you think so, you old Fir Tree?'

'I'm not old at all,' said the Fir Tree. 'There are many much older than I.'

'Where do you come from?' asked the Mice. 'And what do you know?' They were dreadfully inquisitive. 'Tell us about the most beautiful spot on earth. Have you been there? Have you been in the store-room where cheeses lie on the shelves, and hams hang from the ceiling, where one dances on tallow candles, and goes in thin and comes out fat?'

'I don't know that!' replied the Tree; 'but I know the wood where the sun shines, and where the birds sing.'

And then it told all about its youth.

And the little Mice had never heard anything of the kind; and they listened and said,

'What a number of things you have seen! How happy you must have been!'

'I?' said the Fir Tree; and it thought about what it had told. 'Yes, those were really quite happy times.' But then he told of the Christmas-eve, when he had been hung with sweetmeats and candles.

'Oh!' said the little Mice, 'how happy you have been, you old Fir Tree!'

'I'm not old at all,' said the Tree. 'I only came out of the wood this winter. I'm only rather backward in my growth.'

'What splendid stories you can tell!' said the little Mice.

And next night they came with four other little Mice, to hear what the Tree had to relate; and the more it said, the more clearly did it remember everything, and thought, 'Those were quite merry days! But they may come again. Klumpey-Dumpey fell down stairs, and yet he married the Princess. Perhaps I may marry a Princess too!' And then the Fir Tree thought of a pretty little birch tree that grew out in the forest; for the Fir Tree, that birch was a real Princess.

'Who's Klumpey-Dumpey?' asked the little Mice.

And then the Fir Tree told the whole story. It could remember every single word: and the little Mice were ready to leap to the very top of the tree with pleasure. Next night a great many more Mice came, and on Sunday two Rats even appeared; but these thought the story was not pretty, and the little Mice were sorry for that, for now they also did not like it so much as before.

'Do you only know one story?' asked the Rats.

'Only that one,' replied the Tree. 'I heard that on the happiest evening of my life; I did not think then how happy I was.'

'That's a very miserable story. Don't you know any about bacon and tallow candles – a store-room story?'

'No,' said the Tree.

'Then we'd rather not hear you,' said the Rats.

And they went back to their own people. The little Mice at last stayed away also; and then the Tree sighed and said,

'It was very nice when they sat round me, the merry little Mice, and listened when I spoke to them. Now that's past too. But I shall remember to be pleased when they take me out.'

But when did that happen? Why, it was one morning that people came and rummaged in the garret: the boxes were put away, and the Tree brought out; they certainly threw him rather roughly on the floor, but a servant dragged him away at once to the stairs, where the daylight shone.

'Now life is beginning again,' thought the Tree.

It felt the fresh air and the first sunbeams, and now it was out in the courtyard. Everything passed so quickly that the Tree quite forgot to look at itself, there was so much to look at all round. The courtyard was close to a garden, and here everything was blooming; the roses hung fresh and fragrant over the little paling, the linden trees were in blossom, and the swallows cried, 'Quinze-wit! quinze-wit! my husband's come!' But it was not the Fir Tree that they meant.

'Now I shall live!' said the Tree, rejoicingly, and spread its branches far out; but, alas! they were all withered and yellow; and it lay in the corner among nettles and weeds. The tinsel star was still upon it, and shone in the bright sunshine.

In the courtyard a couple of the merry children were playing, who had danced round the tree at Christmas-time, and had rejoiced over it. One of the youngest ran up and tore off the golden star.

'Look what is sticking to the ugly old fir tree,' said the child, and he trod upon the branches till they cracked again under his boots.

And the Tree looked at all the blooming flowers and the splendor of the garden, and then looked at itself, and wished it had remained in the dark corner of the garret; it thought of its fresh youth in the wood, of the merry Christmas-eve, and of the little Mice which had listened so pleasantly to the story of Klumpey-Dumpey.

'Past! past!' said the old Tree. 'Had I but rejoiced when I could have done so! Past! past!'

And the servant came and chopped the Tree into little pieces; a whole bundle lay there, it blazed brightly under the great brewing copper, and it sighed deeply, and each sigh was like a little shot: and the children who were at play there ran up and seated themselves at the fire, looked into it, and cried, 'Puff! puff!' But at each explosion, which was a deep sigh, the Tree thought of a summer day in the woods, or of a winter night there, when the stars beamed; he thought of Christmas-eve and of Klumpey-Dumpey, the only story he had ever heard or knew how to tell; and then the Tree was burned.

The boys played in the garden, and the youngest had on his breast a golden star, which the Tree had worn on its happiest evening. Now that was past, and the Tree's life was past, and the story is past too: past! past! – and that's the way with all stories.

The Christmas Tree

Put out the lights now!
Look at the Tree, the rough tree dazzled
In oriole plumes of flame,
Tinselled with twinkling frost fire, tasselled
With stars and moons – the same
That yesterday hid in the spinney and had no fame
Till we put out the lights now.

Hard are the nights now:
The fields at moonrise turn to agate,
Shadows are cold as jet;
In dyke and furrow, in copse and faggot
The frost's tooth is set;
And stars are the sparks whirled out by the north wind's fret
On the flinty nights now.

So feast your eyes now
On mimic star and moon-cold bauble:
Worlds may wither unseen,
But the Christmas Tree is a tree of fable,
A phoenix in evergreen,
And the world cannot change or chill what its mysteries mean
To your hearts and eyes now.

The vision dies now
Candle by candle: the tree that embraced it
Returns to its own kind,
To be earthed again and weather as best it
May the frost and the wind.
Children, it too had its hour – you will not mind
If it lives or dies now.

C. DAY LEWIS

EVERGREEN

The charming Christmas custom of decorating houses and churches with all the living colours of green branches, red, white and black berries, and any plants that can be induced to flower in midwinter has, like most popular seasonal traditions, a most un-Christian history. To the pagans evergreens were symbols of continuing life when all other trees were bare and brown, and even the sun was dying. Those which bore berries through the worst weather – holly, ivy, mistletoe – were particularly venerated for their fertility. Every religion attached superstitious practices to these mysterious trees that refused to die in the winter.

At the time of the winter solstice, when the sun was at its lowest, they were cut and brought indoors to help the sun to rise again. Northern Europeans brought branches into their homes as refuges for the wood spirits through the worst days of winter. Romans decked their houses with evergreens, and at the January Kalends gave each other green branches and holly, and nailed boughs of laurel, symbolic of victory, to their doorposts.

Mistletoe has particularly violent associations. According to Norse legend, Balder, son of Odin, was slain by a mistletoe dart hurled by the blind god Hödr, deceived by the evil Loki. Balder was

Sentimental scene under the mistletoe. Drawn by M. Jackson, Illustrated London News, *1865.*

returned to life, but the mistletoe was made to swear never to harm another soul. The Druids regarded the Golden Bough as the all-healer. That which grew on the oak was particularly sacred because it was believed to hold the life of the tree through the winter. At the winter solstice – which falls around 22 December – white-robed priests cut it down with a golden sickle, sacrificed two white bulls and, amid great celebration, laid some of the mistletoe on the altar and divided up the rest to be hung above doors. Mistletoe came over the years to be credited with a strange assortment of powers. It was said to be a remedy

Bringing home Christmas. 'The Holly Cart', an illustration by Seymour, dated 1836.

against poisons, to induce fertility in men and animals, to banish evil spirits and to protect the home from thunder and lightning. In Scandinavia mistletoe was the plant of peace and enemies who met under it would lay down their arms and declare a truce. Either this or its associations with fertility may account for the British custom of kissing under the mistletoe. In the old days, the man plucked a berry from the bough each time he kissed a girl. When all the berries were gone, the kissing stopped.

The early Church tried to stamp out the heathen custom of decking homes, halls, even churches with pagan greenery, but was forced to submit and try to attach a Christian significance to every plant. Holly was associated with the Passion,

the leaves representing Christ's crown of thorns and the berries the drops of blood. It was also held to be the symbol of the burning bush in which God appeared to Moses. In Denmark the holly was known as the Kristdorn, or Christ Thorn. Unfortunately for the Church, the Middle Ages attached an entirely new set of heathen superstitions to the holly. It was said to protect against witches and the evil eye. In some districts the prickly-leaved holly was known as 'he' and the smooth-leaved as 'she', and the sort that came into the house at Christmas was held to indicate who would be ruling the roost for the coming year. In early English carols holly stood for the man and clinging ivy for the woman in a ritual battle of the sexes. Ivy, the symbol of Bacchus, remained pagan long after holly became sacred.

In spite of a Christian myth that the Cross was made from mistletoe wood and the plant then shrunk to its present size from shame, mistletoe remained irredeemably pagan and was rarely used in Church decorations. Rosemary for remembrance and friendship, with its attractive scented grey-green leaves, was once one of the most popular Christmas decorations, but fell out of use in the nineteenth century. (More practically, it was used to flavour and decorate the

'The snatched kiss', a pen-and-ink drawing from the turn of the century, by R. Taylor.

boar's head.) Rosemary was believed to have acquired its scent when Jesus' swaddling clothes were hung over it, and its colour in honour of the Virgin, who flung her purple robe over the bush. The tradition of hanging wreaths of holly, evergreen, pine cones and nuts on the front door originated in Scandinavia – probably as symbols of renewal, peace and friendship – and became very popular in the United States. Their round shape discouraged wicked witches and evil spirits from paying seasonal visits.

All sorts of superstitious beliefs attached themselves to the putting up and taking down of the decorations. It was thought unlucky to put them up before Christmas Eve and great care was

(Above) 'The Mistletoe Queen', drawn by F. Offor for Illustrated London News, 1897. (Right) Drawing by Mary Ellen Edwards for Girls' Own Paper, 1881.

taken over their removal, some believing Epiphany to be the most auspicious time, others holding out until Plough Monday or even Candlemas. Holly was burned or buried or given to the cows. Dropping a piece was unlucky. The mistletoe bough was kept until a new one was cut the following year.

The legend that on Christmas Eve trees blossomed and bore fruit led to the old practice in parts of Europe of cutting and bringing indoors branches or even small trees and encouraging them to blossom at Christmas. (Forcing hyacinth bulbs for Christmas or buying hothouse plants is a development of this practice.) In England the old belief is connected with Joseph of Arimathea,

The Meanings of Evergreen

Mistletoe: The all-healer and plant of peace, it induces fertility, banishes evil spirits and protects homes against thunder and lightning.

Holly: Protection against witches and the evil eye. Symbolic of the burning bush in which God appeared to Moses and Christ's crown of thorns.

Yew: Poisonous to men and cattle, but a defence against witches.

Bay: Denotes great power: leaves or sprigs were used as wreaths for Roman poets or conquerors.

Laurel: Protects and purifies. Symbolic of victory, distinction and honour. As with bay, used to wreathe the brows of Roman heroes.

Rosemary: For remembrance and friendship. Believed to have acquired its scent when Jesus' swaddling clothes were hung over it.

Ivy: The sacred plant of Bacchus, believed to protect against drunkenness.

'An Ambuscade', drawn by F. Barnard for the Christmas Number of Illustrated London News, 1893.

whose stave took root at Glastonbury and blossomed every Christmas Day. When the calendar changed in 1752, making Christmas fall twelve days earlier, the flowering of the Glastonbury Thorn at Old Christmas, 6 January, encouraged traditionalists to refuse to recognize the new date. Actually, that variety of thorn flowers naturally twice a year, once usually at Christmas.

The Christmas rose, pure, innocent and growing apparently miraculously from the bare earth at midwinter, featured on early Christmas cards, but is also noted for its black, poisonous roots. As the celebration of Christmas spread to warmer climates, other plants, such as ferns, mosses or palms, were incorporated into the festivities. Early settlers in Australia named all trees they found in bloom at Christmas, Christmas Bush or Christmas Tree. Jamaica enjoys the poinsettia, white euphorbia, red-berried maria and the spathodia. A charming Mexican legend is connected with the poinsettia. In one village there was a custom of putting gifts beside a crèche in the church on Christmas Eve. One small boy with nothing to give knelt to pray in the snow outside and where he knelt a beautiful plant with red leaves grew, which he presented at the crèche. The Mexicans called it the Flower of the Holy Night and it is said to resemble the Star of Bethlehem. The Americans named it after the

man who introduced it to the United States – Dr Poinsett. Recently it has become one of the most popular Christmas plants all over the world – the latest development in the Christmas story.

'The Twenty-Fourth of December', illustration by Miss Jessie MacGregor, Graphic, 1886.

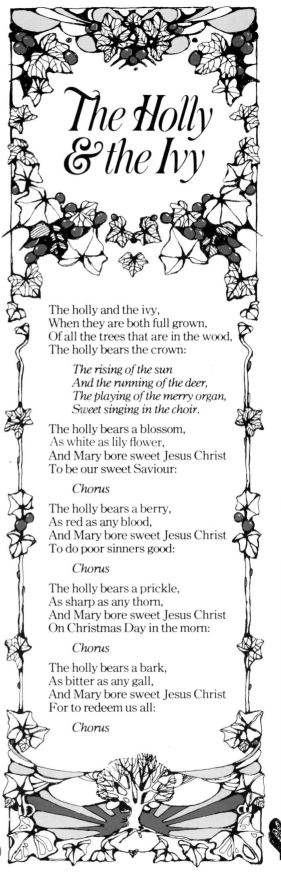

The Holly & the Ivy

The holly and the ivy,
When they are both full grown,
Of all the trees that are in the wood,
The holly bears the crown:

The rising of the sun
And the running of the deer,
The playing of the merry organ,
Sweet singing in the choir.

The holly bears a blossom,
As white as lily flower,
And Mary bore sweet Jesus Christ
To be our sweet Saviour:

Chorus

The holly bears a berry,
As red as any blood,
And Mary bore sweet Jesus Christ
To do poor sinners good:

Chorus

The holly bears a prickle,
As sharp as any thorn,
And Mary bore sweet Jesus Christ
On Christmas Day in the morn:

Chorus

The holly bears a bark,
As bitter as any gall,
And Mary bore sweet Jesus Christ
For to redeem us all:

Chorus

THE CHRISTMAS TREE

The modern Christmas would not be complete without the tree. Glowing with light yet darkly mysterious, glittering with ornaments, topped with a silver star or fairy, for many people it is the very heart of the season. The tree has everything – evergreen for survival, fire and light for everlasting life and the rebirth of the sun and seasonal associations with children, family gatherings and present-giving. Yet the tree is a comparative newcomer to the festivities and was scarcely known until the last century.

Martin Luther has been credited with the creation of the Christmas tree. It is said that one Christmas Eve he was so moved by the sight of the star-lit winter sky through the fir trees that he hurried home and tried to reproduce the sight for his children by decking a tree with candles. Sadly there is no evidence to support this story, but the tree was clearly established in Alsace by 1605, when a citizen wrote: 'At Christmas they set up fir trees in the parlours at Strasbourg and hang thereon roses cut out of many-coloured paper, apples, wafers, gold foil and sweets.'

The Christmas tree did not spring fully fledged into the festivities. Its origins lie in many ancient customs and superstitions. Some experts have traced it back to Egypt, others to the Greek Feast of Light. Romans used to deck their homes with branches and trees at the January Kalends. Northern tribes regarded evergreens as symbols of survival and worshipped a number of trees. When St Boniface completed the Christianization of Germany in the eighth century he toppled the sacred oak of Odin. Finding behind it a small fir tree, he dedicated that to the Holy Child.

Branches or whole trees, such as cherry or hawthorn, used to be brought inside and encouraged to bloom at Christmas. Ceremonial trees figured in many folk customs. In Sweden, young pines stripped of bark and branches were put outside houses at Christmas. On the Greek island of Chios on Christmas morning, tenants used to offer their landlords a pole bound with wreaths, to which were attached flowers, oranges, lemons and strips of coloured paper. In medieval Germany a Paradise play depicted the expulsion of Adam and Eve from Paradise, which was represented by a fir tree hung with apples. When the mystery plays were suppressed in churches the tree found its way into homes and the custom developed of adding to the apples white wafers representing the Holy Eucharist. The Paradise Tree decked with apples and ribbons also appeared on stage in English mystery plays.

Before the Christmas tree became widespread, in many parts of Germany and England wooden

Decorated tree from turn-of-the-century magazine.

Christmas pyramids were decorated, to local custom, with greenery, candles, coloured paper, apples, nuts and small gifts. The Italian counterpart, the 'ceppo' (tree trunk), was substituted in some areas for the Yule log. Shelves of varying sizes were decorated with evergreens, candles, presents and figurines, the supporting pillars wound round with evergreen. On the bottom shelf was a representation of the Stable.

The Christmas tree was slow to spread from its Alsatian home, partly because of resistance to its supposed Lutheran origins. In England it was first referred to in 1789 as 'a charming imported German custom', but it didn't become common until after 1840, when Queen Victoria and Prince Albert set up a tree for their children at Windsor Castle. Princess Helene of Mecklenburg introduced the tree to Paris in the same year, and during the nineteenth century its popularity spread throughout northern Europe. In some peasant communities, such as those of Poland and Finland, it was at first customary to suspend the tree from the ceiling, often upside

Illustration for Hans Andersen's 'The Fir Tree', from Illustrated London News, *1850.*

Drawing by A. Hunt, Illustrated London News, *1876.*

down. The tree was introduced to the United States by the Pennsylvanian Germans and is first mentioned in 1821, but it was a novelty for some years and churches charged admission to see elaborately decorated versions.

Trees were traditionally decorated with nuts, fruits, gingerbread, candies and gilt and paper decorations. Candles first enter the picture in Germany in 1737 with the story of a country lady who lit candles on or around little trees, one for each of her children, and laid presents under them. They were firmly established by the time the tree reached England. Light and fire have ancient connections with winter celebrations, as have evergreens, and it is not surprising that they should get together. Attempts have been made to trace the origin of the use of candles to Hanukkah, the Jewish Feast of Lights, which falls at the end of December, but there seems to be no positive link. The tree, traditionally a spruce, was topped by a Christchild angel, whose hair was often represented by silver and gold thread strung on the branches. More exuberant households added to the decorations almost anything that was edible or could be given away. A tree in mid-nineteenth-century America was hung with 'little horses, whips and wagons, red shoes, collars and handkerchiefs, as well as nuts, fruits and candies'. Over the years the angel evolved into a fairy and sometimes a Bethlehem star took its place. Victorian glass decorations (and later still, mass-produced baubles) took the place of gilded nuts and fruit and, with the advent of electricity, the candles were plugged in.

O Tannebaum

O Tannebaum, o Tannebaum,
  wie treu sind deine Blätter!
Du grünst nicht nur zur Sommerzeit,
  nein, auch im Winter, wenn es schneit.
O Tannebaum, o Tannebaum,
  wie treu sind deine Blätter!
O Tannebaum, o Tannebaum,
  du kannst mir sehr gefallen!
Wie oft hat nicht zur Weihnachtszeit
  ein Baum von dir mich hoch erfreut!
O Tannebaum, o Tannebaum,
  du kannst mir sehr gefallen!
O Tannebaum, o Tannebaum,
  dein Kleid will mich was lehren:
Die Hoffnung und Beständigkeit
  gibt Trost und Krast zu jeder Zeit.
O Tannebaum, o Tannebaum,
  dein Kleid will mich was lehren.

O Christmas Tree, O Christmas tree,
Thy leaves are green forever.
O Christmas tree, O Christmas tree,
Thy beauty leaves thee never.
Thy leaves are green in summer's prime,
Thy leaves are green at Christmas time.
O Christmas tree, O Christmas tree,
Thy leaves are green forever.

'Bringing Home the Christmas Tree', drawn by Alfred Hunt for Illustrated London News, *1882.*

'A Merry Christmas and a Happy New Year to you All.'

Many customs grew up round the tree, particularly in Scandinavia. Traditionally the whole family sallied forth on Christmas Eve to cut and bring home the tree. Now that most people are city dwellers they travel no further than the local market, but the principle is the same. The tree is decorated, often by the grown-ups in secret so as to astonish and delight the expectant children after supper. In Denmark and other Scandinavian countries, family and friends hold hands and circle round the tree singing carols. Many German and Scandinavian families still light real candles–though always keeping a bucket of water handy. In a number of countries presents are stacked under the tree to be distributed on Christmas Eve or Christmas Day.

The Christmas tree used to be a domestic institution, but it has become increasingly openhearted, particularly in America, where the first community tree was erected in Madison Square Garden, New York, in 1912 and where nowadays spruce and firs on front lawns are hung with lights. Norwegian ships throughout the world strap lighted trees to their masts. Giant trees are set up in civic centres everywhere; probably the best known are in New York's Rockefeller Plaza and Trafalgar Square in London, and people gather round to sing carols. The tree has become an expression of friendship. Norway sends one every year to England, Finland to Antwerp and Brussels. The Christmas tree, far from dying out like some older customs, is still evolving and has yet to find its final role; maybe it will come to be a symbol of peace and friendship between nations.

THE YULE LOG

Almost all the superstitions and ceremonies connected with bringing in and lighting the great Yule log, the centre-piece of Christmas in many parts of Europe, are overtly pagan. The Viking Yule was a celebration of the triumph of light over darkness, and the rebirth of the sun at the winter solstice, the darkest time of the year. The origin of the word Yule is debatable. It may derive from the Gothic 'giul', or 'hiul', or the Norse 'rol' or even the Saxon 'hweol', all of which mean 'wheel' and suggest the annual revolution of the sun. Equally, its source may lie with the Gothic 'ol' or 'oel' and the Anglo-Saxon 'geol', all meaning feast, or with the old Norse feast called 'joulo' or 'jol', which was probably named after the head of the Norse gods, Jolnir, better known as Odin.

Whatever its origin, Yule was celebrated with drinking and feasting and fertility rites to ensure a good harvest and a high birth-rate among men and beasts. These rites somehow developed into a feast in honour of the dead, who were believed to come back to haunt the living at the winter solstice. As part of the festivities, oak logs were lit in honour of the god Thor, the implacable foe of a harmful race of demons but a friend to man. More generally, great fires burned to symbolize the sun's survival and its promise of warmth and light. Norse customs were spread throughout Europe by the conquests of the Vikings and became entwined with a Celtic belief in the sacredness of perpetual fire and an assortment of superstitions connected with fires frightening away evil demons, and welcoming and warming the ancestral spirits who dwelt in the hearth– 'focus' in Latin. All these beliefs attached themselves to the log.

Before the advent of the Christmas tree the Yule log played a leading role in the British Christmas. A great log or gnarled root of oak, pine, ash or birch was borne in on Christmas Eve, or drawn in with ivy-covered ropes, children sitting astride it, and amid great frolic and toasting lit with a brand saved from last year's fire. Herrick wrote of the ceremony in the seventeenth century:

Come, bring, with a noise,
My merry, merry boys,
The Christmas Log to the firing:
While my good Dame she
Bids ye all be free,
And drink to your hearts' desiring.

Sometimes corn was sprinkled over the fire or a glass of wine or ale poured on, for good luck in the harvest. Reflecting the belief in the sacredness of perpetual fire, the log was supposed to burn for the full twelve days of Christmas (though some districts insisted merely that it should be lit daily). For the log to go out by itself was a portent of evil and it was very unlucky to give out or borrow a light over the Christmas season, particularly between Christmas Eve and New Year's Day. In Shropshire no one threw ashes out of the house on Christmas Day for fear that they might be thrown in Christ's face.

In Scotland the Yule log was often a piece of birch stripped of its bark. In the Highlands the log was identified with the Cailleach, or spirit of winter. Sometimes a female effigy carved out of wood and known as the Christmas Old Woman was also burnt–perhaps a link with Freya, the Norse god of fertility, who visited hearths at the winter solstice. Some parts of England burnt an ash faggot bound with strips of wood of different thicknesses. In a convivial ceremony, a bowl of cider was drunk as each band snapped in the fire. Sometimes each band was held to represent a pair of lovers and the order in which the bands snapped signified the sequence of weddings. Ash had a special Christian significance as it was said that Christ was first washed and dressed beside an ash fire. The ashes and charcoal from the logs had many magical properties and curative powers. They protected the house from evil and ensured fruitfulness in the land.

Similar practices and beliefs could be found in many parts of Europe, with interesting regional variations. The Serbs and Croats used to fell two or three young oaks on Christmas Eve and the women decorated the trunks with red silk and gold wire, leaves and flowers. As the father of the house carried the logs across the threshold at twilight another member of the family would throw corn or wine over him and the lit wood was similarly treated to ensure a good harvest and healthy beasts.

The northern French know the log as the souche de Noël (souche means tree stump). In Dauphiné it is called the chalendal, and in Provence the calignaou (both words derive from the

'The Yule Log in India – Bringing in the Ice.' Drawing by Adrien Marie for Graphic, 1889.

Roman Kalendae) or the tréfoir. In Provence, in a ceremony similar to that of the Serbs, the whole family used to bring the log in, singing a carol asking for blessings on the house, family and farm. The youngest child poured wine on the log in the name of the Father, the Son and the Holy Ghost and the log was thrown on the fire. Many superstitions attached to the charcoal: put under the bed it protected the house from lightning; incorporated in a plough it made the seed prosper; if women kept fragments until Epiphany, their poultry thrived; and contact with it protected people and animals from many diseases. Instead of Christmas cake French families enjoy the chocolate bûche de Noël, or Christmas log.

The northern Italians called the log ceppo or suc. In one district the blindfolded children of the house used to beat the burning log, then the whole family sang Ave Maria del Ceppo. There is a Christian tradition that the Virgin comes into the houses of poor people while they are at Midnight Mass to warm her newborn baby by the Yule log. In Spain the lads of the village would drag the log through the streets, beating it soundly as they went along. They were given presents of nuts and chocolate by householders along their route. Bulgarians also used to beat the blazing Yule log. Presumably the custom has some connection with driving out evil spirits. In Greece the Yule log was held to avert the Kallikantzaroi, supernatural Christmas visitors who used to terrorize peasants. To the Irish the log was called bloc na Nodlag, or Christmas block. In parts of Germany the block of wood known as the Christbrand was taken off the fire as soon as it was slightly charred and rekindled whenever a storm threatened, as protection against lightning.

Almost all the superstitions and practices connected with the Yule log belong to rural farming communities. Sadly, they faded away as more and more people moved into the cities.

Few domestic fireplaces these days have the capacity to consume a great Yule log, but it is still in accord with the season to light up for Christmas. Nothing can beat the comforting warmth, the cheerful crackle, the old-fashioned smell of a good log fire. The focus of any room, it welcomes friends and family (not just the living but the dead, who return to the family hearth at midwinter). Sadly, the seductive ease of central heating has driven our knowledge of fire-building back into the realms of folklore. Once everyone had their favourite trick to get the fire going or to stop it smoking. Now many families facing the energy crisis and un-boarding their fireplaces for the first time in decades are baffled, and their efforts to create a blazing fire bitterly disappointing.

'The Yule Log', an illustration by Alfred Crowquill, dated 1856.

The first rule is to check the local regulations on smokeless zones. If they give the all-clear, the second is to choose the right logs—some spit like devils, others glow like angels. Oak, if it is old and dry, is hard to beat. It burns slowly with a fierce red glow and smells pleasant, though with an acrid edge that can catch in the throat.

Logs to Burn

Beechwood fires are bright and clear
If the logs are kept a year.
Chestnut only good they say,
If for long 'tis laid away.
Birch and fir logs burn too fast,
Blaze up bright and do not last.
It is by the Irish said
Hawthorn bakes the sweetest bread.
Elm wood burns like churchyard mould,
E'en the very flames are cold.
Poplar gives a bitter smoke,
Fills your eyes and makes you choke.
Apple wood will scent your room,
With an incense like perfume.
Oak and maple, if dry and old,
Keep away the winter's cold.
But ash wood wet, or ash wood dry,
A King shall warm his slippers by.

Beech also burns well but again needs to be dry and well seasoned. The same goes for elm, now the most abundant of fuels. Silver birch guarantees a fiery display, but burns too fast to be economical. All the pines are lively and make excellent kindling, especially larch twigs, but while conifers, particularly cedars, give off a fine aromatic smell, they also spit and crackle like small-arms fire and need a small-mesh fireguard. Apple, pear and cherry are much sought after for their sweet scent. Holly makes good solid logs which can be burnt while still green and which give off a bright, clean flame. Hawthorn also burns when green and produces a lot of heat. Chestnut, willow and poplar come well down the list, with elder last of all. But the finest fuel is undoubtedly ash. The dry twigs which it casts off in abundance in the winter gales are ideal for kindling. A grate piled with seasoned ash logs is a delight to come home to, but they can also be burnt as green as grass.

The logs should be stored in a well-ventilated, waterproof place and used dry, otherwise they will be slow to catch and will smoke eye-wateringly. Fire burns oxygen, so a well-ventilated room or grate—and a recently swept chimney—are the first requirements. There are as many ways of building a fire as there are fire-builders, but for the newcomers more accustomed to manipulating a thermostat than a poker, here is a basic method. Make the foundation out of newspaper sheets rolled up and loosely knotted. Rest kindling wood on the paper so that the pieces rise towards the centre and back of the grate—this encourages the flames to rise and the smoke to go up the chimney. Put small pieces of coal and wood on the kindling. A match to the paper should be enough, but if more drastic action is called for, build the fire on chemical firelighters or use a gas poker or electric fan firelighter. Add more fuel slowly so as not to smother the flames. A well-established fire should have the bigger pieces of wood at the bottom and smaller ones at the top to draw the flames up.

When the smoke has stopped belching out and the logs are really hot and glowing, remember that fire not only warms, it cooks. Crumpets, muffins, even toast, all taste better off the end of a toasting fork. Toasted marshmallows and roast chestnuts are traditional Christmas fare, and potatoes wrapped in foil can be baked in the embers.

If the fire is still lively at bedtime, damp it down with water. Always leave an efficient fireguard round the grate at night, and during the day when there is no one around or if there are small children in the house. For safety's sake, make absolutely sure that any Christmas cards or decorations hung near the fire are securely attached to walls or mantelpiece.

RINGS & WREATHS

Door wreaths, tokens of welcome and friendship, are a recent innovation, but abundant evergreen wreaths, kissing rings and mistletoe balls have been used to decorate homes since before Victorian times. They are simple to make, give a pleasant perfume in a warm room and look much more festive than modern tinsel decorations.

Late nineteenth-century chromo-lithograph by Lizzie Mack.

1 Evergreen wreath hung with toys, bells, hearts and gingerbread.
2 Moss-covered Victorian half kissing ring with a sprig of mistletoe hung from the centre.
3 Ribbon-trimmed mistletoe ball.
4 Candlelit full kissing ring.
5 Classic evergreen Advent wreath with a candle to burn each Sunday of Advent.
6 Evergreen door wreath decorated with cones and gourds.
7 Chinese lantern flowers light up a glossy, dark, evergreen door wreath.
8 Woven corn wreath, ancient symbol of renewal and fertility at the winter solstice.
9 Holly cross, a popular Christmas door decoration in Ireland.
10 Scandinavian Christmas cross of skilfully pared wood.

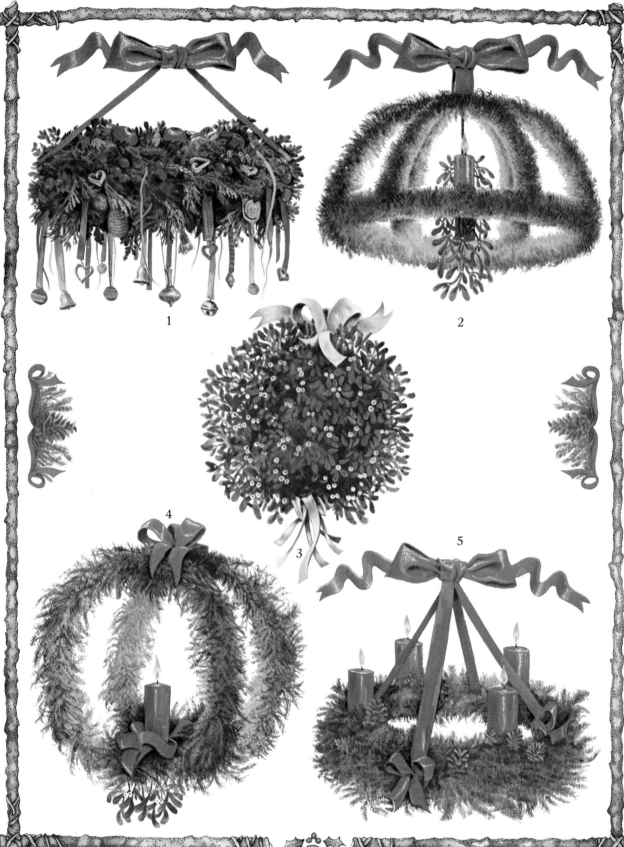

6

7

9

8

10

Making Rings & Wreaths

It takes a little longer to decorate your home with evergreen rings, wreaths and garlands than it does to pin up a few paper chains, but the final effect is infinitely more satisfying and gives a deeper link with the age-old celebrations of Christmas.

CHOOSING EVERGREEN

Most wreaths look more attractive if several different types of foliage are used. Holly, mistletoe, ivy, bay, rosemary, yew, laurel, fir, cypress, box, privet or thyme all give interesting variations of colour and texture. Choose thick, well-leafed branches and if you are buying your evergreen look for foliage which appears freshly cut, bright and glossy and preferably standing in water. If leaves look dry, limp and bedraggled when you buy them they won't last long. Cut the ends of the branches when you get them home, plunge them into deep water and lightly wash the leaves. Leave stems in water as long as possible before making your decorations.

EQUIPMENT REQUIRED

Newspaper to work on; fine and strong grades of wire, preferably covered florists' wire; green gardening string; secateurs; rubber gloves to protect your hands, if you can work in them; wire-cutter pliers; a basic frame for your decoration. You can buy a wreath frame of cane or wire which you can strip and use each year from a good florist, or you can make one by binding together with tape two or three loops of strong wire or wire coat hangers pulled into shape. Bind tightly packed moss or straw on to the basic frame with wire or string to round out the shape and give a good base for the evergreen (fig 1). This base material can be dampened to provide moisture for the cut greenery. The finished base should have a diameter of about 5 cm, rather less for kissing rings, which need a lighter framework.

To make the frame of the kissing ring you will need two circles of cane or four circles of wire bound with tape in pairs as described above. Slide one

fig 1

ring inside the other and bind top and bottom with wire (fig 2). The half kissing ring is more complicated. The easiest solution is to find a lampshade frame of the right shape and use this each year. The alternative is to use a wire or cane circle for the supporting

fig 2

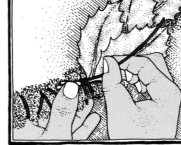

fig 3

base ring and three half-circles of strong wire which are bound together at the top with wire and the ends hooked very firmly round the circular wire base (fig 3). Cover the frames with moss as before but keep the diameter small and the construction light so that the finished decoration is neither heavy nor clumsy-looking. For the mistletoe ball base, pack moss round a ball of damp water-retaining flower-arranging block and wire round firmly (fig 4). The ball should be about 14 cm in diameter.

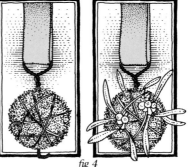

fig 4

TO COVER WREATHS

Cut greenery into lengths 10-16 cm. Have a heap of these at hand and bind them on one at a time, overlapping and closely packed with the foliage all lying in one direction (fig 5). Use florists' wire or green gardening string for this. Remember that a wreath which is intended to hang on a door or wall or to be used as a table decoration will

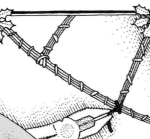

fig 5

not need covering with evergreen all the way round, while one that is to be hung from the ceiling must be well covered all over.

TO DECORATE THE WREATH

When the basic evergreen wreath is complete you can add as many or as few decorations as you wish, but have them wired and ready to use. A few artificial holly berries, which will probably come ready wired, may be useful in case berries fall off the holly. Soft fruit can be wired by pushing a

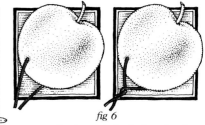

fig 6

strong wire through the fruit and twisting the ends together (fig 6); cones are wired by threading wire around the base and again twisting the ends together (fig 7). Where groups of things

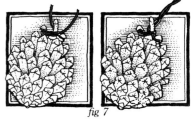

fig 7

such as several little cones or acorns are to be used bind the stems together firmly and twist the remaining wire into a spike as before (fig 8).

With nuts it may be necessary to burn a hole through the shell with a hot skewer (fig 9) to thread the wire

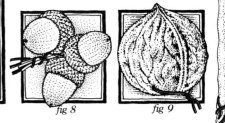

fig 8   fig 9

through. Any bunches of holly or mistletoe you wish to add to the wreath as a special spray or decoration should also be wired around the stems with the ends twisted into a spike (fig 10). When all your decorations are wired and ready push the spiked, twisted ends of the wire firmly into the wreath.

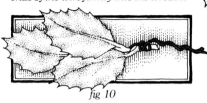
fig 10

RIBBONS AND BOWS
The quickest way of making small bows to dot about a wreath is simply to loop the ribbon in a bow shape and secure in the centre with wire (fig 11).

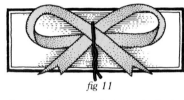
fig 11

Larger bows are best made in two parts, tying the bow first and then wiring the streamers to the back of the knot with a spike to attach it to the wreath. If a ribbon loop and bow is being used to hang a wreath this should also be done in two stages. A loop of the right length is put through the wreath and the ends wired firmly to the back of the separately made bow. In the case of the mistletoe ball or Advent wreath, which are hung on ribbons, strong wire should be threaded through the basic wreath or ball before evergreen is added. The wire is left in a loop, with a twist for strength and sufficient space between the loop and the wreath to allow for the evergreen. The twisted wire is then spiked right through the basic wreath and hooked well in underneath so that it cannot pull through (fig 4). The ribbon is threaded through the loop of wire when the decoration is complete.

CANDLES
Although real candles present a fire hazard many people still like to use them in a decoration rather than the electrical ones. There are fire-retardant sprays which provide some protection

and which can be used on evergreens, but if using candles make sure they are extremely firmly wired on, that they are never left burning when there is no one in the room and that the

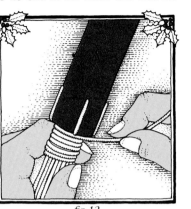
fig 12

flame cannot come into contact with the foliage. The best methods of attaching candles are as follows. Either heat a length of strong wire and push it up through the base of the candle for about 3 cm and secure the remaining

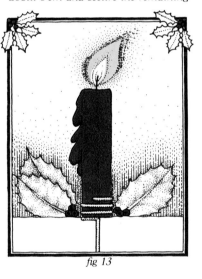
fig 13

spike firmly into the wreath, or place several wires around the base of the candle, bend and bind them together under the candle with wire and twist into a spike (fig 12), or wind a strong piece of wire in a spiral around the base of the candle and spike the end into the wreath as before (fig 13).

Wreaths are often very heavy. Never hang them from the electric light flex.

1 NOVELTY RIBBONED WREATH
Wire little decorations such as straw motifs, hearts, apples and small presents on to a full, bushy evergreen wreath. Hang little toys, bells, sweets and gingerbread from different lengths of multi-coloured ribbons.

2 & 4 VICTORIAN KISSING RINGS
The important thing with both these decorations is to keep the construction as light and neat as possible. If the moss used to cover the frame is in good condition this may be sufficient covering; if adding evergreen, cut sprigs to a length of only about 8 cm to bind on to the base. Foliage must be clipped neatly to prevent any contact with the candle. On the full kissing ring make a pad the size of a tennis ball of tightly packed moss wired at the point where the hoops cross. Flatten this down and wire the candle securely in place. The best type of candle to choose for this decoration would be the kind which burns down inside the centre of the candle. Tie a few sprays of mistletoe with a ribbon, thread with wire and attach underneath the completed decoration. For the half kissing ring it is necessary to use an electric candle fitting in place of a real candle. If the electric candle takes the place of a light bulb the whole decoration makes a charming Christmas light fitting.

3 MISTLETOE BALL
Cut sprigs of mistletoe to approx 15 cm and wire each separately and twist ends into a spike. When all are prepared push spikes firmly into prepared ball, slot a doubled ribbon through the wired loop on the top of the ball and wire another ribbon bow with streamers underneath.

5 ADVENT WREATH
Make a basic wreath binding evergreen all over if wreath is to be hung, leaving the underneath covered only with moss if your Advent wreath is to be used as a table decoration. Wire four candles firmly on to wreath and light one each Sunday of Advent until all four are burning on the fourth Sunday. Loop

doubled ribbon through the prepared wire loops on the wreath and gather the eight ends into a large bow to attach to a hook in the ceiling, taking care that the wreath hangs horizontally. Make separate bows and spike into the wreath where ribbon is attached.

6 CLASSIC DOOR WREATH
Using a wide variety of evergreen make a luxuriantly full wreath and add cones, nuts and gourds all individually wired and spiked into base.

7 CHINESE LANTERN WREATH
Use laurel, bay or other similar dark glossy evergreen leaves for the base of this wreath and add bright flame-coloured lantern flowers, each individually wired and spiked into the wreath. Suspend on a ribbon loop and bow. This wreath would also make a very interesting table centre.

8 CORN WREATH
Full instructions for corn weaving are given on page 36. This wreath makes an unusual door decoration, although it may not survive bad weather very well. It might be preferable to hang it on a wall or inside door or to use it as a table decoration.

9 HOLLY CROSS
This popular door decoration from Ireland is based on two pieces of plywood nailed or bound together with wire. Moss is bound tightly round the shape in the usual way with wire or green string. Masses of holly sprigs are then bound on, working always from the ends of the cross towards the centre, those sprigs most heavily berried being kept for the centre.

10 CHRISTMAS CROSS
This was a traditional door decoration in Scandinavia for St Thomas's day, 21 December; now it is more commonly known simply as a Christmas cross. Two pieces of wood are glued, nailed or jointed together, the wood then being pared delicately with a plane so that the fine curls of wood twist towards the centre of the cross.

GARLANDS & TREES

Garlanding a house is one of the most ancient evergreen traditions. Christmas trees are comparatively new arrivals, but since the last century have become the best loved of all Christmas decorations. Not every home has room for a floor-to-ceiling tree, but table trees can provide an attractive alternative.

Giving out Christmas presents

1 Garlanding surrounds a window, framing the winter scene outside.
2 Small table tree trimmed with scarlet bows and artificial holly berries wired on profusely.
3 Small feathers make an unusual decoration on a tree. Secure with a spot of glue.
4 A host of angels appears through the branches of a table tree above a Nativity scene landscaped below.

ON PAGES 74 & 75

5 A strong colour theme for a Christmas tree with green lights and orange gourds and tangerines.
6 'Homespun' tree with gingerbread shapes and bright rag bows.
7 Frosty tree wreathed in evergreen. Lay sprigs of holly, mistletoe, ivy and laurel between the branches. Cover with artificial frost and snow.
8 Christmas magic tree, with tinsel, toys and a fairy at the top.

1

2

3

4

Weaving Garlands

Traditional evergreen garlands look beautiful around window and door frames, along a mantelpiece, or wound around banisters. In America, Canada and Scandinavia many people decorate their houses outside as well, either with full garlands or simply boughs of evergreen arranged around windows, roof and door. Weaving garlands looks far more difficult than it is, which often deters people from experimenting with this most lovely way of decorating the house. In fact, garlanding needs only patience and a firm hand. First cover a large table with newspaper, then collect together as much evergreen of different types as you can. You will also need rope, about the weight and strength of a child's skipping rope, secateurs, lots of green gardening string and rubber gloves to protect your hands. If you find rubber gloves clumsy to work in, try the finer kind used by hairdressers. They will get punctured and split but will give some protection. Measure the area you wish to garland, looping the rope as you would like the garland to hang, and cut to this length, allowing enough extra rope to tie a strong non-slip loop to hang the finished garland by (fig 1). Tie the loop before starting to weave the garland so that the knot is covered by foliage. Before you start to work on your garland cut a pile of assorted evergreen to lengths of approx 20cm. In bunches of about six sprigs at a time start binding them on to the rope with green string, keeping the foliage

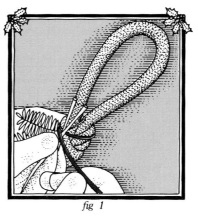

fig 1

packed together and all lying in one direction (fig 2). Be generous with the evergreen; a garland must be full and dense to look its best; mean, stringy garlands look very sad. When your garland is finished add any gourds, fir cones, ribbons or decorations you like, wiring them into place as described on page 68. The finished garland will probably be unexpectedly heavy, so tie or nail it very securely in position using the special loop. To prevent drying, spray lightly with a fine plant spray from time to time as long as the garland is away from electrical fittings, or use an anti-desiccant spray before you start weaving. If you wish to garland a table for a special buffet or supper party the garland should be finer and of non-prickly foliage, such as bay, laurel and fern, so that guests can approach the table safely. Attach the garland securely to a linen cloth, taking care to balance the weight.

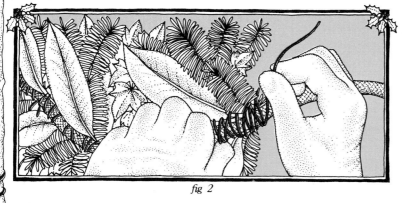

fig 2

Buying & Tending Trees

Before going out to buy your Christmas tree, decide where it is to stand so that you can gauge the height you require and also if the tree has to be perfect all round or just on one side, perhaps if it is to stand in a corner. Many places now sell trees tied up ready to take home, which makes it impossible to see what you are buying, so either ask for the tree to be untied or find a place which sells them standing free. Look for a symmetrical shape, good colour, clean appearance and full foliage. Check the tree for broken branches and bounce it on the ground to see if the branches are fresh and springy. If needles cascade down, the tree is already nearly finished. Look at the ends of the twigs to see how many needles have been lost and run your fingers up the branch; the needles should feel springy and resilient, not brittle or dropping off at the slightest touch.

Many trees are top cuts from trees felled for forestry and many others simply have their roots cut off. If the stump is fresh it may survive, but it is safer to saw it again in a diagonal when you get home and stand it in water. Saw it straight again for stability when you are ready to decorate it. Keep your tree in water, in a cool place, preferably out of doors until the last possible moment. The old practice of decorating the tree on Christmas Eve while the children waited all agog in the next room meant that the tree only had to survive the twelve days of Christmas indoors. Now many people decorate trees weeks before and wonder why they look threadbare and forlorn when Christmas comes.

If you are lucky enough to find a tree with fresh, healthy roots, it will stand a better chance of surviving Christmas with its needles intact. Provided it has been well treated and not yanked from the ground, damaging the roots, with careful handling it should last from year to year. Of course a full-grown tree cannot be dug up again indefinitely, but if you start with a comparatively small tree you stand a good chance of success. If you

have definitely decided to buy a Christmas tree to grow it would be wise to go to a nursery or tree plantation to make your choice. Plant the tree in a large garden tub with strong handles attached so that you can lift it each year. Line the bottom of the tub with broken crocks or stones for drainage and fill with a mixture of peat and garden soil. The tub can be buried in the garden or stand on a patio or balcony until you need it again. The tree's foliage will darken gradually, although the new growth will be lighter. If the surrounding atmosphere is polluted the foliage may need gentle washing before

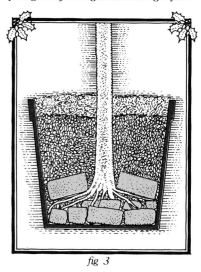

fig 3

you bring the tree indoors. Once installed, water frequently to prevent the tub from drying out in the warm room. If the tree is for one Christmas only, put the stump or roots into a tub and support and weight them with bricks. Fill the tub with wet sand or shingle and cover the top with wet moss to prevent evaporation (fig 3). Place the tree away from the fire or any other room heater and in a position out of the general traffic of the room. Spray with an anti-desiccant to slow down evaporation of moisture from the needles and also a fire-retardant spray as a precautionary measure. Allow branches time to settle if the tree has been tied up.

Decorating the Christmas Tree

Every family has its own ritual for decorating the Christmas tree. In many European countries it is decorated by the adults behind closed doors to be displayed after supper on Christmas Eve to the wonder and amazement of the children. In other countries everyone lends a hand, helping or hindering and generally joining in the fun. For some families the tree is an elegant work of art, for others a glorious chaos of colour, hung with decorations brought out and added to lovingly year after year. However, whichever style or size of tree you choose there are some basic rules to follow for decorating.

1. Install your tree in the right position, leaving enough room to get behind it. The tree should be decorated all round, not just on the side that shows, to give a depth of colour.

2. Make sure that the tree is completely secure and upright in its pot. Trees have been known to topple under the weight of decorations and presents, ripping out electrical wiring and doing considerable damage. Be sure the tree is safe, well watered, sprayed with an anti-desiccant to delay the drying out and loss of needles and sprayed also with a fire-retardant as an extra precaution against accidents.

3. With secateurs and wire clip away or mend any broken twigs or branches which may spoil the shape of the tree.

4. If you are decorating the trunk or tub attend to these first so that the tree is not disturbed when more fragile things have been added.

5. Put the lights on the tree next, having checked them thoroughly first. Nothing is more infuriating than carefully arranging the lights on the tree, mustering the family for the great switch on and nothing happening, then trying to check each bulb through the prickly foliage. Buy your tree lights, or get out the ones you put away carefully the previous year, at least a couple of weeks before you need them. Spread the lights out on the floor and tighten each bulb in turn in its socket. The lights should be connected to a fused plug, so both fuse

and wiring should be checked. Plug in and switch on. Hopefully, the lights will respond glitteringly; if not you must start the laborious job of checking to see which light bulb is the culprit breaking the circuit. Remember, however, that Christmas lights carry the full household voltage even though they look fragile and harmless, so treat them with respect. You should have several good replacement bulbs ready.

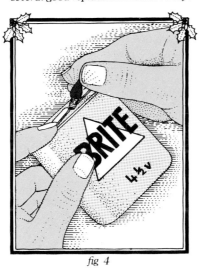

fig 4

There are three ways of checking the bulbs; you can hold each bulb up to a good light, if possible using a strong magnifying glass, to check that the fine filament is unbroken; carefully put a spare bulb which you know to be working into each socket in turn, exchanging it for the bulb in place, until the whole string lights up, switching off the set each time you change a bulb; or take out each bulb in turn and test it with a battery, as in the diagram (fig 4). The second method is best if you fear there may be more than one faulty bulb. If each individual bulb is found to be working and still the string will not light up then, unless you are an electrician, it is best to take the set to a professional as the wires to one of the holders may have become disconnected and re-soldering will be necessary. If you plan to put lights on an outdoor tree

buy some specifically designed for the job and remember that lights which flash on and off can cause interference to your, and your neighbours', television sets. Some Christmas tree lights have an automatic short-circuiting device so that if a bulb fails it is bypassed and the other lights stay on. However the faulty bulb should be replaced as soon as possible. When your lights are in perfect working order switch off and arrange them on the tree, starting at the top and working down and around. Don't bury bulbs in the tree's foliage or decorations or the air will be prevented from circulating, which could cause the bulbs to overheat. Always switch off and unplug the lights at night or when you are not in the house.

6. It is a nice idea to have a small gift on the tree for everyone who visits the house over Christmas. Tree presents should be especially light and attached to the tree. Larger presents should be piled up underneath the tree; if you try to balance them on the branches they will pull the tree out of shape or fall through at the slightest touch, disturbing or breaking other decorations.

7. Decorate the tree from top to bottom and all the way round, not just at eye-level. Tie decorations on firmly with a ribbon bow or use the green plastic S-bend hooks now widely available. Stand back from the tree from time to time to check that the decorations are well distributed.

8. Real candles are always a fire hazard, but many people still prefer them to electric lights. If you are using candles, put them on the tree last, making sure that the holder is securely fastened on the tree and the candle absolutely upright. The flame of the candle should not be able to come into contact with any part of the tree or decoration. Always check that candles are upright each time you relight them. Never leave candles burning if you are out of the room and always have a bucket of water handy in case of accidents. Using a fire-retardant spray on the tree would be particularly valuable if you plan to use candles.

The original Paradise trees were hung with apples and unblessed wafers of the host. By 1820, when the following description of a Christmas tree was published in America, things had changed considerably. It was decorated with 'gingerbread cut in various shapes, stars, hearts, sheep, goats, devils, diamonds, houses, rings. Fruit was also hung on the tree and raisins, strings of almonds, toy baskets filled with nuts, little presents such as handkerchiefs, collars, little red shoes, speckled stockings, little books, dolls, little horses, whips and wagons. Ornaments included: apples, balls, candy, cookies, cranberries, figs, frosting, gilt paper, lemons, oranges, paintings, popcorn, pretzels, rosettes, snow, soldiers, paper ornaments, tapers, tinsel and toys'. This description still gives plenty of ideas for tree decoration. Different countries also have their traditional favourites.

Denmark *People like to make their own decorations, even having a special 'cut and stick' day. Favourites are straw decorations, angels, flags, stars, pine cone birds and squirrels, boats of walnut shells and the unique red and latticed red and white paper hearts.*
Poland *Paper cut-outs are strung around the tree, also toys, apples, nuts, sweets, ribbons and beads.*
Iceland *The children weave colourful little bags to fill with sweets.*
Jamaica *Their Christmas cactus is decorated with gaily painted eggshells.*
Czechoslovakia *Favoured decorations are of paper, straw and papier-mâché.*
Holland and Germany *The custom is to hang the tree with decorated gingerbread shapes and chocolate.*
America *A wealth of different decorations often handed down through generations, the style depending on the original homeland of the family. Especially attractive are stuffed patchwork shapes, gaily coloured rag bows, plain or painted wooden shapes, papier-mâché decorations and amusingly shaped gingerbread, in German or Scandinavian style.*

5

6

7

8

Other Rings & Wreaths

Once you have learned to wire and assemble wreaths you can make any number of variations both for outdoors and indoors. For example, you can wire large, simple, silver Christmas tree baubles on to a basic evergreen wreath, or make a wreath entirely of herbs such as bay, thyme or rosemary and wire on every sweet-smelling thing you can find: dried lavender flowers or rosebuds, a whole nutmeg, dried orange or lemon peel cut into flower shapes, tiny polystyrene balls studded with cloves, and so on. Another idea is a bread wreath baked in the usual way but allowed to dry out completely, then given a couple of coats of varnish and tied with a brightly coloured ribbon or rag bow.

PINE CONE WREATH
One of the most popular door decorations in Scandinavia is the pine cone wreath. Collect together as many different sorts and sizes of pine cones as possible and wire them separately, or in groups if they are very small, in the usual way. You can wire cones either through the top scales or around the base, depending on how open the cone is and the effect you wish to achieve. Twist the ends of the wire together into a spike. Using a wire base covered with moss or straw, arrange the cones in an assorted cluster all the way round, or in graduated sizes with the biggest at the base of the wreath and the smallest at the top.

Spike the twisted ends of the wired cones into the base and finish the wreath with a bright ribbon bow.

APPLE FIR TREE
Another unusual door decoration is the apple fir tree, which originates from Canada. Cut a triangle of thick plywood or blockboard to the size you require for your finished decoration and screw a strong hook into the apex to hang it by. Wire together

several sprigs of fir, spread them out along the base of the triangle to cover the edge of the board, and nail into position. Arrange a pyramid of bright red, shiny apples and nail each apple through to the board to secure. Finish your apple fir tree with a sprinkling of artificial frost.

PLAITED FABRIC WREATHS
Very attractive wreaths with a nice folksy look can be made with printed cotton fabric. To make a plaited ring cut three strips of different prints 130 by 20cm. With right sides together, fold the strips in half widthwise and stitch down the length and across one end. Turn strips right side out, fill softly with padding and stitch end to close. Stitch together one end of all three strips and plait the padded lengths firmly. When the plait is finished, stitch together

the other three ends, curve plait into a ring and stitch both ends of plait together to fasten. Hide join with a large fabric bow.

RAG BOW WREATHS
Rag bow wreaths can be made in two ways, both using a polystyrene or foam base, which you should find in a good craft department or florist's shop. In the simplest version, you cut a pile of 13 cm squares with pinking shears in as many different prints as you can muster. Thread wire through the centre of the square and twist ends together into a spike at the back. Fix the wired squares into the wreath, bunching them as closely together as possible until the whole base is covered. In the second version of the rag bow wreath, a very large number of rag strips are cut with pinking shears in a wide range of prints to a length which will be determined by the

size of the finished bow you would like. Experiment with a few lengths until you find the size that pleases you. Tie the strips into bows, keeping the right side of the fabric showing. Wire the bows through the back of the knot and twist wire into a spike. The bows are then packed tightly around the wreath base until it is completely covered. Both wreaths can be finished with a wide rag bow.

MINIATURE WREATHS
These wreaths can be made to any size you like, to use as small table decorations, to ring candles or candlesticks, or to hang on the wall or the Christmas tree. You can make miniature wreaths as scaled-down versions of normal wreaths using a small wire circle covered with moss and wiring on tiny nuts, acorns, cones, berries, flower heads, seed pods and small evergreen leaves in the usual way. However, if the wreath is only to be seen from one side, for example if it is to lie on a table or hang against a wall,

it is easier to make the wreath in the following way. Cut a circle of thick card and cut a smaller circle from the middle. Cover the remaining ring of card thickly with a rubber solution glue, which will dry transparent, and leave until tacky. Using small ingredients as before, press them firmly into the glue, packed tightly together so that none of the cardboard backing shows. You can do the same thing without removing the centre of the circle and fix a candle into the centre.

Other Garlands & Trees

The classic Christmas tree can become a fairytale ice tree decorated with silver tinsel, artificial snow and frost, white candles, glass icicles and cut glass beads; or something reminiscent of the American pioneers with padded patchwork shapes; or look dramatic with an enormous rich red velvet bow tied at the top, its streamers reaching to the floor. The original Christmas trees were pyramids of apples or wreaths and these can still take the place of a tree in a small room.

THE APPLE PYRAMID

This elegant Christmas pyramid was originally seen in eighteenth-century Williamsburg, Virginia, and is still very popular today in America. Secure and weight a polystyrene cone on a large, lead floristry pin-holder. Wire a pile of sprigs of fir individually, twisting the ends of the wires into spikes, and push some of them, spaced apart, into the cone. Wire some bright red, shiny apples by pushing strong wire through the base of each apple and twisting wires together as before. Spike these in between the fir filling any gaps with more of the wired evergreen. Top the decoration with a pineapple. Secure it on a long double-ended steel knitting needle and push into the top of the cone.

DECORATED BOX TREE

Simple front door box trees can be decorated with small strands of outdoor lights, bunches of gilded nuts or cones, fruit such as apples, oranges or gourds or, as in the illustration, with shiny silver Christmas baubles.

CHRISTMAS WREATH PYRAMID

An elaborate example of a traditional Christmas pyramid, based on an engraving from 1843. Bore holes through a straight branch or a slender section of fir tree trunk approximately 75 cm high from two points to form right-angles at several equidistant points up the length, depending on how many wreaths you wish to attach. The central pole must then be nailed securely through a strong wooden base of sufficient size and weight to balance the height of the pole. Make several evergreen wreaths in the usual way, keeping the construction light and the foliage neat. The wreaths should graduate in size from a miniature wreath for the top of the pyramid to one slightly larger than a normal door wreath for the bottom. Thread two fine wooden rods, of lengths to correspond with the diameter of the various wreaths, through the holes bored up the pole to form a cross support for each wreath. Lay the wreath on the rods and wire to secure. Wire candles in any of the ways suggested on page 69 and attach to the wreaths and the top of the pyramid, taking the greatest care to ensure that the candle flame cannot come into contact with the wreath above. Arrange a mossy landscape on the base.

TABLE GARLANDS

The usual way to garland a table is to attach a looped garland to strategic points on a strong linen tablecloth. An interesting alternative is to put an evergreen wreath in the centre of the table, perhaps circling a candle centrepiece, and run four garlands from the wreath, across the table, to the four corners. These garlands must be made of non-scratch foliage if they are to lie on a polished table.

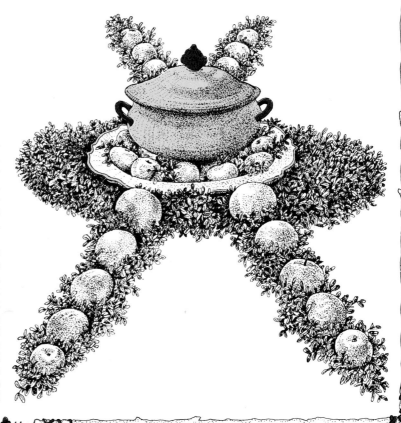

STOCKINGS & SHOES

Children in most countries enjoy the excitement of hanging up a stocking or leaving their shoes on the hearth to be filled with presents during the night by St Nicholas, or Father Christmas. Dutch children who leave their shoes out on St Nicholas Eve, with straw for his horse and an apple for his servant, Black Pete, find the food gone in the morning and sweets, gingerbread and small toys in its place. French children leave a glass of water with their shoes on Christmas Eve to refresh Father Christmas on his travels. In Britain and America children hang stockings on the mantelpiece or at the end of the bed. Traditionally the toe of the stocking was filled with an apple, for good health, the heel with an orange because they were rare and expensive, and a nut. A bag of gold-wrapped chocolate coins commemorates St Nicholas, while a mint-fresh coin symbolizes wealth for the future. A piece of coal wrapped in paper used to be included to indicate warmth in the years to come and salt was for good luck.

1 For warmth on Christmas morning the sock-stockings shown are knitted from a pattern on page 80. Knit one, or make a pair and the lucky child can wear them once they have been emptied of their surprises. Red and green striped stockings have snowy cuffs, pompoms and holly trimmings.

2 Rainbow-striped stockings with brightly contrasting top and toe can be made from any odds and ends of wool.

3 Another version of the pattern looking like party socks and one-button shoes. Make them in bright Christmas colours or try white socks, black shoes and a sparkly button. Cut a felt shape to fit the child's foot and stitch underneath to prolong their life as slipper socks.

4 Bright winter blue stockings with the legs decorated all over with snow-ball pompoms and a snowy cuff, with an outsize pompom on the toe.

1

2

4

3

Stitching Stockings

ILLUSTRATED ON PAGES 78 & 79

MATERIALS:
1 pair needles 9 (5½ mm)
1 medium crochet hook
chunky wool – 1.76 oz for foot/shoe,
5.28 oz for leg, 1.76 oz for turnover

SIZE
The basic stocking measures 22 in
(56 cm) from heel to top of stocking
and 9 in (23 cm) from heel to toe and
should fit a child of 10-12 years. To
make stockings smaller reduce both
needle size and thickness of wool.
3 months – 2 years: 4 ply wool, needles
2 (2¾ mm);3 years – 9 years: double
knitting wool, needles 6 (4 mm)

ABBREVIATIONS:
k=knit; p=purl; st=stitches; sl=slip;
rep=repeat; cont=continue; pr=pair;
c.front=centre front; col=colour;
inc=increase; tog=together.

BASIC STOCKING WITH SHOE
Cast on 51 st in foot colour. Work
two rows in garter stitch
Row 3 inc 1 st, in from each end also
inc 1 st, on each side of centre st
Row 5 as row 3 with 3 st space in
centre
Row 7 as row 3 with 5 st space in
centre
Row 9 as row 3 with 7 st space in
centre. 67 st on needle. Cont in garter
stitch
Row 24 k 39, k 2 tog, turn
Row 25 * sl 1, k 11, k 2 tog turn*
Rep * to * 12 times
Row 37 change colour
Rep * to * 14 times in k 1 p 1 rib
At end of last decrease row knit across
remaining 12 st. Next row rib (37 st).
Cont in rib for 75 rows inc 1 st at each
end of every 10th row.
Row 128 change colour. Cont in rib
for 12 rows.
Row 141 Cast off. Sew seam up back.
STRAP
Pick up 3 st 14 st from seam where
colour changes, k in garter st for 20
rows. Cast off. Sew button through
end of strap to hold in place on other
side of shoe 14 st from seam.
HANGING LOOP
In spare wool pick up 1 st at back
seam of stocking. On crochet hook
make a chain for 16 st. Cast off. Sew
end to stocking to form a loop.

MULTI-STRIPED STOCKING
As for basic stocking, but using 4
colours for the rib. Change colour
every 2nd row. Make 2 pompoms
leaving a long thread on each. Use
this to crochet a 15-in chain. Sew the
end of each chain to c.front of turnover. Tie in a bow.

'SNOWBALL' STOCKING
In blue wool work as basic stocking,
but do not change colour until row
128, then change to white.
Cont in rib for 12 rows.
Row 141 cast off. Sew up seam. Sew
on small white pompoms.

HOLLY LEAF STOCKING
Use red, white fluffy and green wool –
all chunky. In green knit as basic
stocking to row 37.
Row 37 change to red, cont as basic
Row 62 change to green, cont as basic
Row 67 change to red, cont as basic
Row 77 change to green, cont as basic
Row 81 rib 7 st in green, * using red
wool k 1, p 1, k 1, p 1, all in next st,
turn p 4 * turn k 4, turn p 4, turn k 4.
Now sl 2nd, 3rd and 4th st over 1st of
these 4 st*. Bobble berry made. Rib
14 in green rep from * to * on next st,
rib 14 in green, rep from * to * on next
st rib to end of row in green
Row 82 rib
Row 83 rib 6 st in green, on next st rep
* to *
rib 1 st in green, on next st rep * to *
rib 12 st in green, on next st rep * to *
rib 1 st in green, on next st rep * to *
rib 12 st in green, on next st rep * to *
rib 1 st in green, on next st rep * to *
rib 6 st in green
Row 84 rib in green
Row 87 change to red
Row 97 change to green
Row 103 change to red
Row 113 change to green
Row 128 change to white
Row 141 cast off. Sew up back seam.
HOLLY LEAVES
Cast on 5 st in green

Row 1 inc 1 st, rib 2 st, k 2 tog
Row 2 rib
Row 3 as row 1
Row 4 as row 2
Row 5 as row 1
Row 6 cast off.
Sew holly leaves around the berries.
POMPOM
Toe pompom: On two pieces of card,
draw around a saucer and then, in the
centre of the circle, put a cup and draw
around that. Cut around both circles.
Place both rings of card together and
wind wool around them until they are
well covered. Slip scissors between the
outside edges of the rings and cut the
wool all the way round the circumference. Tightly tie a length of wool

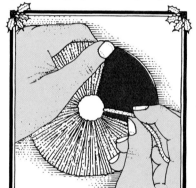

fig 1

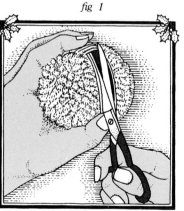

fig 2

between the two layers of card. For
smaller pompoms, use an egg cup and
saucer as a template, or even an egg
cup and large thimble.

La Légende de Saint Nicolas

1
Ils étaient trois petits enfants
Qui s'en allaient glaner aux champs
Ils sont allés et tant venus
Que sur le soir se sont perdus.
Ils sont allés chez le boucher:
– Boucher, voudrais-tu nous loger?

2
– Entrez, entrez, petits enfants,
Y'a de la place assurément.
Ils n'étaient pas sitôt entrés
Que le boucher les a tués,
Les a coupés en p'tits morceaux
Et puis salés dans un tonneau.

3
Saint Nicolas au bout d'sept ans
Vint à passer dedans ce champ,
Alla frapper chez le boucher:
– Boucher, voudrais-tu me loger?
– Entrez, entrez, saint Nicolas,
Y'a de la place, il n'en manqu' pas.

4
Il n'était pas sitôt entré
Qu'il a demandé à souper.
On lui apporte du jambon.
Il n'en veut pas, il n'est pas bon.
On lui apporte du rôti.
Il n'en veut pas, il n'est pas cuit.

5
– Du p'tit salé, je veux avoir
Qu'il y a sept ans qu'est au saloir.
Quand le boucher entendit ça,
Bien vivement il se sauva.
– Petits enfants qui dormez là,
Je suis le grand saint Nicolas.

6
Le grand saint étendit trois doigts,
Les trois enfants ressuscita.
Le premier dit: 'J'ai bien dormi.'
Le second dit: 'Et moi aussi.'
A ajouté le plus petit:
'Je croyais être au Paradis.'

THE GIFT OF THE MAGI

O Henry

NE DOLLAR and eighty-seven cents. That was all. And sixty cents of it was in pennies. Pennies saved one and two at a time by bulldozing the grocer and the vegetable man and the butcher until one's cheeks burned with the silent imputation of parsimony that such close dealing implied. Three times Della counted it. One dollar and eighty-seven cents. And the next day would be Christmas.

There was clearly nothing to do but flop down on the shabby little couch and howl. So Della did it. Which instigates the moral reflection that life is made up of sobs, sniffles, and smiles, with sniffles predominating.

While the mistress of the home is gradually subsiding from the first stage to the second, take a look at the home. A furnished flat at $8 per week. It did not exactly beggar description, but it certainly had that word on the lookout for the mendicancy squad.

In the vestibule below was a letter-box into which no letter would go, and an electric button from which no mortal finger could coax a ring. Also appertaining thereunto was a card bearing the name 'Mr. James Dillingham Young.'

The 'Dillingham' had been flung to the breeze during a former period of prosperity when its possessor was being paid $30 per week. Now, when the income had shrunk to $20, the letters of 'Dillingham' looked blurred, as though they were thinking seriously of contracting to a modest and unassuming D. But whenever Mr. James Dillingham Young came home and reached his flat above he was called 'Jim' and greatly hugged by Mrs. James Dillington Young, already introduced to you as Della. Which is all very good.

Della finished her cry and attended to her cheeks with the powder rag. She stood by the window and looked out dully at a gray cat walking a gray fence in a gray backyard. Tomorrow would be Christmas Day, and she had only $1.87 with which to buy Jim a present. She had been saving every penny she could for months, with this result. Twenty dollars a week doesn't go far. Expenses had been greater than she had calculated. They always are. Only $1.87 to buy a present for Jim. Her Jim. Many a happy hour she had spent planning for something nice for him. Something fine and rare and sterling – something just a little bit near to being worthy of the honor of being owned by Jim.

There was a pier-glass between the windows of the room. Perhaps you have seen a pier-glass in an $8 flat. A very thin and very agile person may, by observing his reflection in a rapid sequence of longitudinal strips, obtain a fairly accurate conception of his looks. Della, being slender, had mastered the art.

Suddenly she whirled from the window and stood before the glass. Her eyes were shining brilliantly, but her face had lost its color within twenty seconds. Rapidly she pulled down her hair and let it fall to its full length.

Now, there were two possessions of the James Dillingham Youngs in which they both took a mighty pride. One was Jim's gold watch that had been his father's and his grandfather's. The other was Della's hair. Had the Queen of Sheba lived in the flat across the airshaft, Della would have let her hair hang out of the window some day to dry just to depreciate Her Majesty's jewels and gifts. Had King Solomon been the janitor, with all his treasures piled up in the basement, Jim would have pulled out his watch every time he passed, just to see him pluck at his beard from envy.

So now Della's beautiful hair fell about her rippling and shining like a cascade of brown waters. It reached below her knees and made itself almost a garment for her. And then she did it up again nervously and quickly. Once she faltered for a minute and stood still while a tear or two splashed on the worn red carpet.

On went her old brown jacket; on went her old brown hat. With a whirl of skirts and with the brilliant sparkle still in her eyes, she fluttered out the door and down the stairs to the street.

Where she stopped the sign read: 'Mme. Sofronie. Hair Goods of All Kinds.' One flight up Della ran, and collected herself, panting. Madame, large, too white, chilly, hardly looked like the 'Sofronie.'

'Will you buy my hair?' asked Della.

'I buy hair,' said Madame. 'Take yer hat off and let's have a sight at the looks of it.'

Down rippled the brown cascade.

'Twenty dollars,' said Madame, lifting the mass with a practised hand.

'Give it to me quick,' said Della.

Oh, and the next two hours tripped by on rosy wings. Forget the hashed metaphor. She was ransacking the stores for Jim's present.

She found it at last. It surely had been made for Jim and no one else. There was no other like it in any of the stores, and she had turned all of them inside out. It was a platinum fob chain simple and chaste in design, properly proclaiming its value by substance alone and not by meretricious ornamentation – as all good things should do. It was even worthy of The Watch. As soon as she saw it she knew that it must be Jim's. It was like him. Quietness and value – the description applied to both. Twenty-one dollars they took from her for it, and she hurried home with the 87 cents. With that chain on his watch Jim might be properly anxious about the time in any company. Grand as the watch was, he sometimes looked at it on the sly on account of the old leather strap that he used in place of a chain.

When Della reached home her intoxication gave way a little to prudence and reason. She got out her curling irons and lighted the gas and went to work repairing the ravages made by generosity added to love. Which is always a tremendous task, dear friends – a mammoth task.

Within forty minutes her head was covered with tiny, close-lying curls that made her look wonderfully like a truant schoolboy. She looked at her reflection in the mirror long, carefully, and critically.

'If Jim doesn't kill me,' she said to herself, 'before he takes a second look at me, he'll say I look like a Coney Island chorus girl. But what could I do – Oh! what could I do with a dollar and eighty-seven cents?'

At 7 o'clock the coffee was made and the frying-pan was on the back of the stove hot and ready to cook the chops.

Jim was never late. Della doubled the fob chain in her hand and sat on the corner of the table near the door that he always entered. Then she heard his step on the stair away down on the first flight, and she turned white for just a moment. She had a habit of saying little silent prayers about the simplest everyday things, and now she whispered: 'Please God, make him think I'm still pretty.'

The door opened and Jim stepped in and closed it. He looked thin and very serious. Poor fellow, he was only twenty-two – and to be burdened with a family! He needed a new overcoat and he was without gloves.

Jim stopped inside the door, as immovable as a setter at the scent of quail. His eyes were fixed upon Della, and there was an expression in them that she could not read, and it terrified her. It was not anger, nor surprise, nor disapproval, nor horror, nor any of the sentiments that she had been prepared for. He simply stared at her fixedly with that peculiar expression on his face.

Della wriggled off the table and went for him.

'Jim, darling,' she cried, 'don't look at me that way. I had my hair cut off and sold it because I couldn't have lived through Christmas without giving you a present. It'll grow out again – you won't mind, will you? I just had to do it. My hair grows awfully fast. Say "Merry Christmas!" Jim,

and let's be happy. You don't know what a nice – what a beautiful, nice gift I've got for you.'

'You've cut off your hair?' asked Jim, laboriously, as if he had not arrived at that patent fact yet even after the hardest mental labor.

'Cut it off and sold it,' said Della. 'Don't you like me just as well, anyhow? I'm me without my hair, ain't I?'

Jim looked about the room curiously.

'You say your hair is gone?' he said, with an air almost of idiocy.

'You needn't look for it,' said Della. 'It's sold, I tell you – sold and gone, too. It's Christmas Eve, boy. Be good to me, for it went for you. Maybe the hairs of my head were numbered,' she went on with a sudden serious sweetness, 'but nobody could ever count my love for you. Shall I put the chops on, Jim?'

Out of his trance Jim seemed quickly to wake. He enfolded his Della. For ten seconds let us regard with discreet scrutiny some inconsequential object in the other direction. Eight dollars a week or a million a year – what is the difference? A mathematician or a wit would give you the wrong answer. The magi brought valuable gifts, but that was not among them. This dark assertion will be illuminated later on.

Jim drew a package from his overcoat pocket and threw it upon the table.

'Don't make any mistake, Dell,' he said, 'about me. I don't think there's anything in the way of a haircut or a shave or a shampoo that could make me like my girl any less. But if you'll unwrap that package you may see why you had me going a while at first.'

White fingers and nimble tore at the string and paper. And then an ecstatic scream of joy; and then, alas! a quick feminine change to hysterical tears and wails, necessitating the immediate employment of all the comforting powers of the lord of the flat.

For there lay The Combs – the set of combs, side and back, that Della had worshipped for long in a Broadway window. Beautiful combs, pure tortoise shell, with jewelled rims – just the shade to wear in the beautiful vanished hair. They were expensive combs, she knew, and her heart had simply craved and yearned over them without the least hope of possession. And now, they were hers, but the tresses that should have adorned the coveted adornments were gone.

But she hugged them to her bosom and at length she was able to look up with dim eyes and smile and say: 'My hair grows so fast, Jim!'

And then Della leaped up like a little singed cat and cried, 'Oh, oh!'

Jim had not yet seen his beautiful present. She held it out to him eagerly upon her open palm. The dull precious metal seemed to flash with a reflection of her bright and ardent spirit.

'Isn't it a dandy, Jim? I hunted all over town to find it. You'll have to look at the time a hundred times a day now. Give me your watch. I want to see how it looks on it.'

Instead of obeying, Jim tumbled down on the couch and put his hands under the back of his head and smiled.

'Dell,' said he, 'let's put our Christmas presents away and keep 'em a while. They're too nice to use just at present. I sold the watch to get the money to buy your combs. And now suppose you put the chops on.'

The magi, as you know, were wise men – wonderfully wise men – who brought gifts to the Babe in the manger. They invented the art of giving Christmas presents. Being wise, their gifts were no doubt wise ones, possibly bearing the privilege of exchange in case of duplication. And here I have lamely related to you the uneventful chronicle of two foolish children in a flat who most unwisely sacrificed for each other the greatest treasures of their house. But in a last word to the wise of these days let it be said that of all who give gifts these two were the wisest. Of all who give and receive gifts, such as they are wisest. Everywhere they are wisest. They are the magi.

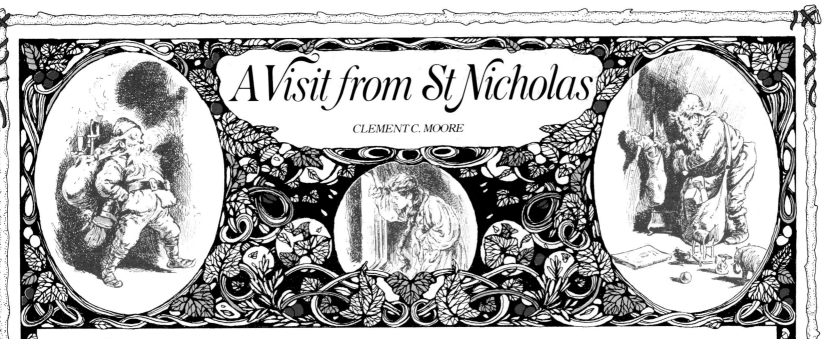

A Visit from St Nicholas

CLEMENT C. MOORE

'Twas the night before Christmas, when all through the house
Not a creature was stirring, not even a mouse;
The stockings were hung by the chimney with care,
In hopes that St Nicholas soon would be there;
The children were nestled all snug in their beds,
While visions of sugar-plums danced in their heads;
And Mamma in her kerchief, and I in my cap,
Had just settled our brains for a long winter's nap,
When out on the lawn there arose such a clatter,
I sprang from the bed to see what was the matter.
Away to the window I flew like a flash,
Tore open the shutters and threw up the sash.
The moon on the breast of the new-fallen snow
Gave the lustre of midday to objects below,
When, what to my wondering eyes should appear,
But a miniature sleigh, and eight tiny reindeer,
With a little old driver, so lively and quick,
I knew in a moment it must be St Nick.
More rapid than eagles his coursers they came,
And he whistled, and shouted, and called them by name:
Now, Dasher! now Dancer! now Prancer and Vixen!
On, Comet! on, Cupid! on, Donner and Blitzen!
To the top of the porch! to the top of the wall!
Now dash away! dash away! dash away all!'
As dry leaves that before the wild hurricane fly,
When they meet with an obstacle, mount to the sky,
So up to the house-top the coursers they flew,
With the sleigh full of toys, and St Nicholas too.

And then, in a twinkling, I heard on the roof
The prancing and pawing of each little hoof.
As I drew in my head, and was turning around,
Down the chimney St Nicholas came with a bound.
He was dressed all in fur, from his head to his foot,
And his clothes were all tarnished with ashes and soot;
A bundle of toys he had flung on his back,
And he looked like a pedlar just opening his pack.
His eyes – how they twinkled! his dimples how merry!
His cheeks were like roses, his nose like a cherry!
His droll little mouth was drawn up like a bow,
And the beard of his chin was as white as the snow;
The stump of a pipe he held tight in his teeth,
And the smoke it encircled his head like a wreath;
He had a broad face and a little round belly,
That shook when he laughed, like a bowlful of jelly.
He was chubby and plump, a right jolly old elf,
And I laughed when I saw him, in spite of myself;
A wink of his eye and a twist of his head
Soon gave me to know I had nothing to dread.
He spoke not a word, but went straight to his work,
And filled all the stockings; then turned with a jerk,
And laying his finger aside of his nose,
And giving a nod, up the chimney he rose;
He sprang to his sleigh, to his team gave a whistle,
And away they all flew like the down of a thistle.
But I heard him exclaim, ere he drove out of sight,
Happy Christmas to all and to all a good night.

CHRISTMAS

EDIEVAL CHRIST-MAS was a glorious public spectacle, lasting for several weeks, in which everyone played a role. Nowadays Christmas is a private affair with no universally accepted pattern. National and religious traditions link people's celebrations but for the most part Christmas customs have come to rest within the family.

Decorations for the tree, the Christmas menu, the carols sung and stories told are family practices preserved and handed on from generation to generation. Taken round the world by emigrants and missionaries, these traditions have adapted to hotter climes and merged with local customs – just as the early Church imposed its own interpretations on pagan practices. In Jamaica the cactus makes a fine Christmas tree. In Brazil Christmas is carnival time. In Australia sensible people eat their roast turkey cold with salad. In Japan children in kimonos perform Nativity plays.

The mood of Christmas celebrations varies from culture to culture. For some, it is a time for quiet, reverence and fasting – the revelry and presents are saved for New Year or Epiphany. For others, Christmas is the most joyous festival of the year, marked by feasting and fun. Christmas Eve is the most important day for many nationalities, but in the Anglo-Saxon tradition it is merely the prologue to Christmas Day. In many lands the holiday has shrunk to a single day, but in the Southern Hemisphere it falls in the middle of the long summer holidays. Even the date of Christmas varies, with some Eastern

'Christmas Morning' drawn by A. Forestier. From the Illustrated London News, Christmas, 1896.

Orthodox churches still insisting on celebrating Old Christmas on 6 January.

Everywhere Christmas Eve is the day when weeks of preparation, spiritual and practical, are finally completed. In spite of the far-flung celebrations of Christmas and the diversity of the cultures it draws on, a surprising range of practices and beliefs are common to many lands. Most people attach great importance to

cleanliness, of body and home, at the festive season. This was even more significant in the days before constant hot water and vacuum cleaners. In rural areas of countries as far apart as Jamaica and Ireland, the week before Christmas is spent sweeping, repairing and whitewashing farms and yards. The last Sunday before Christmas is still called Dirty Sunday in Norway. Houses are thoroughly cleaned and everything that can be polished gleams. In the old days everyone, including the animals, had their annual bath. In Finland everyone who can find time goes for a Christmas sauna. Clean clothes, or even new clothes, are commonly worn at Christmas. In Iceland anyone who did not have a new garment of some sort was believed to fall victim to the 'Christmas cat', which ate up his Christmas dinner.

Animals as well as humans are paid extra attention in honour of their presence at the manger and presumably in the unexpressed, but distinctly pagan, hope that this will encourage them to produce well in the coming year. In some parts of Poland families pay a ceremonial visit to the farm animals, taking the leftovers from Christmas supper with them. Norwegian farmers used to paint tar crosses over the doors of farm buildings on Christmas Eve to ward off evil spirits, and animals in many lands are treated to especially rich food and drink. Legendary stories are told about animals: that at midnight on Christmas Eve cattle kneel down and adore the newborn King, or that animals gain the power of speech, though it brings bad luck to hear them speaking. Bees are said to wake from their winter sleep and hum – in northern England they used to go further and hum a

'Uncle William's Christmas Presents' by John Gilbert. Illustrated London News, *1856.*

Christmas hymn. Midnight on Christmas Eve is considered a most auspicious time for divining the future.

On Christmas Eve throughout the world, under a blazing sun or surrounded by ice and snow, the house is decorated, the tree and the crib set up, the last cards despatched, and candles and fires lit. The Christmas tree is one of the most recent, and now one of the most widespread, of seasonal traditions, and in the absence of the Norway Spruce, traditional to northern Europe, almost any tree is substituted and decked with stars and presents, sweet-meats, lights and baubles. In countries that celebrate Christmas in cold midwinter, holly, mistletoe, ivy and evergreens are cut and brought indoors. People in hotter climates decorate their homes with all the flowers and shrubs in bloom. In Catholic countries treasured figures of the Holy Family and their attendants are unwrapped and lovingly installed in and around the crib.

In country areas where large fireplaces survive, the Yule log is still cut and borne in amid singing and dancing to be blessed with corn or wine or oil before being lit to burn through the Christmas season. When darkness falls on Ireland the tall Christmas candle, usually red and decorated with holly sprigs or ribbon, is lit and placed in the window to guide the Holy Family to shelter. Candles play a particularly important

part in the dark, cold Christmases of northern Europe, where, in accord with the old belief that Christmas is a celebration of the dead as well as the living, it is the custom to visit the church-yard on Christmas Eve and put lighted candles on the graves of relatives.

Straw used to figure prominently at Christmas and is a clear link with pagan practices, though the Christian explanation is that it commemorates Christ's first resting place. Straw crosses and mobiles are used in decorations. Many Scandinavian families still hang out a sheaf of oats for the birds at Christmas. In Poland a few blades of hay are placed under the white linen cloth. In the old days straw used to be spread over the floor and a sheaf each of wheat, rye, oats and barley was placed in the four corners of the room.

On Christmas Eve, in countries where gifts are exchanged at Christmas, and these days that includes most countries, the family retires to separate rooms to do the last-minute wrapping. Every country, whether it belongs to the feasting or fasting tradition, has special food to prepare and last-minute jobs to do in the kitchen. Absent members of the family and old friends who join the family circle at Christmas are welcomed home on Christmas Eve. The signal is given for the start of Christmas – often quite literally. In Finland it is the Christmas proclamation of peace which is given from the

cathedral in Turku, Finland's oldest town, at midday. In Norway church bells at 5 pm send the last people on the streets scuttling home. In Orthodox homes in Russia and in Poland children watch for the first star to appear. Then everyone exchanges greetings and breaks bread before starting the traditional supper.

Those countries that celebrate Christmas as a quiet time of family devotion tend to allocate gift-bringing duties to characters who appear before or after Christmas – St Nicholas, Befana or the Three Kings, though these days most children hope for Santa Claus to visit them as well. But in households which are expecting a visit from Santa, tomtes and nisser, the Christ-kind or the Weihnachtsman, excitement builds up throughout the Christmas Eve meal. In Germany, Scandinavia, Switzerland and Austria the tree is revealed after supper in all its candle-lit glory. Gifts are exchanged, carols sung, the gospel read and stories told. If the windows are opened the family may be lucky enough to hear on the cold night air carols sung by star boys or carol singers going from house to house. In Scandinavian countries families form a ring round the tree and sing carols together.

The Christmas Eve Midnight Mass plays the central part in the celebrations in those countries where Christmas is still essentially a religious festival. In Italy and France, Spain and Belgium and distant parts of the globe where their influence is felt, whole families, right down

'Christmas Comes but Once a Year': A scene at the Evelina Hospital by C.J. Staniland.

to the smallest, sleepiest child attend church. In Belgium mass is followed by an exchange of presents, in France by a meal called the Réveillon, a sumptuous feast with pâté and oysters and other delicious foods. French Canadians often follow their Réveillon with party games and dancing until dawn. Church-going is also central to the celebrations in Jamaica and Ireland, where midnight mass and the dawn service vie for popularity. Those who attend the dawn masses in the Philippines can stave off hunger pangs by tasting the local delicacies on the stalls in the churchyard. Midnight masses have also become increasingly popular in recent years in Protestant countries.

In the robust cultures of South America, Christmas is often a time for revelry and dressing up. Brazil has a strong Carnival tradition of Christmas folk plays, dances, music and games involving all the townspeople. Mexican families enact the 'posadas', a ritual procession and play dramatizing Mary and Joseph's search for a room in an inn ('posada' means an inn). In the Peruvian capital there is a Christmas bull fight and in Colombia Christmas Eve is celebrated with fancy-dress revelry. The Jonkunnu band and dancers play a treasured part in the Jamaican Christmas and on Christmas morning Jamaican families attend concerts which are usually variety shows of song, dance and comedy. In the Philippines beautiful ladies in colourful costumes dance a pantomime of the Lord's Nativity.

In those countries where everyone spent Christmas Eve eating and drinking, singing and dancing and opening presents, Christmas Day is for quiet family gatherings and informal visits and attending church. Some countries, though, are reluctant to give up. The Danes, after enjoying a particularly full Christmas Eve, wake up to

A German Christmas tree, decorated with candles, by A. Muttenthaler, 1865.

a boisterous and sociable Christmas Day, when they commonly enjoy a two-hour lunch with family and friends and then walk it off in the snow. Hungarians feast again on Christmas Day and French families gather round another well-spread table with poultry traditionally at the centre and the chocolate Christmas log or Bûche de Noël to round things off. Icelanders can indulge in card-playing – banned on Christmas Eve. In Holland, where Christmas is essentially a season of peace and goodwill, best spent quietly at home, the Dutch eat their Christmas dinner in the evening of Christmas Day.

In the Anglo-Saxon tradition, Christmas Day is the most important of the festive season and is always spent at home with the family. The day starts distressingly early when the children discover that the stockings they left at the end of their beds have been filled mysteriously during the night by Father Christmas. Family presents are taken from under the tree and opened during the morning, before or after church service, if the family attends. Roast turkey followed by a flaming Christmas pudding is the traditional Christmas meal, usually eaten at late lunchtime, and finished off with cracker-pulling, paper hats and mottoes, port and Stilton cheese for the adults and nuts and chocolate for the children. The Queen's Christmas Day broadcast enjoys a wide audience after lunch and then the more awake members of the family go for a walk or play parlour games. The day often finishes with ghost stories or carol singing.

The English tradition is dominant in English-speaking Canada, in the United States, where many of the traditions have merged with other influences and been re-exported to England, and in all parts of the world where British settlers have established themselves. In spite of temperatures in the hundreds and the unmistakeably summer sound of cricket ball on bat, many Australians try to reproduce the Christmas they knew in an earlier homeland. But if the hot roast turkey and the scarlet-robed Father Christmas seem out of place the great family gatherings are in the right mood for the season. South African Christmas dinner – a spread of roast lamb, chicken pie, roast sucking pig and fresh ripe fruit and vegetables – might be eaten to the accompaniment of a deafening midsummer thunderstorm.

By the end of Christmas Day most people will have eaten and drunk too much and seen enough of their family to last them for some time. Many go back to work the following day. For others there is at least one more holiday left.

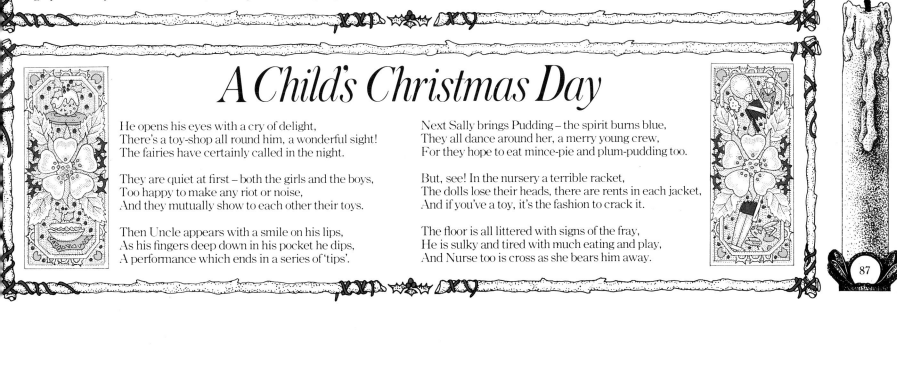

A Child's Christmas Day

He opens his eyes with a cry of delight,
There's a toy-shop all round him, a wonderful sight!
The fairies have certainly called in the night.

They are quiet at first – both the girls and the boys,
Too happy to make any riot or noise,
And they mutually show to each other their toys.

Then Uncle appears with a smile on his lips,
As his fingers deep down in his pocket he dips,
A performance which ends in a series of 'tips'.

Next Sally brings Pudding – the spirit burns blue,
They all dance around her, a merry young crew,
For they hope to eat mince-pie and plum-pudding too.

But, see! In the nursery a terrible racket,
The dolls lose their heads, there are rents in each jacket,
And if you've a toy, it's the fashion to crack it.

The floor is all littered with signs of the fray,
He is sulky and tired with much eating and play,
And Nurse too is cross as she bears him away.

NATIVITY CRIBS

Shortly before Christmas 1223, St Francis of Assisi wrote to his friend John Velita, the lord of Greccio, 'I would fain make memorial of that Child who was born in Bethlehem, and in some sort behold with bodily eyes His infant hardships; how He lay in a manger on the hay, with the ox and the ass standing by.' On Christmas Eve the local people, bearing torches and singing hymns, made their way up the rocky hillside above the village to join St Francis and his brethren. The hay and the manger were ready, the ox and the ass were led in, and the scene of the nativity was re-enacted in a joyful and moving ceremony that brought home to the congregation Christ's humble birth.

St Francis and his followers popularized the presepio, or crib, but they did not invent the custom. In early Christmas ritual, mass was celebrated over a 'manger' in which the consecrated host was laid. In the eighth century Pope Gregory III placed 'a golden image of the Mother of God embracing God our Saviour, in various gems' in Santa Maria Maggiore in Rome, a fourth-century church dedicated to the new festival of Christmas. The clergy in early liturgical drama re-created the scene at Bethlehem with the altar representing the manger.

St Francis' simple example was followed with enthusiasm by other churches. The cribs became larger, more elaborate and realistic. The shepherds came to adore in familiar but most un-Biblical settings – amid ruined castles, classical temples and Tyrolean mountains. Whole villages and towns were constructed, complete with figures dressed in contemporary costume representing all aspects of everyday life (one group of nuns in the eighteenth century clothed their angel in wasp waist and powdered wig). These presepi were not just fine examples of the craftsmen's art: they illustrated the story of the Nativity in a way that everyone could understand. The early German custom of cradle rocking forged even closer links between the Infant Jesus and ordinary people. The crib became a cradle and at first the priests, later the congregation, rocked it to soothe the Child.

Protestant countries banished the crib custom, but echoes of it survived in other Christmas traditions. In parts of England a 'vessel-cup' – a glass-lidded box containing dolls dressed as the Virgin Mary and the Infant Jesus – was carried from house to house during Advent. Mary, Joseph and Jesus dolls, sometimes arranged to form a manger scene, hung from the centre of the Kissing Bunch.

Christmas Eve in a German family. A child offers gifts to the Infant Jesus in the crib.

Nativity plays performed by schoolchildren everywhere are a link with the early liturgical dramas. The centuries-old connection between acting and the crib is also maintained in other ways. In Belgian villages and towns men, women, children, and sheep and lambs present living tableaux of the manger scene. In Hungary children dressed as angels or shepherds carry a crib from house to house, acting scenes from the Bible story. In many countries children's marionette theatres enact the story of the birth of Jesus. At Les Baux in Provence, France, a newborn lamb is blessed during a colourful festive ceremony on Christmas Eve.

Cribs are still constructed in all their glory in Catholic countries, particularly in Italy, their country of origin. Highly elaborate presepi, complete with lighting effects, mechanical turntables and animated figures, are set up in churches and town squares – traditionally they are erected on Christmas Eve and dismantled at Epiphany. Humble gifts are left beside the crib while children go from church to church to gaze at the Nativity scenes. Many cribs are designed with more love than skill, but others are works of art. One of the best examples can be found in the church of San Giovanni a Carbonara in Naples, famous since the fifteenth century for its wood carvings of the Nativity. Santa Maria Maggiore boasts the oldest presepio. In the Italian tradition the Three Kings are kept apart from the other characters and are moved a little nearer the crib each day until their arrival at Epiphany. In many churches at Midnight Mass on Christmas Eve the Infant is taken from the crib and held by the priest for the adoration of the people.

Historically the crib was intended for public display, but during this century it has also become a domestic institution. Often the figures of the Holy Family, the Kings, angels and shepherds are family treasures, carefully wrapped and stored from year to year, while the household's crib is as much an exhibition of creativity as of reverence. In even the poorest Italian homes children construct a Nativity scene from twigs and moss, pebbles and paper. Clay figures of the Holy Family and their attendants are sold all over Italy. Every Spanish home also has its crib. The Portuguese make cribs of painted wooden figures and moss. At midnight on Christmas Eve the father slips the Christ Child into the manger while the children's attention is distracted. In Germany the 'krippe' is often placed under the tree, so combining two traditions. Small figures called 'santons', or little saints, made of unbaked painted clay, surround the 'crêches' of southern France. They not only depict the traditional Christmas figures, but village characters dressed as they were a century ago, going to worship the Child.

Catholic emigrants took the crib tradition to North and South America. In Peru, gaily painted boxes open up to reveal the stable peopled by little figures in peasant costume. Sometimes these theatrical scenes are confined to the lid, leaving room in the box for religious objects. Latin American cribs sometimes follow the tradition of incorporating scenes from contemporary life and include guns and tanks. In America, the Pennsylvania Dutch manger scene or 'putz' is an elaborate landscaped winter scene which may fill a room and include mill wheels, villages and bridges as well as the Holy Family. At Bethlehem, Pennsylvania, which was founded by Moravians from central Europe, a vast community putz is revealed each Christmas Eve. One called for twelve bushels of moss and forty Christmas trees among other spectacular effects. In many American cities live sheep and cattle graze in large crêches constructed in public places. More recently the crib, for some reason the last of the rejected Catholic Christmas customs to be rehabilitated, has been accepted in English homes and churches, where it has added a new thread to the Christmas tapestry.

Making Cribs

In most Italian and Spanish homes, making or assembling a crib has always been a central part of Christmas and the custom has spread widely during this century. Making a crib can be as simple or as complicated as you wish it to be. The traditional crib shown here can be made by children.

Choose a strong cardboard box and lay it on its side so that it opens towards you. Fold the bottom of the box in to strengthen the base and the top back to support the thatched roof.

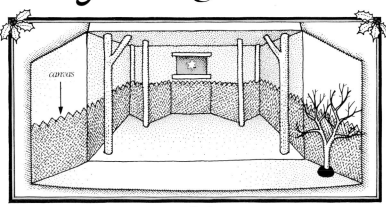

canvas

fig 2

Trim the side flaps down as shown in fig 1 and open them out. Cut a cardboard semicircle as wide as the box with the flaps open to give an extension to the stable (fig 2) on which you can stand figures. Cut a window in the centre back of the box. Coat the box inside and out, including the flaps and extension, with thick black poster paint. Glue blue crêpe paper behind the window opening and stick on a silver or gold card star. If you cut a second window out of a piece of black painted card, glue it over the window

opening still leaving a small space between the two, and glue blue crêpe paper to this extended window instead, you can achieve the effect of light coming through. Thatch the roof with overlapping bundles of straw tied with garden twine, attached by threading wire through the bundles and into the cardboard, as if sewing. The apex of the roof is a long roll of straw attached in the same way along the flap edge (fig 3). Insert two canes, slightly longer than the height of the box, through holes in the top back corners and push

lid and roof
cut
cane
bottom of box

fig 1

fig 3

into the roll of straw to give the roof a good pitch. Fold two oblong pieces of card in half and glue into the corners of the box to make stalls for animals. Fray the top edge of a strip of canvas (fig 2) and glue along the inside of the box from flap to flap, covering the stalls. Cut two canes to the height of the box and wedge between floor and ceiling at the corners of the stalls and glue into position. Prune two rustic-looking branches to form supports for the front of the crib and fix into place with Plasticine. Prop doors open, put extension in place and cover floor and extension with piles of straw. Arrange bunches of twigs or dried flowers inside the stable to give atmosphere and add traditional Nativity figures.

MAKING NATIVITY FIGURES

Thin card cones form the base of the figures with slits cut to take the arms (fig 4). The arms are cardboard strips which can be slotted through. Heads

fig 4

can be made with cotton craft balls or ping-pong balls with a hole cut where they are to be glued on to the cone. Paint faces on the balls and use wool or string to make hair. The basic clothes are cut as caftans with arms and body cut in one piece. Wrap them around the cardboard shapes and stitch or glue into position. Use fabric suitable for the character: canvas or hessian for Joseph or the shepherds and velvet for the kings. Give each one a generous cloak. Crooks or gifts can be placed in their hands, or the cardboard hands can be glued together as if in prayer. Animals can be cut out in cardboard and covered with fur or felt, with beads for eyes and manes of wool.

The Oxen

Christmas Eve, and twelve of the clock.
'Now they are all on their knees,'
An elder said as we sat in a flock
By the embers in hearthside ease.

We pictured the meek mild creatures where
They dwelt in their strawy pen,
Nor did it occur to one of us there
To doubt they were kneeling then.

So fair a fancy few would weave
In these years! Yet, I feel,
If someone said on Christmas Eve,
'Come; see the oxen kneel

'In the lonely barton by yonder coomb
Our childhood used to know,'
I should go with him in the gloom,
Hoping it might be so.

THOMAS HARDY

PERUVIAN CRIB

Attractive, gaily painted cribs from Peru incorporate figures from everyday life as well as those from the traditional Nativity scene. The figures are arranged as a tableau in a hinged wooden box, into which are fitted wooden platforms of graduating height. The outside of the box and the doors are painted in bright naive patterns. Small pots of emulsion paint would probably be ideal for this. The inside is painted bright blue for the sky and the floor of the box and platforms green or brown to represent the earth. Allow the paint to dry for 24 hours before putting figures inside. These can be made easily in self-hardening modelling clay. The figures are crudely shaped, rather flat to fit into the box and with a smooth base to glue securely on to the platforms. Allow two days for the figures to dry completely. Add faces and costumes with bright water colours, enamel or acrylic modelling paint. Paint halos and wings in gold. When the paint is dry give the figures a coat of modelling varnish and glue into position on the platforms. Touch up the tableau with gold where you place the manger and add a star.

PROVENCAL SANTONS

In Provence, in the south of France, small terracotta figures called 'santons', or little saints, surround the crêche. These represent traditional Nativity figures, peasants and characters from Provençal folklore. The santons can be shaped in self-hardening modelling clay. Long skirts act as support, but toothpicks can be used to stiffen legs, to push through the body to hold it erect and to push through the top of the head into the body to hold the head on securely. Twisted wire gives a good frame to shape the arms on. All the body joints should be smoothed over carefully with a wet finger. Add costumes to the figures, working moist clay finely to

make folds in skirts, cloaks, shawls or smocks. Mark detail such as facial features, basketwork or fringes with a knife or toothpick. Allow the models to dry for at least two days then paint and coat with varnish. For animal figures, a basic cardboard cut-out will help give a good shape. The santons should be set in a rural scene. Arrange a landscape of pebbles, moss, little plants and twigs or plant a meadow of corn or grass seed a little before Christmas.

CAROLS

Angels sang the first carol at Christ's Nativity, but the early Church, austere and puritanical, frowned on such unseemly merriment. While mummers, elaborately dressed and masked, performed traditional folk plays, and minstrels in baronial halls sang of feasting and pagan customs, churchgoers heard only stately Latin hymns. Carols swept in on the same fourteenth-century tide of humanism and emancipation that led to the miracle plays and St Francis' crib. The word 'carol' comes from the old French term for a ring dance and many early carols were simply new words to old folk songs and dances. Carols were, and are, simple, joyful and memorable songs in the common tongue, their words homely and their images vivid and down to earth.

Carol singing soon joined hands with other popular Christmas customs, pagan as well as religious. In England, convivial wassailers carried the wassail bowl of steaming ale from house to house and sang seasonal songs in the hope that their neighbours would replenish the contents. The custom was continued in the eighteenth and nineteenth centuries by 'waits', or watchmen who serenaded householders at Christmas and then returned on Boxing Day for their tips. The police took over their guardianship duties, but visiting carol singers continued to be called waits. The Victorian revival of interest in Christmas led to new carols being composed, old ones rediscovered and carol singing becoming increasingly popular.

In Britain the waits are traditionally pictured gathered round a lantern, but in many parts of Europe 'star singers' undertake the job of singing from house to house. They carry a great star in memory of the Star of Bethlehem and sometimes dress up as the Magi and other figures from the Nativity – perhaps a remnant of old Epiphany plays. With some modifications the practice extends from Italy to Iceland. In Poland the cardboard star is made to revolve like a pinwheel, and one or two of the boys may wear a goat mask. A goat figure, originally the personification of the devil, also appears in Sweden, where the rest of the star boys, dressed in white, act out short biblical scenes and sing songs. In Norway in olden times the star boys, dressed as the Magi in colourful brocade costumes, used to carry large illuminated stars through the streets. An even older ritual involved participants donning demon masks and going from house to house making mischief. Tyrolean star singers used to have to stamp on the snowy fields to

Star singers going carol singing in Bucharest, Romania, 1848.

promote a good crop before they received any hospitality. In Romania the wooden star was adorned with frills, little bells and a manger scene. On the Sunday before Christmas, Swiss star singers dressed as Mary and Joseph, angels, shepherds and the wise men, perform the Christmas story and sing carols. The Tierna boys in Finland raise large sums of money for charity with their play about the Three Kings. On Christmas Day, some Spanish villages used to elect 'mayorales' for the coming year who would go from house to house singing traditional Christmas chants and collecting an egg in return for their efforts.

In Jamaica the Christmas music tradition is carried on by Jonkunnu dancers, bands of masked men wearing bright satin costumes, who dance in the streets to a musical accompaniment. One dancer appears in black with a tail to represent the devil and scares small children. In Brazil, dancers and musicians go from village to village performing the Dance of the Three Wise Men. An abundance of dance and drama survives in Mexico and South America. Throughout Scandinavia the medieval meaning of carols as ring dances is still upheld by many families who circle the tree on Christmas Eve to sing traditional songs.

Emigrants took carol singing customs with them to the New World. The English tradition predominates in the United States, but several practices seem to blend in Alaska. Singers carrying both a lantern and a star go from house to house, at some point clashing with a rival group who try to destroy the star – a symbol of Herod

chasing Christ. In Vancouver, Canada, decorated carol ships tour the waterways. Australia has established open-air Carols by Candlelight as a popular Christmas custom. Started in Melbourne as a small, charitable money-raising venture, it now attracts a huge audience of candle-bearers, who, at midnight, usher in Christmas Day with *Auld Lang Syne*.

Probably the most popular carol in the world today is *Silent Night*, composed hurriedly on Christmas Eve 1818 in the Austrian village of Oberndorf. Father Josef Mohr, the parish priest, had discovered to his horror that the church organ would not play that evening, either because of rust or because mice had eaten the bellows cloth. At once he wrote the words of a Christmas song and asked his friend, organist and schoolmaster Franz Grüber, to set them to music to be sung by the choir accompanied on a guitar. Grüber worked so fast that *Silent Night* was completed in time for a rehearsal before Midnight Mass. The carol was copied by the organ mender, taken up by strolling singers and within thirty years had achieved worldwide popularity. As for the writers, Mohr died penniless and Grüber spent the last years of his life fighting to prove that he had composed the music. In England the carolling custom almost died out following the Puritan suppression of Christmas. The majority of today's most popular carols originated, or were adapted, in the nineteenth century. *O Come All Ye Faithful* and *Hark the Herald Angels Sing*, for instance, acquired their modern form in the middle of the last century, while *O Little Town of Bethlehem, Away in a Manger* and *We Three Kings* were composed in America around the same time.

Carol singing has become increasingly large scale and organized. Carol services and concerts are well attended, but nowadays the only reminder of lantern-lit waits are naughty children who ring the doorbell after one ragged verse of *O Come All Ye Faithful*. There is nothing to stop musically inclined groups of family and friends learning some carols, rehearsing them, and taking to the streets to give pleasure to themselves and to others. In return they might even be rewarded with wine and mince pies by those they visit. Groups planning to collect for charity should learn the rules from their local police station and contact the charity of their choice for collecting tins well before Christmas. Thinking about others is very much in the mood of Christmas – but so is singing favourite carols for the simple pleasure of it.

RISE UP SHEPHERD, AND FOLLOW

There's a star in the east on
                          Christmas morn;
Rise up, shepherd, and follow,
It will lead to the place where the
                          Saviour's born,
Rise up, shepherd, and follow.

Rise up, rise up, rise up,
        shepherd, and follow;
Follow the star to Bethlehem,
        Rise up shepherd, and follow.

Leave your sheep, leave your sheep
        and leave your lambs;
Leave your sheep, leave your sheep,
        leave your ewes and rams;

Chorus

If you take a good heed to the angel's
                          words;
You'll forget all your flock, you'll
                          forget your herds;

Chorus

ABOUT THE ARRANGEMENTS

Most of the carols have been arranged for three parts: melody line, bass and in-between harmony. This makes the carols slightly easier to play, but at the same time gives the enthusiast a chance to arrange the carols for a small instrumental group. A cello, bassoon or baritone will be able to tackle the bass in most instances, and a viola, violin or clarinet the middle voice. If the music is being arranged for clarinet it must be taken up a tone to allow for transposition. (For example, if the carol is written in F, write the music up a note in the key of G.) Baritone players usually will prefer to read in the treble clef, so the music must be written an octave and a tone higher. (F, fourth line up in the bass clef, will become G, second line up in the treble clef.)

Some carols will take less kindly to being arranged for these small resources. Examples are Il est né, which only needs the lightest of accompaniments – tambourine and guitar would do – and at the other extreme, Adeste, Fideles, which needs full treatment from the keyboard – piano or organ.

Guitar chords have been indicated on the music. Where possible these match the piano harmonizations, but where the harmonies would have demanded unusually difficult guitar chord changes, the guitar parts have been left at as close approximations as possible.

92

Arrangements of the carols for this book by Derek Walters

Rise Up Shepherd, and Follow

Negro Spiritual

Away in a Manger

Anonymous

Dolce

A- way in a man- ger, no crib for a

F   B♭   F   F   D7

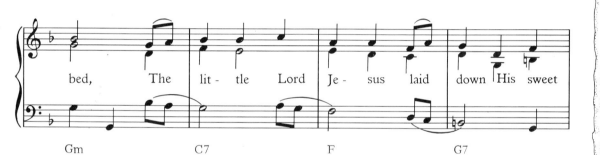

bed, The lit- tle Lord Je- sus laid down His sweet

Gm   C7   F   G7

head. The stars in the bright sky looked down where He

C   C7   F   B♭   F   F7   D7

lay, The lit- tle Lord Je- sus a- sleep on the hay.

Gm   C   C7   F   Gm   C7   F

Carol singers gather round a lantern. Detail from Illustrated London News, *1848*

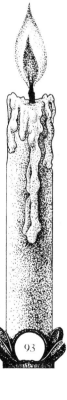

AWAY IN A MANGER

Away in a manger, no crib for a bed,
The little Lord Jesus laid down His
           sweet head.
The stars in the bright sky looked down
           where He lay,
The little Lord Jesus asleep on the hay.

The cattle are lowing, the Baby awakes,
But little Lord Jesus no crying He
           makes.
I love Thee, Lord Jesus, look down from
           the sky,
And stay by my side until morning is
           nigh.

Be near me, Lord Jesus, I ask Thee to
           stay
Close by me for ever, and love me, I
           pray.
Bless all the dear children in Thy tender
           care,
And fit us for heaven, to live with Thee
           there.

93

SILENT NIGHT

Silent night, holy night.
All is calm, all is bright.
Round yon Virgin Mother and Child,
Holy Infant so tender and mild,
Sleep in heavenly peace,
Sleep in heavenly peace.

Silent night, holy night!
Shepherds quake at the sight!
Glories stream from heaven afar,
Heavenly hosts sing Alleluia!
Christ the Saviour is born,
Christ the Saviour is born.

Silent night, holy night!
Son of God, love's pure light;
Radiant beams from Thy holy face,
With the dawn of redeeming grace.
Jesus, Lord at Thy birth,
Jesus, Lord at Thy birth.

STILLE NACHT

Stille Nacht, heilige Nacht!
Alles schläft, einsam wacht
Nur das traute, hochheilige Paar.
Holder Knabe im lokkigen Haar,
Schlaf in himmlischer Ruh,
Schlaf in himmlischer Ruh.

Stille Nacht, heilige Nacht!
Hirten erst kund gemacht.
Durch der Engel Halleluja
Tönt es laut von fern und nah:
Christ der Retter ist da,
Christ der Retter ist da.

Stille Nacht, heilige Nacht!
Gottes Sohn, o wie lacht
Lieb' aus deinem göttlichen Mund,
Da uns schlägt die rettende Stund,
Christ in deiner Geburt,
Christ in deiner Geburt.

SAINTE NUIT

Sainte nuit, à minuit,
Le hameau dort sans bruit;
Dans l'étable repose un enfant
Que sa mère contempl' en priant;
Elle a vu le Sauveur,
Dans l'Enfant de son coeur.

A minuit, dans la nuit,
Un espoir vous conduit,
Pauvres pâtres craintifs et pieux,
Qui dormiez sous la voûte des cieux,
Lorsque l'hymne divin,
A retenti soudain.

Sainte nuit, douce nuit!
O splendeur qui reluit!
De tendresse ta bouche sourit,
O Jésus! Ta naissance nous dit:
'Le Fils vous est donné,
Un Sauveur vous est né.'

Silent Night

Josef Mohr

Dolce

Stil - le Nacht, hei - li-ge Nacht! Al - es schläft, ein - sam wacht
Si - lent night, ho - ly night. All is calm, all is bright.
Saint - e nuit, à — mi-nuit, Le ha-meau dort sans bruit;

pp

Led. *Led. *Led. G7 *similè
C C

Nur das trau - te, hoch-hei - li-ge Paar. Hol - der Kna-be im lok-ki-gen Haar,
Round yon Vir - gin Moth-er and Child, Ho - ly In-fant so ten-der and mild,
Dans l' é - ta-ble re - pose un en - fant Que sa mè-re con-tem-pl'en priant;

F C F C

Schlaf in himm-li-scher Ruh, — Schlaf — in himm-li-scher Ruh.
Sleep in heav-en-ly peace, — Sleep — in heav-en-ly peace.
Elle a vu le Sau - veur, — Dans — l'En-fant de son coeur.

G7 C C C G7 C

Puer Nobis

English words by Percy Dearmer

Allegro*

p

Pu-er no-bis nas-cit-ur, rec-tor an-ge-lor-um. In hoc mun-do pas-cit-ur, Do-
Un-to us a boy is born, King of all cre-a-tion. Came he to a world for-lorn, The

D   A7   D   G   F#m   Em   D

mi-nus Do-min-o — — — — — rum.
Lord of ev'-ry na — — — — — tion.

A7   Bm   A7   D

Yorkshire carol singers carrying bunches of evergreen. Illustrated London News, 1864.

PUER NOBIS

Puer nobis nascitur,
Rector angelorum.
In hoc mundo pascitur,
Dominus Dominorum.

In praesepe ponitur
Sub foeno asinorum
Cognoverunt Dominum
Christum regem coelorum.

Hinc Herodes timuit
Magno cum dolore,
Et pueros occidit,
Infantes cum livore.

Qui natus de virgine
Die hodierna
Ducat nos cum gratia
Ad gaudia superna.

O et A et A et O
Cum cantibus in choro,
Cum canticis et organo,
Benedicamus Domino.

UNTO US A BOY IS BORN

Unto us a Boy is born,
King of all creation,
Came He to a world forlorn,
The Lord of ev'ry nation.

Cradled in a stall was He
With sleepy cows and asses;
But the very beasts could see
That He all men surpasses.

Herod then with fear was filled:
'A prince', he said, 'in Jewry,'
All the little boys he killed
At Bethlem in his fury.

Now may Mary's Son, who came
So long ago to love us,
Lead us all with hearts aflame
Unto the joys above us.

Omega and Alpha He!
Let the organ thunder,
While the choir with peals of glee
Doth rend the air asunder.

Once in royal David's city
Stood a lowly cattle shed,
Where a mother laid her baby
In a manger for His bed.
Mary was that mother mild;
Jesus Christ her little child.

He came down to earth from heaven
Who is God and Lord of all,
And His shelter was a stable,
And His cradle was a stall;
With the poor and mean and lowly
Lived on earth our Saviour holy.

And through all His wondrous
                          childhood
He would honour and obey,
Love and watch the lowly maiden,
In whose gentle arms He lay:
Christian children all must be
Mild, obedient, good as He.

For He is our childhood's pattern,
Day by day like us He grew;
He was little, weak and helpless,
Tears and smiles like us He knew;
And He feeleth for our sadness,
And He shareth in our gladness.

And our eyes at last shall see Him,
Through His own redeeming love;
For that Child so dear and gentle
Is our Lord in heaven above;
And He leads His children on
To the place where He is gone.

Not in that poor lowly stable,
With the oxen standing by
We shall see Him, but in heaven,
Set at God's right hand on high;
When like stars His children
                          crowned
All in white shall wait around.

Once in Royal David's City

Mrs C. F. Alexander

'Two Views' by A. Forestier. Contrasting
Victorian life styles, from the Illustrated
London News, 1897.

The First Nowell

Traditional

Grazioso

The first — No - well the — an - gel did say Was to
A7   D   A Bm7 G   G A7 G   D   G

cer - tain poor shep-herds in fields as they lay; In— fields — where —
G A7 G   D G A7   D   A7   D   A7   D

they lay, — keeping their sheep, On a cold win - ter's night — that
A7 D G   A7 G D4-3   G   A7 G   D G A7

was — so deep: No - well, — no - well, no -
D A   A7   D   A7   Bm   A7   D

well, no - well. Born is the King — of Is - ra - el!
G   D A A7 G A7 G   D G A7 Bm D A7   D

A group of carol singers with violin accompaniment, 1863.

THE FIRST NOWELL

The first Nowell the angel did say
Was to certain poor shepherds in fields
                             as they lay;
In fields where they lay, keeping their
                                 sheep,
On a cold winter's night that was so deep:

   Nowell, nowell, nowell, nowell,
   Born is the King of Israel!

They looked up and saw a star,
Shining in the east, beyond them far;
And to the earth it gave great light,
And so it continued both day and night:

   Chorus

And by the light of that same star,
Three wise men came from country far;
To seek for a king was their intent,
And to follow the star wherever it went:

   Chorus

This star drew nigh to the north-west;
O'er Bethlehem it took its rest,
And there it did both stop and stay,
Right over the place where Jesus lay:

   Chorus

Then entered in those wise men three,
Full reverently upon their knee,
And offered there, in His presence,
Both gold and myrrh and frankincense:

   Chorus

Then let us all with one accord
Sing praises to our heavenly Lord,
That hath made heaven and earth of
                               naught,
And with His blood mankind hath
                               bought:

   Chorus

IN DULCI JUBILO

In dulci jubilo
Nun singet und seid froh!
Unsers Herzens Wonne
Liegt in praesepio,
Und leuchtet als die Sonne
Matris in gremio.
Alpha es et O! *(rep)*

O Jesu parvule,
Nach dir ist mir so weh!
Tröst' mir mein Gemüte,
O puer optime
Durch alle deine Güte
O princeps gloriae.
Trahe me post te! *(rep)*

O Patris caritas!
O Nati lenitas!
Wir wären all verloren
Per nostra crimina;
So hat er uns erworben
Coelorum gaudia.
Eia, wären wir da! *(rep)*

Ubi sunt gaudia?
Nirgend mehr denn da!
Da die Engel singen
Nova cantica,
Und die Schellen klingen
In Regis curia.
Eia, gualia! *(rep)*

IN DULCI JUBILO

In dulci jubilo
Now sing with hearts a-glow,
Our delight and pleasure
Lies in praesepio,
Like sunshine is our treasure
Matris in gremio.
Alpha es et O! *(rep)*

O Jesu parvule,
For thee I long alway;
Comfort my heart's blindness
O puer optime,
With all they loving kindness,
O princeps gloria.
Trahe me post te! *(rep)*

O Patris caritas!
O Nati lenitas!
Deeply were we stainèd
Per nostra crimina;
But thou for us hast gainèd
Coelorum gaudia.
O that we were there! *(rep)*

Ubi sunt gaudia?
In any place but there?
There are angels singing
Nova cantica,
And there the bells are ringing
In Regis curia.
O that we were there! *(rep)*

In Dulci Jubilo

English words by Percy Dearmer

Angels from the Realms of Glory

English words by J. Montgomery

Les ang-es dans nos cam-pagn-es Ont é-ton-né
Et l'éch-o de nos montagn-es Re-dit ce chant
An-gels, from the realms of glo-ry, Wing your fllight o'er
Ye who sang cre-a-tion's sto-ry, Now pro-claim Mes-

l'hymne des cieux;
mé-lo-dieux:
all the earth;
si-ah's birth.

Glor — — — — —

— ia in ex-cel-sis De-o, Glor — — —

— — — ia in ex-cel-sis De - o.

ANGELS FROM THE REALMS OF GLORY

Angels, from the realms of glory,
Wing your flight o'er all the earth;
Ye who sang creation's story,
Now proclaim Messiah's birth.

Gloria in excelsis Deo ... (rep)

Shepherds in the fields abiding,
Watching o'er your flocks by night,
God with man is now residing;
Yonder shines the infant Light.

Gloria in excelsis Deo ... (rep)

Sages, leave your contemplations;
Brighter visions beam afar;
Seek the great Desire of Nations;
Ye have seen His natal star.

Gloria in excelsis Deo ... (rep)

Saints before the altar bending,
Watching long in hope and fear,
Suddenly the Lord, descending,
In His temple shall appear.

Gloria in excelsis Deo ... (rep)

Though an infant now we view Him,
He shall fill His Father's throne,
Gather all the nations to Him;
Every knee shall then bow down.

Gloria in excelsis Deo ... (rep)

LES ANGES DANS NOS CAMPAGNES

Les anges dans nos campagnes
Ont étonné l'hymne des cieux;
Et l'écho de nos montagnes
Redit ce chant mélodieux:

Gloria in excelsis Deo ... (rep)

Bergers, pour qui cette fête?
Quel est l'objet de tous ces chants?
Quel vainqueur, quelle conquête
Mérite ces cris triomphants?

Gloria in excelsis Deo ... (rep)

Ils annoncent la naissance
Du libérateur d'Israël,
Et, pleins de reconnaissance,
Chantent en ce jour solennel:

Gloria in excelsis Deo ... (rep)

Bergers, loin de vos retraites
Unissez-vous à leurs concerts
Et que vos tendres musettes
Fassent retentir dans les airs:

Gloria in excelsis Deo ... (rep)

Cherchons tous l'heureux village
Qui l'a vu naître sous ses toits,
Offrons-lui le tendre hommage
Et de nos coeurs et nos voix!

Gloria in excelsis Deo ... (rep)

IL EST NÉ, LE DIVIN ENFANT

Il est né, le divin Enfant,
Jouez, hautbois, résonnez,
              musettes;
Il est né, le divin Enfant;
Chantons tous son avènement!

Depuis plus de quatre mille ans,
Nous le promettaient les Prophètes;
Depuis plus de quatre mille ans,
Nous attendions cet heureux temps.

    Chorus: Il est né …

Ah! qu'il est beau, qu'il est
              charmant,
Que ses grâces sont parfaites!
Ah! qu'il est beau, qu'il est
              charmant,
Qu'il est doux le divin Enfant!

    Chorus

Une étable est son logement,
Un peu de paille, sa couchette,
Une étable est son logement,
Pour un Dieu, quel abaissement!

    Chorus

O Jésus! O Roi tout puissant!
Tout petit enfant que vous êtes,
O Jésus! O Roi tout puissant!
Régnez sur nous entièrement!

    Chorus

HE IS BORN, HOLY CHILD DIVINE

He is born, Holy Child divine,
Loud let us sing to greet His coming;
He is born, holy child adored,
Sound the pipes, let the trumpets play.

We have waited a thousand years
Since the prophets' first foretelling;
We have waited a thousand years,
Hail, our new-born Lord this day.

    Chorus: He is born …

How the light about Him shines!
He is perfect, He is enchanting;
How the light about Him shines,
Sweetly casting fear away.

    Chorus

Starlit is His humble crib,
Ox and ass beside Him sleeping;
Starlit is His humble crib;
See His throne, a bed of hay.

    Chorus

Baby Jesus, new-born Lord,
Bells are ringing, we are singing,
Baby Jesus, new-born Lord,
Live within our hearts, we pray.

    Chorus

Il est né, le divin Enfant

English words by Cordelia Chitty

Hark! The Herald Angels Sing

Charles Wesley

Hark! the her-ald an-gels sing,— Glo-ry to the new-born King;

G   D   G   D   G   Cmaj7 G D7 G

Peace on earth and mer-cy mild, — God and sin - ners re - con - ciled.

G   D   Em   A7   Bm7 A7 D A7   D A7 D

Joy - ful, all ye na - tions rise,— Join the tri - umph of the skies,—

G D G Em Am7 Bm G D   G D7 G   C A9 G D

With th'an-ge- lic host pro - claim: 'Christ is born in Beth-le - hem.'

C Cmaj7 C E7   Am E7 Am Am7 C6 Bm G   Em7 D G

Hark! the her-ald an-gels sing, — Glo-ry to the new-born King.

E F#m7 E E7   Am E Am Am7 C6 D7 G   Em D G

'A Christmas Carol' drawn by Dickens's celebrated illustrator, Phiz. Illustrated London News, 1855.

HARK! THE HERALD ANGELS SING

Hark! the herald angels sing,
Glory to the new-born King;
Peace on earth and mercy mild,
God and sinners reconciled.
Joyful, all ye nations rise,
Join the triumph of the skies,
With th'angelic host proclaim:
'Christ is born in Bethlehem.'

Hark! the herald angels sing,
Glory to the new-born King.

Christ, by highest heaven adored;
Christ, the everlasting Lord;
Late in time behold Him come,
Offspring of a virgin's womb.
Veiled in flesh the Godhead see;
Hail the incarnate Deity!
Pleased as Man with man to dwell,
Jesus our Emmanuel!

Chorus

Hail the heaven-born Prince of Peace!
Hail the Sun of Righteousness!
Light and life to all He brings,
Risen with healing in His wings.
Mild, He lays His glory by,
Born that man no more may die,
Born to raise the sons of earth,
Born to give them second birth.

Chorus

O du fröhliche, O du selige
Gnaden bringende Weihnachtszeit!
Welt ging verloren,
Christ ist geboren,
Freue, freue dich, o Christenheit!

O du fröhliche, o du selige
Gnaden bringende Weihnachtszeit!
Christ ist erschienen
Uns zu versühnen,
Freue, freue dich, o Christenheit!

O du fröhliche, o du selige
Gnaden bringende Weihnachtszeit!
Himmlische Heere
Jauchzen dir Ehre,
Freue, freue dich, o Christenheit!

Setting off to church on a cold, snowy Christmas morning. Illustrated London News, 1894.

O THOU JOYFUL INFANT HOLY

O thou joyful Infant holy,
Christmas fills our souls with joy;
Men at last can cease to mourn,
Christ the Son of God is born,
Christians praise the holy Boy.

O thou joyful Infant holy,
Christmas fills our souls with joy;
God has sent His Son to earth
To redeem us by His birth,
Christians praise the holy Boy.

O thou joyful Infant holy,
Christmas fills our souls with joy;
High above, the stars look down
On a King without a crown,
Christians praise the holy Boy.

102

O Du Fröhliche

von Herder
English words by Romana Unger-Hamilton

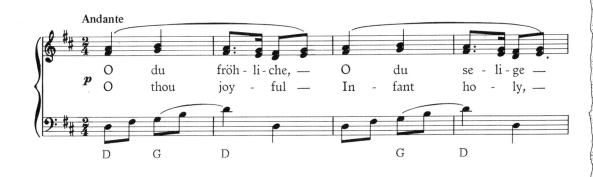

O du fröh-li-che, — O du se-li-ge —
O thou joy-ful — In-fant ho-ly, —

D   G   D   G   D

Gna-den — brin-gen-de Weih-nachts-zeit!
Christ-mas fills our — souls with joy;

D   A   E7   A   A   E7   A

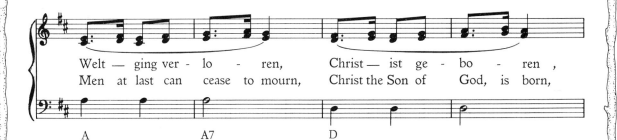

Welt — ging ver-lo-ren, Christ — ist ge-bo-ren,
Men at last can cease to mourn, Christ the Son of God, is born,

A   A7   D

Freu-e, — freu-e dich, O Chri-sten-heit!
Christ-ians — praise — the — ho-ly Boy.

Bm7   G   Bm7   A6-7   D   A7   D

We Three Kings

Dr J.H. Hopkins

Singing carols in church as Christmas approaches. Victorian engraving, 1865.

WE THREE KINGS

We three kings of orient are.
Bearing gifts we traverse afar.
Field and fountain, moor and mountain
Following yonder star.

O star of wonder,
Star of night,
Star with royal beauty bright,
Westward leading, still proceeding,
Guide us to thy perfect light.

Melchior:
Born a King on Bethlehem's plain,
Gold I bring to crown Him again,
King for ever, ceasing never,
Over us all to reign.

Chorus

Caspar:
Frankincense to offer have I,
Incense, owns a Deity nigh,
Prayer and praising, all men raising,
Worship Him, God most high.

Chorus

Balthazar:
Myrrh is mine, its bitter perfume,
Breathes a life of gathering gloom.
Sorrowing, sighing, bleeding, dying,
Sealed in the stone-cold tomb.

Chorus

Glorious now behold Him arise,
King and God and Sacrifice!
Heaven sings, Alleluia,
Alleluia, the earth replies.

Chorus

Es ist ein' Ros' entsprungen,
Aus einer Wurzel zart.
Als uns die Alten sungen;
Aus Jesse kam die Art.
Und hat ein Blümlein bracht,
Mitten im kalten Winter,
Wohl zu der halben Nacht.

Das Röslein, das ich meine,
Davon Isaias sagt:
Hat uns gebracht alleine
Marie, die reine Magd.
Aus Gottes ew'gem Rat
Hat sie ein Kind geboren,
Wohl zu der halben Nacht.

Das Blümeline so kleine,
Das duftet uns so süss,
Mit seinem hellen Scheine,
Vertreibt's die Finsternis.
Wahr' Mensch und wahrer Gott,
Hilft uns aus allem Leide,
Rettet von Sünd und Tod.

THERE IS A FLOWER

There is a flower springing,
From tender roots it grows,
From Eden beauty bringing,
From Jesse's stem a rose.
On his green branch it blows.
A bud that in cold winter
At midnight will unclose.

Pure Mary, maiden holy,
The dream by prophets seen,
Who in a stable lowly
Above her Child did lean
So gentle and serene:
This was Esaias' vision,
The tree of living green.

To Mary, rose of heaven,
With loving hearts we say
Let our sins be forgiven,
And grief be turned away
Upon this Christmas Day:
To Jesus, Child of winter,
For grace and hope we pray.

Country waits singing carols for a cup of ale. Illustrated London News, 1850.

Es ist ein' Ros'

English words by Ursula Vaughan Williams

Grazioso

Es ist ein' Ros' ent-sprung-en, Aus ein-er Wur-zel zart,
There is a flow-er spring-ing, From ten-der roots it grows,

C C7 F Gm F C F Bb F C C7 sus4-7 F

Als uns die Alt-en sung-en; Aus Jess-e kam die Art. Und hat ein Blümlein
From Ed-en beau-ty bring-ing, From Jess-e's stem a rose. On his green branch it

C C7 F Gm F C F Bb F C C7 sus4-7 F F C G7

bracht, Mit-ten im kalt-en Win-ter, Wohl zu der halb-en Nacht.
blows. A bud that in cold win-ter At mid-night will un-close.

C C7 F Gm Am7 Dm7 Am Gm Am C GmBb F C7 F

Noël Nouvelet

English words by Cordelia Chitty

Andantino

No-ël nou-ve - let, No - ël chant-ons i - ci;
Joy-ful-ly we sing, to praise the new No-ël.

Em A7 Em A7 Bm4 B7 Em7 A7

De - vo - tes gens, cri - ons à Dieu mer - ci.
Raise to God glad voi - ces all ye who love Him well.

Em A7 Em A7 Bm4 B7 Em7 A7 Em

Chant - ons No - ël pour le Roi nou-ve - let,
Sing we in praise of Christ the new-born King.

Em Bm Am Bm Em Cm7 Bm Cm7 B(maj)

No - ël nou-ve - let, No - ël chant-ons i - ci!
Joy-ful-ly we sing, To praise the new No - ël.

Em A7 Em A7 Bm4 Em B7 Em A7 Em

NOEL NOUVELET

Noël nouvelet, Noël chantons ici;
Dévotes gens, crions à Dieu merci.
Chantons Noël pour le Roi nouvelet,

Noël nouvelet, Noël chantons ici!
(Repeat chorus after each verse.)

Quand m'éveillai et eus assez dormi,
J'ouvris les yeux, vis un arbre fleuri
Dont il sourtait un bouton vermeillet.

D'un oiselet après le chant ouïs
Qui, aux pasteurs disait: 'Partez d'ici;
En Bethléem trouverez l'Agnelet.'

En Bethléem, Maire et Joseph vis,
L'âne et le boeuf, l'Enfant couché parmi.
La crèche était, au lieu d'un bercelet.

L'étoile y vis, qui la nuit éclaircit,
Qui, d'orient dont elle était sortie,
En Bethléem les trois rois conduisait.

L'un portait l'or, l'autre le myrrhe aussi,
L'autre l'encens qu'il faisait bon senti:
Du Paradis semblait le jardinet.

THE NEW NÖEL

Joyfully we sing, to praise the new Noel.
Raise to God glad voices all ye who love
Him well.
Sing we in praise of Christ the New Born
King.

Joyfully we sing,
To praise the new Noel.
(Repeat chorus after each verse.)

Waking from deep sleep that lasted
many hours
I beheld a tree, it was adorned with
flowers.
Upon this tree a scarlet bud did bloom.

Notes of joy I heard, a bird lifted up its
voice:
'Shepherds leave your flocks, depart
now and rejoice!
In Bethlehem the Lamb of God awaits'.

In Bethlehem, I saw the Holy New Born
Child;
Ass and oxen watched with Joseph and
Mary mild;
Cradle He lacked, so in a manger lay.

I looked to the east, and there I saw a
star;
Lighting up the night, it brought kings
from afar.
To Bethlehem with gifts they made their
way.

One king brings Him myrrh, another
frankincense,
To the Child the third king gifts of gold
presents,
Round him, like blossoms of Paradise
laid.

Adeste, fideles,
Laeti triumphantes;
Venite, venite in Bethlehem.
Natum videte
Regem angelorum.

Venite, adoremus,
Venite, adoremus,
Venite, adoremus, Dominum.

Deum de Deo,
Lumen de Lumine,
Parturit virgo mater,
Deum verum,
Genitum, non factum:

Chorus

Cantet nunc hymnos
Chorus angelorum;
Cantet nunc aula caelestium:
Gloria
In excelsis Deo!

Chorus

Ergo qui natus
Die hodierna,
Jesu, tibi sit gloria:
Patris aeterni
Verbum caro factum:

Chorus

O COME, ALL YE FAITHFUL

O come, all ye faithful,
Joyful and triumphant;
O come ye, O come ye to Bethlehem.
Come and behold Him,
Born the King of Angels:

O come, let us adore Him,
O come, let us adore Him,
O come, let us adore Him, Christ the
Lord.

God of God,
Light of Light,
Lo! He abhors not the virgin's womb;
Very God
Begotten, not created:

Chorus

Sing, choirs of angels,
Sing in exultation,
Sing, all ye citizens of heaven above;
Glory to God
In the highest:

Chorus

Yea, Lord, we greet thee,
Born this happy morning,
Jesu, to Thee be glory given;
Word of the Father,
Now in flesh appearing:

Chorus

Adeste, Fideles

English words by the Reverend Francis Oakeley

Christmas Day in the Workhouse

GEORGE R. SIMS

1

It is Christmas Day in the Workhouse,
And the cold bare walls are bright
With garlands of green and holly,
And the place is a pleasant sight:
For with clean-washed hands and faces,
In a long and hungry line
The paupers sit at the tables,
For this is the hour they dine.

2

And the guardians and their ladies,
Although the wind is east,
Have come in their furs and wrappers,
To watch their charges feast;
To smile and be condescending,
Put pudding on pauper plates,
To be hosts at the workhouse banquet
They've paid for – with the rates.

3

Oh, the paupers are meek and lowly
With their 'Thank'ee kindly, mum's';
So long as they fill their stomachs,
What matter it whence it comes?
But one of the old men mutters,
And pushes his plate aside:
'Great God!' he cries; 'but it chokes me!
For this is the day *she* died.'

4

The guardians gazed in horror,
The master's face went white;
'Did a pauper refuse their pudding?'
'Could their ears believe aright?'
Then the ladies clutched their husbands,
Thinking the man would die,
Struck by a bolt, or something,
By the outraged One on high.

5

But the pauper sat for a moment,
Then rose 'mid a silence grim,
For the others had ceased to chatter,
And trembled in every limb.
He looked at the guardians' ladies,
Then, eyeing their lords, he said,
'I eat not the food of villains
Whose hands are foul and red:

6

'Whose victims cry for vengeance
From their dank, unhallowed graves.'
'He's drunk!' said the workhouse master.
'Or else he's mad, and raves.'
'Not drunk or mad,' cried the pauper, ·
'But only a hunted beast,
Who, torn by the hounds and mangled,
Declines the vulture's feast.

7

'I care not a curse for the guardians,
And I won't be dragged away.
Just let me have the fit out,
It's only on Christmas Day
That the black past comes to goad me,
And prey on my burning brain;
I'll tell you the rest in a whisper, –
I swear I won't shout again.

8

'Keep your hands off me, curse you!
Hear me right out to the end.
You come here to see how paupers
The season of Christmas spend.
You come here to watch us feeding,
As they watch the captured beast.
Hear why a penniless pauper
Spits on your paltry feast.

9

'Do you think I will take your bounty,
And let you smile and think
You're doing a noble action
With the parish's meat and drink?
Where is my wife, you traitors –
The poor old wife you slew?
Yes, by the God above us,
My Nance was killed by you!

10

'Last winter my wife lay dying,
Starved in a filthy den;
I had never been to the parish, –
I came to the parish then.
I swallowed my pride in coming,
For, ere the ruin came,
I held up my head as a trader,
And I bore a spotless name.

11

'I came to the parish, craving
Bread for a starving wife,
Bread for the woman who'd loved me
Through fifty years of life;
And what do you think they told me,
Mocking my awful grief?
That "the House" was open to us,
But they wouldn't give "out relief."

12

'I slunk to the filthy alley –
'Twas a cold, raw Christmas eve –
And the bakers' shops were open,
Tempting a man to thieve;
But I clenched my fists together,
Holding my head awry,
So I came to her empty-handed,
And mournfully told her why.

13

'Then I told her "the House" was open;
She had heard the ways of *that*,
For her bloodless cheeks went crimson,
And up in her rags she sat,
Crying, "Bide the Christmas here, John,
We've never had one apart;
I think I can bear the hunger, –
The other would break my heart."

14

'All through that eve I watched her,
Holding her hand in mine,
Praying the Lord, and weeping
Till my lips were salt as brine.
I asked her once if she hungered,
And as she answered "No,"
The moon shone in at the window
Set in a wreath of snow.

15

'Then the room was bathed in glory,
And I saw in my darling's eyes
The far-away look of wonder
That comes when the spirit flies;
And her lips were parched and parted,
And her reason came and went,
For she raved of her home in Devon,
Where our happiest years were spent.

16

'And the accents, long forgotten,
Came back to the tongue once more,
For she talked like the country lassie
I woo'd by the Devon shore.
Then she rose to her feet and trembled,
And fell on the rags and moaned,
And, "Give me a crust – I'm famished –
For the love of God!" she groaned.

17

'I rushed from the room like a madman,
And flew to the workhouse gate,
Crying, "Food for a dying woman!"
And the answer came, "Too late."
They drove me away with curses;
Then I fought with a dog in the street,
And tore from the mongrel's clutches
A crust he was trying to eat.

18

'Back, through the filthy by-lanes!
Back, through the trampled slush!
Up to the crazy garret,
Wrapped in an awful hush.
My heart sank down at the threshold,
And I paused with a sudden thrill,
For there in the silv'ry moonlight
My Nance lay, cold and still.

19

'Up to the blackened ceiling
The sunken eyes were cast –
I knew on those lips all bloodless
My name had been the last;
She'd called for her absent husband –
O God! had I but known! –
Had called in vain, and in anguish
Had died in that den – *alone*.

20

'Yes, there, in a land of plenty,
Lay a loving woman dead,
Cruelly starved and murdered
For a loaf of the parish bread.
At yonder gate, last Christmas,
I craved for a human life.
You, who would feast us paupers,
What of my murdered wife?

21

'There, get ye gone to your dinners;
Don't mind me in the least;
Think of the happy paupers
Eating your Christmas feast;
And when you recount their blessings
In your smug parochial way,
Say what you did for *me*, too,
Only last Christmas Day.'

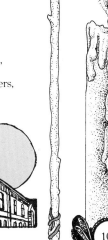

THE THREE LOW MASSES
Alphonse Daudet

TWO TRUFFLED turkeys, Garrigou?'

'Yes, your Reverence, two magnificent turkeys stuffed with truffles. I know, because I helped stuff them. The skin had been stretched so tightly you would have thought it was going to burst as it was roasting....'

'Jesus-Maria! How I do love truffles! Give me my surplice. Quickly, Garrigou.... And what else did you see in the kitchen, besides the turkeys?...'

'Oh, all sorts of good things... since midday they've done nothing but pluck pheasants, larks, pullets, grouse. Feathers flying everywhere... Then they brought eels, carp, trout from the pond and....'

'How big – the trout, Garrigou?'

'As big as that, your Reverence... Enormous!'

'Merciful heavens! You make me see them... Have you put the wine in the altar-cruets?'

'Yes, your Reverence, I've put the wine in the altar-cruets.... But wait and see! It doesn't compare with what you'll be drinking soon, after Midnight Mass. You should see inside the dining-room at the château: decanters blazing bright with wines of all colours.... And the silver dishes, the carved dining-table, the flowers, the candelabra!... Never will there be a Christmas midnight supper like it. Monsieur le Marquis has invited all the nobility of the neighbourhood. You will be at least forty at table, not counting the bailiff and the scrivener. Ah, you are indeed fortunate to be among them, your Reverence! Just from having sniffed those beautiful turkeys, the smell of the truffles is following me everywhere.... Myum!'

'Come now, my son. Let us guard ourselves against the sin of gluttony, especially on the eve of the Nativity. Off with you, quickly. Light the candles and ring the bell for the first Mass; it is nearly midnight already, and we mustn't be late.'

This conversation took place one Christmas Eve in the year of grace sixteen hundred and something, between the Reverend Father Balaguère, formerly Prior of the Barnabites, at present Chaplain to the Lords of Trinquelage, and his little clerk Garrigou, for you must know that the devil, on that very evening, had assumed the round face and nondescript features of the young sacristan, the better to lead the reverend father into temptation and make him commit the terrible sin of gluttony. So, whilst the supposed Garrigou (Hem! hm!) was vigorously jingling the bells of the baronial chapel, the reverend father was hastening to clothe himself in his chasuble in the little sacristy of the château and, already troubled in spirit by all these gastronomic descriptions, he was repeating to himself as he dressed,

'Roast turkeys... golden carp... trout as big as that!...'

Outside, the night wind was blowing, spreading the music of the bells, and gradually lights were appearing in the darkness along the slopes of Mont Ventoux, on the top of which rose the age-old towers of Trinquelage. The families of the tenant-farmers were coming to hear Midnight Mass at the château. They sang as they climbed the incline in groups of five or six, the father in front, lantern in hand, the women swathed in their long, brown cloaks under which the children huddled for shelter. In spite of the hour and the cold, all these good folk walked cheerfully, sustained by the thought that when they came out from Mass there would be tables laid for them down in the kitchens, as there were every year. Now and then, on the steep slope, a nobleman's carriage preceded by torch bearers would twinkle its windows in the moonlight, or a mule would trot along tinkling its bells, and by the light of the mist-enveloped lanterns, the tenants would recognize their bailiff and salute him as he passed.

'Good evening, good evening, Master Arnoton!'

'Good evening, good evening, friends!'

The night was clear, the stars gleamed bright in the cold air; the north wind and a fine frozen snow, glancing off the clothes without wetting them, faithfully maintained the tradition of a white Christmas. At the very summit of the slope rose their destination, the château, with its enormous mass of towers and gables, its chapel spire rising into the bluish-black sky, and, at all its windows, little lights that twinkled, bobbing back and forth, and looking, against the dark background of the building, like sparks flashing in the ashes of burnt paper.... Once one was beyond the drawbridge and the postern-gate, to reach the chapel it was necessary to cross the outer courtyard, full of carriages, valets and sedan chairs, all brightly lit by the flames of torches and by the blazing kitchen fires. All around could be heard the chinking click of the turnspits, the clatter of pans, the clink of crystal and silver being set out in preparation for a feast; from up above, a warm vapour which smelt of roast meat and potent herbs used for complicated sauces made not only the tenants, but the chaplain, the bailiff, everybody say: 'What a fine Christmas supper we are going to have after Mass!'

Dingdong-dong!... dingdong-dong!...

So the Midnight Mass begins. In the chapel of the château, a cathedral in miniature, with interlaced arches and oak wainscoting high up the walls, tapestries have been hung, all the candles lit. And the people! The costumes! See first, seated in the carved stalls surrounding the chancel, the Lord of Trinquelage, in salmon-coloured taffeta, and near him all the invited nobility. Opposite, kneeling on prie-Dieus hung with velvet, are the old Dowager Marchioness in her gown of flame-coloured brocade and the young Lady of Trinquelage, wearing on her head the latest fashion of the Court of France: a high tower of fluted lace. Further back, their faces shaved, and wearing black with vast pointed wigs, can be seen the bailiff Thomas Arnoton and the scrivener Master Ambroy, striking two solemn notes among the gaudy silks and brocaded damasks. Then come the fat majordomos, the pages, the grooms, the stewards, the housekeeper with all her keys hung at her side on a fine silver chain. Further back, on benches, are the servants, the maids, and the tenants with their families. And last of all, at the very back, right against the door which they open and shut discreetly, are the scullions who slip in, between sauces, to snatch a little of the atmosphere of the Mass and to bring the smell of the supper into the church, festive and warm with all its lighted candles.

Is it the sight of the scullions' little white caps which distracts the officiating priest? Might it not rather be Garrigou's little bell, that mocking little bell which shakes at the foot of the altar with such infernal haste and seems to keep saying:

'Let's hurry! Let's hurry! The sooner we're finished, the sooner we'll be at supper.'

The fact is that each time this devilish little bell rings, the chaplain forgets his Mass and thinks only of the midnight supper. He imagines the scurrying cooks, the kitchen stoves blazing like blacksmiths' forges, the steam escaping from half-open lids, and, beneath that steam, two magnificent turkeys, stuffed, taut, bursting with truffles....

Or still more, he sees pages passing in files carrying dishes surrounded with tempting odours, and he goes with them into the great hall already prepared for the feast. Oh, paradise! He sees the immense table blazing with lights and laden from end to end with peacocks dressed in their feathers, pheasants spreading their wings, flagons the colour of rubies, fruit dazzling bright among green branches, and all the marvellous fish Garrigou was talking about (yes! – Garrigou, of course) displayed on a bed of fennel, their scales pearly as if just from the sea, with bunches of sweet-smelling herbs in their huge

nostrils. So real is the vision of these marvels that it seems to Father Balaguère that all these wonderful dishes are served before him on the embroidered altar-cloth, and once – or twice – instead of 'Dominus vobiscum!' he catches himself saying 'Benedicite'. Apart from these slight mistakes, the worthy man recites his office most conscientiously, without missing a line, without omitting one genuflection, and all goes very well until the end of the first Mass; for, as you know, the same priest must celebrate three consecutive Masses on Christmas Day.

'One over!' says the chaplain to himself with a sigh of relief; then without wasting a moment, he signs to his clerk, or him who he thinks is his clerk, and –

Dingdong-dong!... Dingdong-dong!...

So the second Mass begins, and with it begins also the sin of Father Balaguère.

'Quick, quick, let's hurry!' Garrigou's little bell cries to him in its shrill little voice, and this time the unfortunate priest abandons himself completely to the demon of gluttony, hurls himself on the missal and devours the pages with the avidity of his over-stimulated appetite. Frantically he kneels, rises, makes vague signs of the cross, half-genuflects, cuts short all his gestures in order to finish the sooner. He scarcely extends his arms at the Gospel, or beats his breast at the Confiteor. It is between the clerk and himself who will jabber the quicker. Verses and responses patter pell-mell, buffeting each other. Worlds half-pronounced without opening the mouth which would take too much time, die away in a baffling hum.

'Oremus ps... ps... ps...'

'Mea culpa... pa... pa...'

Like hurrying wine-harvesters treading the grapes, both splatter about in the Latin of the Mass, sending splashes in all directions.

'Dom... scum!... says Balaguère.

'...Stutuo...,' replies Garrigou; and all the time that damned little bell is ringing in their ears, like those bells they put on post-horses to make them gallop quicker. Obviously at this pace a Low Mass is quickly got out of the way.

'Two over!' says the chaplain quite out of breath; then, red and sweating, without pausing to recover, he rushes down the altar steps and...

Ding dong!... Ding dong-dong!...

So the third Mass begins. It is not far now to the dining hall; but, alas, the nearer the midnight supper approaches, the more the unfortunate Balaguère feels himself seized by a gluttonous madness of impatience. He even sees more distinctly the golden carp, the roast turkeys.... There!... Yes, and there!... He touches them... he... Oh, merciful heavens!... the dishes are steaming, the wines

are ambrosial, and, shaking itself madly, the little bell is shrieking at him:

'Quick, quick! Be more quick!'

But how could he go more quickly? His lips are scarcely moving. He is no longer pronouncing the words.... Unless he cheats the good God completely and omits part of the Mass.... And that is exactly what the wretched man does! Falling deeper into temptation, he begins by skipping one verse, then two, then the Epistle is too long so he doesn't finish it; he skims through the Gospel, passes over the Creed, jumps the pater, bows distantly to the Preface, and thus by leaps and bounds hurls himself into eternal damnation, closely followed by the infamous Garrigou (vade, retro, Satanus!) who co-operates splendidly, holding up his chasuble, turning the pages two at a time, knocking over the desks, upsetting the altar-cruets, and ceaselessly shaking that tiny little bell, louder and louder, quicker and quicker.

The startled faces of the congregation are a sight to behold! Obliged to join in a Mass conducted in dumb-show by a priest whose words they can't hear, some stand up as others are kneeling, or sit when others are rising. And every succeeding part of this extraordinary service results in a confused variety of postures on all the benches. The Star of the Nativity, journeying up there across the sky towards the little stable, paled with apprehension at the sight of such disorder.

'The priest is going too quickly... you can't keep up with him,' the old Dowager grumbles, shaking her coif angrily.

Master Arnoton, his large steel spectacles on his nose, searches in his prayer-book, wondering where the deuce they are up to. But, on the whole, all these worthy folk are themselves also thinking of the supper, and are not sorry the mass is going at top speed. And when Father Balaguère, his face shining radiantly, turns towards the congregation and shouts at the top of his voice: 'Ite, missa est,' the whole chapel replies, as one voice, with a 'Deo Gratias' so merry and so lively you would have thought they were already at table responding to the first toast.

Five minutes later, the nobles were taking their seats in the great hall, the chaplain in the midst of them. The château, bright with lights in every room, was reverberating with songs, shouts, laughter, uproar everywhere; and the venerable Father Balaguère was plunging his fork into the wing of the grouse, drowning remorse for his sin under floods of wine and rich meat gravy. The unfortunate holy man drank so much and ate so much, he died of a stroke that night without even having time to repent. In the morning, he arrived in heaven still all in a stupor

after the night's feasting and I leave you to ponder over the reception he was given.

'Get out of My sight, you wicked Christian!' the Sovereign Judge, Master of us all, said to him, 'Your lapse from virtue is so great it outweighs all the goodness of your life. You stole from Me a Midnight Mass. Well, you will pay it back three-hundred fold. You will not enter Paradise until you have celebrated three hundred Christmas Masses in your own chapel and in the presence of all those who sinned with you and by your fault.'

… Such, in truth, is the legend of Father Balaguère, as you will hear it told in the land of olives. Today the Château de Trinquelage no longer exists, but the chapel still stands on the summit of Mont Ventoux, in a clump of holly oaks. Its disjointed door bangs in the wind, its threshold is overgrown with weeds; there are nests in the corners of the altar and in the recesses of the huge casement windows from which the coloured glass has long since disappeared. Yet it is said that at Christmas every year a supernatural light hovers among these ruins, and that peasants, going to Mass and the midnight supper in the church since built below, see this ghost of a chapel lit with invisible candles which burn in the open air even in wind and snow. You may laugh if you will, but a local vine-grower named Garrigue, a descendant no doubt of Garrigou, has assured me that one Christmas Eve, being slightly drunk, he had lost his way on the mountain near Trinquelage; and this is what he saw… Until eleven o'clock, nothing. Suddenly, towards midnight, a peal of bells sounded high in the steeple, an old peal not heard for many many years and seeming to come from many leagues away. Soon after, on the path leading upwards, he saw lights flickering, faint shadows moving. Under the chapel porch there were footsteps, voices whispering:

'Good evening, Master Arnoton!'

'Good evening, good evening, friends!'

When everyone had entered, my vine-grower, who was very brave, approached softly, looked through the broken door, and saw a strange sight. All these people he had seen passing were ranged in rows around the chancel, in the ruined nave, as if the ancient benches were still there. Beautiful ladies in brocade with coifs of lace, handsome noblemen bedecked from head to foot, peasants in flowered jackets such as our grandfathers wore; everything appeared faded, dusty, old and tired. From time to time night birds, the residents now of the chapel, woken by all the lights, came swooping around the candles whose flames burned erect yet nebulous, as if hidden behind a thin veil. And what amused Garrigue greatly was a certain person wearing large steel spectacles who kept shaking his tall black wig on which one of these birds stood, entangled, silently flapping its wings. At the far end, a little old man no taller than a child was kneeling in the centre of the chancel, shaking despairingly a little, tongueless, soundless bell; while a priest clothed in old gold moved back and fro before the altar reciting prayers no word of which could be heard… It was, most surely, Father Balaguère saying his third Low Mass.

Ballade of Christmas Ghosts

ANDREW LANG

Between the moonlight and the fire
In winter twilights long ago,
What ghosts we raised for your desire,
To make your merry blood run slow!
How old, how grave, how wise we grow!
No Christmas ghost can make us chill,
Save those that troop in mournful row,
The ghosts we all can raise at will!

The beasts can talk in barn and byre
On Christmas Eve, old legends know.
As year by year the years retire,
We men fall silent then I trow,
Such sights hath memory to show,
Such voices from the silence thrill,
Such shapes return with Christmas snow,
The ghosts we all can raise at will.

Oh, children of the village choir,
Your carols on the midnight throw!
Oh, bright across the mist and mire,
Ye ruddy hearths of Christmas glow!
Beat back the dread, beat down the woe,
Let's cheerily descend the hill;
Be welcome all, to come or go,
The ghosts we all can raise at will!

Envoy

Friend, sursum corda, soon or slow
We part, like guests who've joyed their fill;
Forget them not, nor mourn them so,
The ghosts we all can raise at will.

CHRISTMAS FEASTING

Christmas feasts have ranged from the sublime to the ridiculous, from the gorgeously exotic to the plain disgusting, according to custom, availability and wealth. Gilded peacocks, boars' heads with apples in their mouths and elaborate sweetmeats were set before medieval kings. Early settlers in Australia gamely tried to reproduce the English plum pudding under the boiling summer sun after tucking into braised kangaroo. Smoked elephant and fried locusts have graced the table of at least one African adventurer and during the Siege of Paris in 1870 one party dined off roast cat. Whatever the menu, the season is marked by a sturdy determination to prepare and eat something special, a spirit of overwhelming hospitality, a remarkably tenacious adherence to national and family custom and a quite extraordinary greed.

Eating at Christmas has a sacramental quality. As well as the ceremonial breaking of bread and sipping of wine there are pagan rituals connected with ensuring the next year's harvest. In Poland crumbs are saved to be 'sewn' in spring. In most countries animals are given special food. Evil or naughty spirits have to be appeased – the Danish and Norwegian nisser and Swedish tomtes get up to all sorts of mischief if they are not left bowls of rich porridge. In Serbia

'Bringing in the Peacock', an exotic Christmas dish from The Graphic, Christmas, 1881.

pistols were fired before the sucking pig was cooked and again when it was ready, while Siberians left a portion of their feast on a candle-lit window-sill to cheer any escaped prisoner who happened to be passing in the night.

But meals of the season have developed as much from practical considerations as religious and superstitious beliefs. In northern Europe the annual slaughter of animals that could not be kept through the winter was followed by feasting. This originally took place in November – 'blot-monath' or sacrifice month – but as agricultural methods improved the feast gradually merged with Christmas and the New Year. The great consumption of meat at Christmas also reflects ancient sacrificial elements. Catholic fasting customs on the eve of the Nativity and in the weeks before account for the quantity of fish eaten out of season and in places where it is not readily available.

The shape and ingredients of a wide variety of cakes, breads, biscuits and puddings are symbolic to both Christians and heathens. Gluttony – though on a much smaller scale now than in the past – governs the richness and quantity of food. Climate and season influence the range and type of foods served, as to availability and economic considerations. All these strands

combine to create a rich and interesting range of Christmas menus. Whatever other Christmas traditions a nation may forsake, those connected with food, however unpalatable, are fiercely preserved.

The wild boar used to be the favoured sacrificial animal – sacrificed by the Scandinavians to Freya, goddess of love and fertility. The boar's head with an apple or orange in its mouth was the traditional centrepiece of the nobleman's Christmas table. Today the pig, the boar's anaemic relative, still plays a prominent part in most countries' Christmas feasts in the form of roast pork, sausages, ham or brawn.

The Christmas ham is the main dish on Finnish tables, served with a cabbage or beetroot salad, and casserole dishes of carrots, liver, swedes or candied potatoes – thus making a ceremonial virtue out of a seasonal necessity. On Christmas Eve in Sweden many families go through the ritual of 'doppa y grytan' – eating bread dipped in the ham water. Ham served with red or green cabbage is usually part of the meal. Norwegians are more likely to eat their pork roast or smoked. Scandinavian tables also traditionally carry 'lutfisk' or dried split cod – an unappetizing relic of Catholic fast days when fresh fish was not available – and herring and

Christmas in the jungle, complete with traditional plum pudding and port, 1878

Stirring the Christmas pudding is a time for making wishes, 1876.

A busy Christmas market scene with seasonal food on sale. 1836.

other smörgasbord dishes. A hot or cold rice pudding begins or ends the meal. It contains one almond, which wins the finder a small present, perhaps a marzipan pig. The Swedish believe that whoever gets the almond will marry within a year.

The pre-Christmas fasting traditions of Catholics rarely lead to actual suffering. The Polish 'wigilia', the Christmas Eve meal, is meatless because Advent is a period of fasting, but is none the less opulent. It consists of an odd number of dishes – nine or eleven – which should all represent hard work and the produce of the farmer's land. Mushrooms, wheat or millet, dried fruit, peas and cabbage, herring and carp, together with sweet dishes are commonly served. Fasting Hungarians tuck into grilled or jellied carp or a fried fish. Stuffed baked carp in a rich sauce is usual in Czechoslovakia. Cured hake or ling was eaten in Ireland (although richer foods brought from the great Christmas market were eaten before night prayers). Strictly Orthodox Russians fast for six weeks before Christmas and break their fast with a dish called 'kutya' when the first star appears on Christmas Eve. This dish is traditional in many Eastern European countries, but ingredients vary from region to region. In southern Russia it is made with boiled rice and raisins, honey and walnuts, in central Russia with cooked whole wheat, honey, poppyseed, sultanas and walnuts. In some areas the porridge is said to signify the straw in the Bethlehem stable; the fruit, the body; and the honey, the blood of the Infant Jesus. In old Armenia, after the Christmas Eve service, fried fish, lettuce and spinach were served – Mary is thought to have eaten spinach the evening before Christ's birth. Lithuanians share an unconsecrated wafer to symbolize love, harmony and good will. Ukrainians eat a twelve-course meal to commemorate the twelve apostles. Fasting nations make up for Christmas Eve deprivations on Christmas Day when a Russian menu, for instance, might include goose or duck plus the inevitable ham. Fish also features on the Christmas Eve menus further south, where a wider variety of seafood is available. Coastal Italians, for instance, may feast on eels, octopus and squid. The French break their fast after Midnight Mass with a meal called the Réveillon. This is a generous spread – often cold – consisting of oysters, pâtés, boudins, special black or white sausages, and the finest examples of the charcutier's art, game or poultry, a salad, cheeses and desserts. The main dish varies from district to district: Alsatians enjoy goose, Burgundians and Parisians, turkey. On Christmas Day the family gathers for another meal usually based on poultry of some kind.

The centrepiece of the Christmas feast, as opposed to the Christmas Eve fast, is meat – traditionally the best the family can afford. Spaniards tuck into roast sucking pig, truffled turkey with chestnuts or roast lamb. Icelanders choose ptarmigan. Austrians and Germans prefer goose. The Dutch favour roast hare, venison or goose; the Belgians, game, rabbit or hare. Unfortunately these national favourites are being increasingly displaced by turkey, long the festive bird of Britain and the United States. The turkey reached England from the New World in the first half of the sixteenth century and by the early nineteenth century flocks of them were being driven down from Norfolk daily for the London Christmas markets. Before the turkey, English festive boards had groaned under the weight of geese – a German import – swans, roast peacocks and great joints of beef.

European Christmas is particularly rich in cakes, breads, pies and biscuits, many of which appear only during the festive season and have some sort of sacrificial or sacramental significance. No English Christmas scene would be complete without the blazing plum pudding, traditionally spherical but now, for convenience, usually pudding-basin shaped, and topped with a sprig of holly. The pudding began life as a frumenty, a Christmas fasting dish made of hulled wheat boiled in milk and seasoned with spices, cinnamon and sugar. Meat and eggs, spirits and dried fruits were added over the years until a plum porridge emerged. Gradually the meat was dropped, the mixture thickened and the plum pudding we know today, rich with nuts, fruit and alcohol, emerged, complete with holly, symbol of everlasting life, and burning brandy, a reminder of the rebirth of the sun. Lucky charms or coins are traditionally added when all the family gather to stir the pudding mixture on Stir-Up Sunday – the Sunday before the first Sunday of Advent when the Collect for the day begins, 'Stir up, we beseech thee, O Lord, the wills of thy faithful people.'

The other surviving English sweetmeat of the season is mince pie, made originally from minced meat and known as 'shrid' or 'shredded' pie. Before the Reformation the oval sunken lid was taken to represent the manger and often held a pastry baby. The Puritans were deeply offended by such idolatry and banned the eating of mince

'Bringing in the Boar's Head', an illustration from Harper's Monthly, *1873.*

'Skirmishing Against Turkey' from 'A Dream of Christmas Dinner' by Thomas Worth, 1874.

'A Dream of Christmas Night', an illustration from Boy's Own Annual.

pies. When mince pies reappeared after the Restoration, they were round in shape. In some parts it was regarded as unlucky to refuse a mince pie, while good luck came to anyone who ate one on each of the twelve days of Christmas.

In Sweden and Denmark the Yule Boar – a loaf shaped like a boar and made from the corn of the last sheaf of the harvest – stood on the table throughout Christmas. This loaf was said to be the corn spirit embodied in pig form. Anyone eating a popular Norwegian biscuit shaped like a goat had to bray like one and the crumbs were said to have magical curative powers. Gingerbread biscuits cut like pigs, stars and Christmas trees, saffron-flavoured bread, tarts shaped like stars and half-moons and filled with jam are common throughout Scandinavia at Christmas.

Russians traditionally tuck into pastries called 'hvorost' ('branches') and a fruit cake called 'mazurka'. Hungarians usually follow their carp with 'beigli' – a pastry filled with grated walnuts and poppyseed. Poland also has a poppyseed cake and families ceremonially break holy wafers on Christmas Eve when the first star appears. In Czechoslovakia a fruit stew called 'masika' is served with a slice of plaited white Christmas bread. The traditional Rumanian cake is the 'turte' – layers of thin dough sandwiching melted sugar or honey and walnuts. The Serbo-Croatian cake is the 'kolach' – a ring-shaped coffee cake with three candles in the centre, the first of which is lit on Christmas Eve. The cake is eaten at Epiphany.

German Christmas markets stock a vast range of decorated spiced cakes, biscuits and gingerbreads; among the best known are 'lebkuchen' with raisins, nuts and candied lemon and orange peel, and 'stollen' – a sort of fruit loaf. German peasants used to believe that bread baked at Christmas, particularly if moistened with Christmas dew, had magical powers. An

elaborately iced 'Christ Bread' – 'Christopsomo' – is traditional in Greece, while Spain and Italy specialize in a sort of nougat called 'turron' or 'torrone'. Italy has a number of traditional cakes, but 'panetone' – a dome-shaped fruit cake from Milan – is the most popular. Christmas sweets traditionally contain nuts and honey because eating nuts was believed to encourage the earth to be more fertile and honey was given in ancient Rome to make the new year sweet. France's Christmas cake is the Bûche de Noël – a chocolate log. Belgium specializes in pancakes and, as a Christmas dinner sweet course, a Yule log topped with a fondant baby.

All nationalities took their feasting custom with them when they settled in far-off lands. Australians persevered with roast turkey – though many now prefer it cold with salad. Canadians of English extraction also roast a turkey, while French-speaking Canadians serve meat pies at their Réveillon and German Canadians may choose goose, duck or sucking pig. South Africans sit down to lamb or sucking pig and the fresh fruits and vegetables of the summer. In Jamaica, instead of eating twelve mince pies for luck, twelve pieces of particularly rich and alcoholic Christmas pudding are consumed. All the old national traditions are preserved in the United States – often after they have fallen into disuse in their countries of origin.

Nations stick stubbornly and conservatively to their traditional festive food – and none more so than the English to their turkey and plum pudding – but Christmas food is so varied and interesting that there is endless scope for experiment. And the Christmas season is now long enough to try the feasts of other nations without sacrificing your own favourites. While other Christmas customs are in danger of becoming drearily uniform throughout the world the traditions of eating are rich and robust and so easy to reproduce.

The glorious climax of the traditional English Christmas dinner is the arrival of the Christmas plum pudding in brandy and set alight. 'Bringing in the Pudding', 1891.

BREAD

A warm, family table dressed in the traditional Polish style with straw to commemorate the stable at Bethlehem, the table covered with the very best fine white linen cloth. Place corn wreaths around the candles. Wooden napkin holders, carved in a festive star shape, and pottery goblets echo the rural theme. In the old days a whole sheaf of corn used to cover the table, now a few symbolic blades suffice.

1 On the table and in the basket, poppyseed plaits of mild, milky bread, brushed with egg and sprinkled with poppyseeds.

2 An attractive star design modelled in a rather crisp bread. The same recipe can be used to make any type of Christmas design. The bread is brushed with egg and rolled in poppyseeds.

3 Plaited wholewheat wreath, decorated with a bread or fabric bow. These braided bread wreaths are often allowed to dry completely, given a coat of varnish and used as wall decorations.

4 Walnut and date loaf, rich and fruity. Loaves like these are traditionally symbolic of the fertility of the earth.

5 Scandinavian Julekake, a rich, spicy, honey-flavoured fruit bread in an unusual twisted spiral shape, and brushed with a honey glaze.

6 Initials made from the same recipe as the star design. Make one for each guest as an interesting way to indicate seating at the table.

7 Salt sticks, crisp bread sticks, piquant and savoury, are rolled in crunchy sea salt.

8 Muffins are traditionally English. They are made with a yeast dough but cooked on a griddle or heavy frying pan. Serve hot with butter; add jam, if you wish.

9 Vanochka is a Czechoslovakian Christmas loaf, elaborately braided and filled with fruit and nuts.

10 Raisin braid is a rich, sweet, spicy fruit bread of Bohemian origin.

4

5

6

7

8

9

10

115

Recipes for Bread

Notes on breadmaking: All yeast mentioned is fresh yeast. If dried yeast is used half the quantity will be enough. Kneading the bread is a laborious job. It can take 15-20 minutes to bring dough to the 'smooth and elastic' stage, but it is important not to give up too soon. Rising times are approximate and will depend on the warmth of the room.

1 POPPY SEED PLAIT
3 cups (450 g) all-purpose flour
1 tbs (15 g) granulated sugar
1 oz (30 g) fresh yeast
1 egg, beaten
1 egg yolk, beaten
¾-1 cup (175-225ml) warm milk
1 teaspoon salt
½ cup (115 g) butter, melted
For the topping
1 egg, beaten
½ oz (15 g) poppyseeds

Sift the flour into a large bowl. In a smaller bowl put a quarter of the sifted flour with the sugar, yeast, egg and egg yolk well beaten and the warm milk. Beat to a smooth batter entirely free of lumps. Cover the bowl with a cloth and allow to stand for five minutes. Add this mixture to the flour with the salt, melted butter and enough of the warm milk to make a stiffish but pliable dough. Turn out on to a floured board and knead well until it is smooth and elastic. Put the dough into a large greased plastic bag covered with a cloth and allow to rise until it has doubled in size. Put the dough back on the floured board and punch down. Divide the dough into three pieces, roll these into long ropes, and plait them. Put the plait on a greased baking sheet, wetting the ends of the plait and forming a point at each end. Brush the top of the plait with an egg well beaten with a teaspoon of water and a pinch of salt. Cover with greased wrap and allow to rise for a further period until well risen. Brush again with egg and sprinkle with poppyseeds. Bake in a hot oven 425°F (220°C, Gas Mark 7) for 10 minutes and then at 375°F (190°C, Gas Mark 5) for a further 40-50 minutes. The loaf will sound hollow when it is done. Cool on a wire rack and cut when cold.

2 & 6 BREAD STAR AND LETTERS
4½ cups (700 g) all-purpose flour
1½ teaspoons salt
½ oz (15 g) fresh yeast
1 teaspoon granulated sugar
⅝ cup (150 ml) warm milk
¼ cup (55 g) butter, melted
1¼ cups (275 ml) warm water
For the topping
1 egg, beaten
1 oz (30 g) poppyseeds

Sift the flour and salt into a large bowl. Cream the yeast and sugar with some of the warm milk. Mix the rest of the milk with the melted butter and add both mixtures to the flour together with enough of the warm water to make a fairly stiff dough. Knead the dough on a floured board until smooth and elastic. Put the dough to rise in a large, well-greased plastic bag covered with a cloth and allow to rise until it has doubled in size, approximately one hour. Taking the dough a little at a time, keeping the rest covered, roll into long snakes and use these to form the initials and star, using a little water where you need to join the pieces. Put the star or the letters on a greased baking sheet, brush with beaten egg and sprinkle with poppyseeds. Cover with greased wrap and allow to rise for half an hour. Bake in a hot oven 450°F (230°C, Gas Mark 8) for 15-20 minutes.

3 CHRISTMAS WHOLE WHEAT WREATHS
Quantities sufficient for 2 wreaths
4 cups (590 g) all-purpose flour
1 tablespoon salt
2⅝ cups (340 g) whole wheat flour
1 tablespoon soft dark-brown sugar
1 oz (30 g) fresh yeast
⅛ cup (30 g) butter, melted
2½ cups (550 ml) warm water
For the topping
1 egg, beaten
1 oz (30 g) sesame seeds

Sift the white flour with the salt into a large bowl and add the whole wheat flour. Mix the sugar, yeast and four tablespoons of the water together and leave for five minutes to dissolve. Stir this liquid into the flour together with the melted butter and enough of the warm water to make a good dough. Knead the dough on a floured board for about 15 minutes until it is smooth and elastic. Place the dough in a large greased plastic bag covered with a cloth and leave to rise until double in size. Punch down the dough and divide it into two equal pieces. Return one piece to the plastic bag. Grease a large baking sheet and the outside of a 6 in round cake pan. Take a piece the size of a large hen's egg from the dough and divide the rest into three equal pieces. Roll these into long ropes 28 in long and plait them together. Put the plait on the baking sheet round the cake pan. Wet the ends of the plait and push them together. Roll the fourth piece of dough and make a bow, attaching it to the loaf where the two ends of the plait meet, using a little water to stick the bow on to the loaf. Cover with greased wrap and allow to rise for about 30 minutes in a warm place. Repeat this process with the other half of the dough. When the loaves are well risen paint them with beaten egg and sprinkle with sesame seeds. Bake in a hot oven, 400°F (200°C, Gas Mark 6) for 10 minutes and then at 375°F (190°C, Gas Mark 5) for a further 20-30 minutes. When done the loaves will sound hollow. If both the loaves are cooked at the same time reverse the baking sheets on their shelves halfway through the cooking and give them a further five minutes if necessary. Cool on wire racks.

4 DATE AND WALNUT LOAF
1½ cups (225 g) self-rising flour
½ teaspoon salt
½ cup (115 g) granulated sugar
½ cup (115 g) butter
3 oz (85 g) walnuts, chopped
⅜ cup (85 g) dates, chopped
2 eggs, beaten
⅜ cup (85 ml) milk

Sift the flour, salt and sugar into a bowl. Add the butter cut in small pieces and rub it into the flour. Add the walnuts and dates and mix in the well-beaten eggs and enough of the milk to make a mixture of a dropping consistency. Put this into a greased bread pan 4 in by 8 in. Bake in a moderate oven 350°F (180°C, Gas Mark 4) for 50-60 minutes. Test with a skewer and cook for a further 5-10 minutes if it does not come out clean. Cool for 10 minutes in the pan, remove and cool. Ice the loaf with 1 egg white beaten until frothy, mixed with 2 oz (55 g) confectioners' sugar and ½ teaspoon lemon juice.

5 SCANDINAVIAN CHRISTMAS BREAD (JULEKAKE)
1½ cups (225 g) all-purpose flour
2½ cups (225 g) rye flour
½ teaspoon salt
⅜ cup (55 g) sultanas
⅜ cup (55 g) candied peel, chopped
2 teaspoons ground cardamom or caraway seeds
1 orange, rind and juice
¾ oz (20 g) fresh yeast
2 tbs (30 g) granulated sugar
2 tablespoons (30 g) butter
3 tablespoons runny honey
1 egg, beaten
¾-1 cup (175-225 ml) warm water or half water, half Guinness
For the topping
1 tablespoon runny honey
1 tablespoon water

Sift the flour and salt into a large warm bowl and add the sultanas, chopped peel, crushed cardamom or caraway seeds, the orange peel and the sugar. Dissolve the yeast in ¼ cup (60 ml) of the warm water. Melt the butter and honey together and allow to cool. Add this, the yeast mixture, orange juice and the beaten egg to the bowl of flour and mix together with enough water, or water and Guinness, to make a manageable dough. Turn on to a floured board and knead until the dough is smooth and elastic. Place the dough in a large greased plastic bag covered with a cloth and allow to rise for one hour, or until doubled in bulk. Knead the dough again, divide it into two pieces and roll these into long snakes. Starting at the edge of a 9in spring-sided cake tin that has been well buttered, coil the dough round and round to the centre, joining the second piece with a little water to the end of the first. Cover with plastic wrap and allow to rise until almost level with the top of the pan. Bake in a moderately hot oven, 375°F (190°C, Gas mark 5) for 10 minutes and then at 325°F (170°C, Gas Mark 3) for a further 40-50 minutes. Glaze the loaf with honey mixed with a little water when it is cooked and leave to cool on a wire cake rack.

7 SALTSTICKS

2¼ cups (340 g) all-purpose flour
1 teaspoon salt
2 tablespoons (30 g) butter
½ oz (15 g) fresh yeast
1 egg
¾ cup (175 ml) warm water
For the topping
1 oz (30 g) coarse sea salt

Sift the flour and salt into a large bowl and rub in the butter. Dissolve the yeast in three tablespoons of warm water. Beat the egg and add this together with the yeast mixture and most of the rest of the water to the flour and salt and mix well. Turn out on to a floured board and knead well until smooth and elastic. Put the dough in a large greased plastic bag, cover with a cloth and allow to rise for about ¾-1 hour. Punch down the dough and divide it into 20-24 equal pieces. Roll out each piece into a pencil shape 10 in long and put them 1 in apart on two greased baking sheets. Allow to rise covered with greased wrap for 15 minutes. Brush the sticks with warm water and sprinkle with the sea salt. Bake in a moderately hot oven, 400°F (200°C, Gas Mark 6) for 10-15 minutes until golden brown. Cool on a wire cake rack. If you would like the bread sticks crisp like Italian bread sticks leave them in the oven at its lowest setting for a further 45-60 minutes until they are hard.

8 MUFFINS

3 cups (450 g) all-purpose flour
1 teaspoon salt

⅓ oz (10 g) fresh yeast
1 teaspoon granulated sugar
1-1¼ cups (225-275 ml) warm milk
1 egg, beaten
2 tablespoons (30 g) butter, melted

Sift the flour and salt into a large bowl. Cream the yeast and sugar with three tablespoons of the warm milk and let it stand in a warm place until it is frothy. Stir the yeast mixture into the flour together with the beaten egg and the melted butter and enough of the warm milk to make a soft dough. Turn the dough on to a floured board and knead until soft and elastic. Place the dough in a large greased plastic bag covered with a cloth and put in a warm place for about one hour, until it has doubled in size. Turn the dough back on to the floured board, punch it down and divide it into 16 pieces. Roll out each piece into a circle 2¾ in across and ⅜-¾ thick. Cover the muffins with a piece of greased wrap and allow to rise again for 15-20 minutes. Cook them gently a few at a time on a greased griddle or in a heavy frying pan for just under 10 minutes on each side. When they are cooked keep them warm until they are all ready, pull them apart using two forks, butter them and serve immediately. It is important not to cut them with a knife as this will make them 'sad' in the middle. Any muffins not required can be split and toasted the next day.

9 CZECHOSLOVAKIAN CHRISTMAS PLAIT (VANOCHKA)

3 cups (450 g) all-purpose flour
1 teaspoon salt
½ cup (115 g) vanilla sugar
2 egg yolks, beaten
1 oz (30 g) fresh yeast
1¼ cups (275 ml) warm milk
3 tbs (30 g) chopped mixed peel
3 tbs (30 g) sultanas
½ cup (115g) butter, melted
2 oz (55 g) flaked almonds
For the topping
2 egg whites, beaten
pinch salt
1-2 tablespoons flaked almonds
   or 1 oz (30 g) poppyseeds

Sift the flour and salt into a large bowl. In a smaller bowl put a quarter of the sifted flour, 2 tbs (30 g) of the sugar, the two egg yolks, the yeast and

half the warm milk. Beat well to a smooth batter entirely free of lumps. Cover the bowl with a cloth and allow to stand until light and spongy. Meanwhile soak the peel and the sultanas in the rest of the warm milk. Add the butter, the almonds and the soaked fruit to the sifted flour together with the yeast mixture and enough of the warm milk to make a manageable dough. Knead this well on a floured board until smooth and elastic. Put the dough in a large greased plastic bag covered with a cloth and allow to rise until doubled in size. Punch down the dough on the floured board and divide it into eight equal pieces. Put four pieces back in the plastic bag while you roll the other four into long ropes. Plait these starting in the middle (fig 1). Damp the ends with water and pinch together to prevent them separating. This section forms the base of the loaf. Place this on a greased baking sheet and brush with the egg whites beaten a little with a pinch of salt. Make another plait with three of the remaining pieces of dough and place

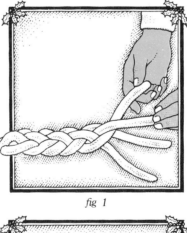

fig 1

fig 2

this firmly on top of the base (fig 2). Brush this also with egg white. Divide the last piece of dough in half and roll into two thin ropes (fig 2). Twist these together and press along the top of the last plait and brush with egg white. If the first two plaits look at all dry give them another coat of egg white and sprinkle the loaf with poppyseeds or flaked almonds. Cover with greased wrap and allow to stand again until well risen. Bake in a moderate oven 350°F (180°C, Gas Mark 4) for 40-50 minutes, until golden brown. Halfway through the cooking, if the loaf is decorated with almonds, cover the loaf loosely with a piece of greaseproof paper to prevent the almonds burning. Cool the loaf on a wire rack before slicing it.

10 FRUIT BRAID

3 cups (450 g) all-purpose flour
¼ cup (55 g) granulated sugar
1 oz (30 g) fresh yeast
¾ cup (175 ml) warm milk mixed
   with ⅜ cup (85 ml) water
1 teaspoon salt
1 teaspoon mixed spice
1 teaspoon cinnamon
1⅛ cups (170 g) mixed raisins,
   sultanas and chopped candied peel
¼ cup (55 g) butter, melted
1 egg, beaten
For the topping
2 tablespoons runny honey

Mix ¾ cup (115 g) of the flour with a teaspoon of the sugar. Blend yeast with a little milk and water, stir into remaining liquid and add to flour and sugar. Beat and leave for 15 minutes, until bubbles form. Add rest of flour, salt, sugar, mixed spice and cinnamon, fruit, peel and melted butter to yeast mixture and stir in beaten egg. Mix until a soft dough forms. Knead until smooth and elastic on a floured board. Put in a large greased plastic bag, cover with a cloth and leave until doubled in size. Place dough on floured board, divide into three, rolling each piece into a rope about 1 foot long. Plait these together, sealing ends with a little water. Place on a greased baking tray, cover with greased plastic wrap and leave until doubled in size. Bake at 425°F (220°C, Gas Mark 7) for 25-30 minutes. Cool and glaze with honey.

MEAT, POULTRY, GAME & FISH

A classic table of polished wood is decorated with a magical collection of cut glass candlesticks in the centre, and creamy candles flickering and reflecting in the gleaming surface and the old silver tableware. Starched white linen napkins and mats are decorated with ivy wreaths to give original and appropriate place settings for a formal Christmas dinner.

1 Sucking pig on a bed of rosemary, garlanded with a wreath of bay leaves.

2 Roast pheasant decorated with its tail feathers in the traditional way. Serve with game chips, bread sauce and roast chestnuts.

3 In many countries fish is served on Christmas Eve as a reminder of the old Christmas fast. One of the most interesting fish dishes is devilled carp with its sweet, spicy sauce as served by many families of Czechoslovakian origin.

4 Roast duck, garnished with sharp baked apples stuffed with prunes.

5 Traditional ham decorated with pineapple and served Scandinavian style with sweet, glazed, new potatoes, a creamy mustard sauce and red cabbage.

6 Rich goose with savoury apple stuffing and served with sliced apples cooked in butter or in the French style with boudins.

7 Boudins are almost always served at the French Christmas feast, the Réveillon. Boudins, either black or white, are served with turkey or goose, either surrounding the fowl or piled decoratively high on a silver salver.

8 On the table, the traditional turkey served English style with forcemeat and chestnut stuffing, bacon rolls, stuffing balls, bread or cranberry sauce, roast potatoes and sprouts with chestnuts or almonds.

1

2

3

4

5

6

7

8

119

Recipes for Main Courses

1 SUCKING PIG

10-12 lb (4.5-5.5 kg) sucking pig
½ cup (125 ml) olive oil
salt and pepper
1 large potato
1 red apple
rosemary and bay leaves
parsley or watercress
For the stuffing
1 cup (115 g) soft white breadcrumbs,
    grated
½ cup (115 g) butter
1 medium onion, chopped
3 sticks celery, chopped
kidneys from the sucking pig
liver from the sucking pig
1 orange
½ lemon, rind and juice
salt and pepper
sage leaves or rosemary

Make sure that the pig is not too big for your oven. Ask the butcher to prepare the pig for easy carving. It should be chined on either side of the backbone from the inside and the leg joints should be disjointed. To prepare the pig for roasting wipe it inside and out with kitchen paper. Prepare the stuffing. Grate the breadcrumbs. Melt the butter in a saucepan and sauté the chopped onion and celery. When they begin to look transparent add the chopped kidneys and liver and cook until they are browned. Stir in the breadcrumbs, grated orange, lemon peel and juice, salt, pepper and either rosemary or sage. Peel the grated orange and put the orange segments into the stuffing too. Fill the body of the pig with this stuffing and sew up the pig, using thin string. Rub the outside of the pig with oil and sprinkle with salt and pepper. Tie the legs underneath the pig and wrap the ears and tail in greased aluminium foil to prevent burning. Put a potato in the mouth to keep it open. Put the sucking pig on a rack over the largest roasting pan that will fit into the oven. If it is too small line the shelf of the oven with aluminium foil. If the pig is so long that it will touch the sides of the oven, protect it with more greased foil. Cook the pig in a very hot oven, 450°F (230°C, Gas Mark 8) for 15 minutes. Paint the pig with some of the remaining olive oil and turn the oven down to 375°F (190°C, Gas Mark 5) and cook for a further 2-2½ hours, painting with olive oil every half-hour or so. Remove the pig to a large, hot serving dish and rest it in a warm place for 15-20 minutes. Remove the foil from the ears and tail of the pig, and take the potato from the mouth. Serve the sucking pig with a red apple in the mouth and rosemary or watercress round it on the dish. Put a wreath of rosemary and bayleaves round the neck. Serve with a sharp-tasting apple sauce. Serves 12-14.

SHARP APPLE SAUCE

4 large cooking apples
2 tablespoons (30 g) butter
1 tablespoon sugar
pinch ground cloves

Peel and core and slice the apples. Rinse them and put into the saucepan with a little water. Cover closely and cook over a medium heat until the apples are soft and fluffy. Beat the apples with a fork, adding the butter, sugar and a pinch of ground cloves.

2 ROAST PHEASANT

2 plump young pheasants
2 shallots
½ cup (115 g) butter, softened
4-6 slices bacon
salt and pepper
2 tablespoons flour

Wipe the pheasants inside and out with a clean damp cloth. Put inside each bird a shallot, 2 tbs (30 g) butter and a little salt and pepper. Rub the rest of the butter over the breasts of the pheasants, tie the bacon across them and put in a roasting tin. Cover the birds loosely with aluminium foil and roast in a fairly hot oven, 400°F (200°C, Gas Mark 6) for 30 minutes. Remove the foil and the bacon and baste well, dredge the breasts of the birds with flour and return to the oven for a further 10-15 minutes until nicely browned. Turn off the oven and rest the birds on the serving dish in the oven for 15 minutes while you make the gravy. Serves 4-6.

BREAD SAUCE

1⅞ cups (425 ml) milk
1 onion
3 or 4 cloves
6 peppercorns
½ teaspoon salt
1 bayleaf
pinch mace or nutmeg
¾ cup (85 g) soft white breadcrumbs
2 tablespoons (30 g) butter
2 tablespoons heavy cream

Heat the milk in a saucepan with the onion, cloves, peppercorns, salt, bayleaf and spice. Keep the mixture hot, but not quite boiling for 10 minutes and then take off the heat and keep warm for a further 20 minutes. Strain the milk into the top of a double boiler and add the breadcrumbs, butter and cream. Stir gently and cook over boiling water for 10 minutes until the sauce thickens. Adjust the seasoning and keep hot until ready to serve.

3 DEVILLED CARP

3-4 lb (1.5-2 kg) carp
4 tablespoons red wine vinegar
¼ cup (55 g) butter
1 carrot
1 onion
1 oz (30 g) piece of celeriac
3 sprigs parsley
1 bayleaf
6 peppercorns
pinch each allspice, thyme, mace and
    ginger
½ lemon, rind only
salt and pepper
2½ cups (550 ml) brown ale
1 cup (115 g) gingerbread crumbs
2 tablespoons redcurrant jelly
1 tablespoon pale, soft brown sugar
6 prunes, stoned
½ oz (15 g) almonds, chopped
2 tablespoons (15 g) raisins

If possible collect the blood of a freshly killed carp and mix with 2 tablespoons of the vinegar. Clean the fish and rinse it in cold water, leave it to soak in water with the remaining 2 tablespoons of vinegar. Finely chop the carrot, onion and the celeriac and sauté gently with the butter in a heatproof casserole until the onion begins to colour a little. Add the herbs, spices, lemon rind, salt, pepper, ale and the gingerbread crumbs. Dry the fish and put it in the casserole and simmer very gently for 15-20 minutes. Remove the fish carefully to an oval ovenproof dish and strain the sauce over it. Add the rest of the ingredients and cook in a low oven, 300°F, (160°C, Gas Mark 2) for a further 30 minutes. Remove from the oven and cool. Reheat on the following day, adjust seasoning to taste and serve. Serves 6.

4 ROAST DUCK

4-5 lb (2 kg) duck
salt and pepper
1 tablespoon flour
1 tablespoon olive oil
For the stuffing
¼ cup (55 g) butter
1 onion, chopped
duck's liver
2 small cooking apples, grated
8 prunes or apricots, stoned and
    chopped
1 cup (115 g) soft white breadcrumbs
salt and pepper
handful of parsley, chopped

To make the stuffing, soften the chopped onion in the butter, stir in the chopped liver, and when this is browned, add the grated apples, prunes or apricots, breadcrumbs, seasoning and parsley. Mix well together and put the stuffing into the body of the duck. Truss the duck, prick its breast well all over with a thin skewer or darning needle, rub with olive oil and sprinkle with flour, salt and pepper.

Rest the duck on a suitable rack over a roasting pan and roast in a moderate oven, 350°F (180°C, Gas Mark 4) for 30 minutes. Baste well and continue cooking for about a further two hours, basting often. When the duck is cooked put it on a serving dish and rest for 15-20 minutes. Serves 3.

GARNISH – APPLES STUFFED WITH PRUNES

⅞ cup (170 g) brown sugar
½ cup (125 ml) red wine
½ cup (125 ml) water
½ lemon, rind only
3 tablespoons redcurrant jelly
6 small cooking apples
6 prunes or apricots, stoned

Put the sugar, red wine, water, lemon rind and redcurrant jelly in a saucepan and simmer for a moment until the jelly is melted. Peel and core the apples and stuff them with the stoned prunes or apricots. Put them in the liquid and poach gently, basting from time to time until they are cooked, but still firm. Put them in a dish and pour the syrup over them.

5 CHRISTMAS HAM

12-16 lb (6-7 kg) ham
1 quart (1 litre) dry cider
1⅝ cups (370 ml) cider vinegar
1 oz (30 g) whole cloves
1 lb (450 g) soft, light brown sugar
2 tablespoons French mustard
2 teaspoons ground cloves
1 egg, beaten
For decoration
fresh pineapple

Soak the ham in a large pan of cold water for 12-24 hours, changing the water two or three times. Remove the ham and scrub with a stiff brush. Wipe it dry with kitchen paper and put in a pan with the cider and the cider vinegar and enough cold water to cover the ham. Bring to the boil, skim and lower the heat. Partially cover the pan and simmer. Cook the ham for 20-25 minutes per pound until the small bone beside the shank bone is loose and easy to pull out. Cool the ham in the cooking liquid until it can be handled. Put the ham in a large roasting pan. Ease the skin off with a small, sharp knife. Score the fat in a diamond pattern and insert a clove at each intersection. Mix the brown sugar, mustard, ground cloves and the beaten egg, adding some water to make a stiff paste. Spread the paste on to the ham and decorate with small cubes of fresh pineapple, held on with pieces of toothpick. Pour a few spoonfuls of the cooking liquid into the pan and put

the ham into a hot oven, 400°F (200°C, Gas Mark 6) for 20 minutes. Baste the ham twice with the liquid until the glaze is richly browned. Serve with mustard sauce.

MUSTARD SAUCE

1¼ cups (280 ml) heavy cream
4 tablespoons French mustard
pinch salt

Whip the cream until soft peaks form and add the mustard and salt. Whip for a moment or two longer so that the mustard is thoroughly blended with the cream. Put the sauce in a serving dish and stand in a cool place to allow the flavour to develop.

6 ROAST GOOSE

8-10 lb (3.5-4.5 kg) goose
salt and pepper
1-2 tablespoons flour
For the stuffing
1 lb (450 g) onions
8 oz (225 g) cooking apples
4 cups (450 g) white breadcrumbs
salt and pepper
2 teaspoons French mustard
4-6 sage leaves

To make the stuffing boil the onions in water until they are soft. Drain well and chop them. Peel and core the apples and cut them in quarters. Mix the onions, apples, breadcrumbs together and add the seasoning, chopped sage leaves and the mustard. Wipe inside the goose with kitchen paper. Put the stuffing into the body cavity and truss the goose with string. Prick the breast of the bird all over with a thin skewer or darning needle. Rub into the skin, salt, pepper and some flour and put the goose on a rack over a large roasting pan. Cook in a moderate oven, 350°F (180°C, Gas Mark 4) for 25 minutes per pound (450 g). Baste the goose with the fat that runs from the breast and drain any excess fat from the pan after the first hour. If the wings brown too fast cover them with foil. When the goose is cooked, rest it in a warm place for 15-20 minutes. Serve the goose with apples and grilled boudins. French boudins noirs are a fine, spicy version of the traditional black 'blood' pudding. Boudins blancs have a milder filling. Serves 6-8.

7 APPLES AND BOUDINS

2 lb (900 g) eating apples
¾ cup (115-170 g) unsalted butter
boudins or blood pudding
2-3 tablespoons olive oil

Peel, core and slice the apples into rings. Fry them in the butter until they are just cooked, but not disintegrating. Keep them in a warm oven. Paint the boudins with a little olive oil and prick them well. Cook under a medium hot grill. Leave whole or cut into pieces and arrange them on a dish or with the apple rings round the goose.

8 ROAST TURKEY

10-14 lb (4.5-6 kg) turkey
salt and pepper
1-2 tablespoons flour
½ cup (115 g) butter, softened
For the Chestnut stuffing
2 lb (900 g) chestnuts, cooked and
  peeled
2 oz (55 g) sausage meat
1 cup (115 g) brown breadcrumbs
1 teaspoon mixed herbs
¼ cup (55 g) butter, melted
For the Forcemeat
2 cups (225 g) soft white breadcrumbs
¾ cup (170 g) butter
1 turkey liver, chopped
4 oz (115 g) ham, chopped
2 tablespoons parsley
1 teaspoon thyme
1 lemon, peel and juice
1 clove garlic
1 egg

Wipe the turkey inside with kitchen paper. Prepare the two stuffings. Prick, bake or boil the chestnuts until they split and peel them. Break the chestnuts in half and mix them with the other ingredients. Use this stuffing for the neck end of the bird.

Make the forcemeat. Melt the butter and stir into the breadcrumbs, add the finely chopped ham and liver, herbs, lemon peel and juice, crushed garlic and the egg well beaten. Use this stuffing for the body of the bird. Do not pack it in too tightly, but use any left over to make forcemeat balls. Cook these on the shelf below the turkey, basting them with a little turkey fat. Cook them until they are golden brown and serve on the dish with the turkey. When the turkey is stuffed, truss it and rub the breast with some

butter. Sprinkle with flour, salt and pepper. Wrap the wings and legs with aluminium foil and put the turkey on a rack over a large roasting pan and put in a hot oven 400°F (200°C, Gas Mark 6) for 20 minutes. Baste the bird and turn down the oven to 350°F (180°C, Gas Mark 4) and cook for 20 minutes per pound. Baste often and remove the foil from the wings and legs towards the end of the cooking time. If the bird is browning too fast put a piece of foil loosely over the top to protect the breast. When the turkey is done put it on a warm serving dish and keep it warm in a low oven while you make the gravy. Serve with bacon rolls, made with rindless slices of bacon curled round and held with a toothpick, and cooked in the oven with the forcemeat balls. Serves 8-12.

CRANBERRY SAUCE

1 lb (450 g) fresh cranberries
1⅞ cups (425 ml) water
1½ cups (225-280 g) light soft brown
  sugar
1 orange, juice and rind

Rinse the cranberries and put them in a saucepan with the water. Bring to the boil and simmer until they split. Continue to cook for a few minutes more and then add the sugar, orange rind and juice. Stir well and simmer until the sauce is thick. Put into a serving dish and serve cold.

MAKING GRAVY

The method of making gravy is similar for most poultry or game. Rinse giblets, with the exception of the liver, and place them in a small saucepan with an onion, a carrot, salt, pepper and a bouquet garni. Cover with water and simmer slowly. When the meat has cooked place it on a serving dish and pour off as much fat as possible from the roasting pan. Add a glass of red or white wine to the remaining juices and cook over a medium heat to deglaze the pan, scraping any sediment from the bottom. Mix 3 teaspoons of softened butter with 3 teaspoons of flour and add this gradually to the pan with any juices which have collected in the serving dish. Stir well and cook until sauce is glossy and slightly thickened. Keep covered until required and serve in a hot sauce boat.

CAKES & PUDDINGS

A festive holly theme makes a bright and traditional Christmas table. A generous mound of holly and other evergreen with red ribbon bows and candles forms the centrepiece. Holly decorates the crackers, makes a bed for mince pies and, of course, tops the Christmas pudding. The holly cloth could be a printed design, or stencilled on paper, or even embroidered as a family heirloom.

1 Almond trifle with crushed macaroons, held in a case of biscuits. If the case seems insecure tie it with a gold ribbon and decorate with Christmas baubles.

2 Port wine jelly, rich looking and rich tasting. Serve with clotted cream and small sweet biscuits.

3 Bûche de Nöel, the traditional French Christmas log of light chocolate cake rolled with cream, liqueur and nuts and coated with chocolate butter icing to look like bark. Decorate with a candle and dredged icing sugar.

4 Snowball of icecream filled with candied fruits and nuts, coated with cream and decorated with more fruit.

5 Cranberry water ice makes a pretty and refreshing change from heavy Christmas food.

6 Ginger meringues piled high and decorated with crystallized ginger.

7 On the table, traditional Christmas pudding flamed with brandy and served with brandy or rum butter. Individual mince pies can be made from prepared mincemeat. If you wish to mix your own, make it earlier in the year when the new dried fruits come into the shops.

8 Panetone, the light, sweet Italian Christmas yeast cake.

9 Bavarois Clermont, a creamy custard with chestnut purée in an elaborate mould. Decorate with whipped cream and marrons glacés.

10 Christstollen, the traditional German Christmas fruit loaf, decorated with fruit and nuts and sifted icing sugar.

122

7

8

9

10

123

Recipes for Cakes & Puddings

1 ALMOND TRIFLE
2½ cups (600 ml) heavy cream
2 tablespoons (30 g) granulated sugar
¾ cup (175 ml) sherry or brandy
4 oz (115 g) chopped almonds
4 oz (115 g) almond macaroons
For case
2 packets Boudoir cookies
1 egg white, beaten
For topping
1¼ cups (280 ml) heavy cream
4 oz (115 g) whole blanched almonds

On a plate suitable for serving the trifle, place an 8 in cake pan with a removable bottom, to make it easy to lift when the case is set. Stand Boudoir cookies vertically round outside of pan, securing the first with a knob of butter and sticking others together by dipping edges of cookies in beaten egg white. Tie round with broad tape and leave to dry. An hour before serving remove pan. Whip cream, sugar and liqueur until it almost forms peaks. Fold in chopped almonds and crushed macaroons. Fill case and pipe top with whipped cream and spike with blanched almonds. Leave to chill. Remove tape just before serving.

2 PORT WINE JELLY
2 oranges, juice and rind
1 cup (225 ml) water
8 tbs (55 g) powdered gelatine
3¾ cups (840 ml) Ruby Port
½ nutmeg, grated
¼-⅜ cups (55-85 g) granulated sugar

Measure the orange juice and make up to 1¼ cups (280 ml) with cold water. Put half this liquid into a bowl and sprinkle in the gelatine to soften. Put the remaining orange juice and water, the port, orange peel, grated nutmeg and sugar into a saucepan and stir over a low heat until the sugar has dissolved. Bring to the boil and simmer for 5 minutes. Pour through a fine strainer. Put some of the hot liquid into the gelatine and stir until dissolved. Combine this with the rest of the liquid. Pour into a damp mould and allow to set in a cool place. Turn the jelly out on to a moist plate.

3 BÛCHE DE NOËL
6 eggs
⅝ cup (140 g) granulated sugar
3 oz (85 g) cooking chocolate, melted
1 tablespoon rum or brandy
¼ teaspoon cream of tartar
4 oz (115 g) ground almonds
1 teaspoon baking soda
1 tablespoon warm water
For the filling
1¼ cups (280 ml) heavy cream
2 oz (55 g) chopped hazelnuts
1 tablespoon Grand Marnier
For the topping
⅜ cup (85 g) unsalted butter
1⅜ cups (170 g) icing sugar, sifted
3 oz (85 g) cooking chocolate, melted

Beat the egg yolks with the sugar until pale and light. Put the chocolate and the rum or brandy in a bowl over a saucepan of hot water and warm over a gentle heat. Whisk the egg whites with the cream of tartar until they are stiff. Mix the ground almonds, the melted chocolate and the baking soda with the egg yolks, adding the warm water. Fold two tablespoons of the egg white into this and then fold this mixture into the egg whites a little at a time, using a metal spoon. Pour the mixture into a large 11 in × 16 in baking pan lined with baking parchment. Cook at 350°F (180°C, Gas Mark 4) for 20-25 minutes, testing with a skewer to make sure that the cake is cooked in the middle. Let the cake cool in the pan for 10 minutes and then turn out on to greaseproof paper sprinkled with confectioners' sugar. Remove the paper carefully from the bottom of the cake and let it cool completely. Roll up the cake with the fresh paper and wrap in a cloth until ready to fill. Unroll the log and fill with the cream whipped with liqueur and hazelnuts. Cover with chocolate butter icing made by creaming the butter and confectioners' sugar and adding the melted chocolate. Run a fork along the surface to make it look like the bark of a tree. Confectioners' sugar and holly leaves could be used for decoration. Keep chilled until required.

4 CHRISTMAS SNOWBALL
3⅛ cups (700 ml) milk
6 egg yolks
1⅛ cups (255 g) vanilla sugar
1⅜ cups (200 g) chopped glacé fruit
2 tablespoons Kirsch, Grand Marnier or Cointreau
1¼ cups (280 ml) heavy cream
For the coating
1¼ cups (280 ml) heavy cream
5½ tbs (45 g) confectioners' sugar
1 tablespoon liqueur
3 oz (85 g) blanched toasted nuts or 3 oz (85 g) glacé fruit

Bring the milk just to the boil and allow to cool. Beat the egg yolks with the sugar until pale and fluffy and gradually add the warm milk, beating well. Put this custard into a double boiler and stir continuously over a gentle heat until it coats the back of a wooden spoon. Put in a bowl to cool, stirring from time to time to prevent a skin forming. Put the chopped glacé fruits to soak in the liqueur. When the custard is cold whip the cream to soft peaks and fold this into the custard. To make a snowball shape put the mixture into two hemispherical bowls and freeze for one hour. Remove from the freezer and beat well, add half quantity of the fruit and liqueur to each bowl and return to the freezer. Beat again after one hour and once again if necessary. Turn out of moulds and put cream between two halves to form ball. Coat with cream beaten with confectioners' sugar and a tablespoon of liqueur. Decorate with more glacé fruit or blanched and toasted nuts. Keep cold until ready to serve.

5 CRANBERRY SORBET
½ lb (225 g) fresh cranberries
3¼ cups (900 ml) water
1½ cups (340 g) granulated sugar
1 teaspoon lemon juice
2 tablespoons vodka or gin

Wash and drain the cranberries and put them with the water into a large enamel or stainless steel saucepan. Bring them to the boil on a high heat, cover and simmer for 10-12 minutes until the cranberries are soft. Put the cranberries and their juice through a wire sieve, using pressure to extract all the juice. Stir in the sugar and the lemon juice. Cool and add vodka or gin. Pour into two ice-trays and place in the freezing compartment of the refrigerator for 3-4 hours, stirring well every half-hour or so. If possible, half an hour before serving put the mixture into a blender until fluffy. Freeze in the trays until required. The alcohol prevents the ice freezing hard.

6 GINGER MERINGUE
3 large egg whites
pinch salt
1⅜ cups (170 g) confectioners' sugar
½-1 teaspoon ground ginger
For the filling
1¼ cups (280 ml) heavy cream
1 tablespoon preserved ginger syrup
2 oz (55 g) preserved ginger, chopped

Whip the egg whites with a pinch of salt until stiff peaks form. Add half the sifted sugar and the ginger and whip until mixture is stiff again. Gently fold in the rest of the sifted sugar with a metal spoon. Line a baking sheet with baking parchment and put tablespoonsful of the mixture 1 in apart or use a piping bag with a large serrated nozzle to make rosettes. Bake at the bottom of a cool oven, 150°F (70°C, Gas Mark ¼) for 2½-3 hours. Cool the meringues on a wire cake rack. Store in an airtight tin until one hour before serving. Whip the cream, add the ginger syrup and chopped preserved ginger and sandwich the meringues together in pairs. Decorate with more preserved ginger, and pile on a serving dish.

7 CHRISTMAS PUDDING
Quantities to make 2 puddings
¾ cup (115 g) self-rising flour
2 cups (225 g) white breadcrumbs
1 cup (225 g) suet
2¼ cups (340 g) stoned raisins
1½ cups (225 g) currants
6 oz (170 g) apple, peeled and grated
⅝ cup (115 g) soft brown sugar
¾ cup (115 g) candied peel, chopped

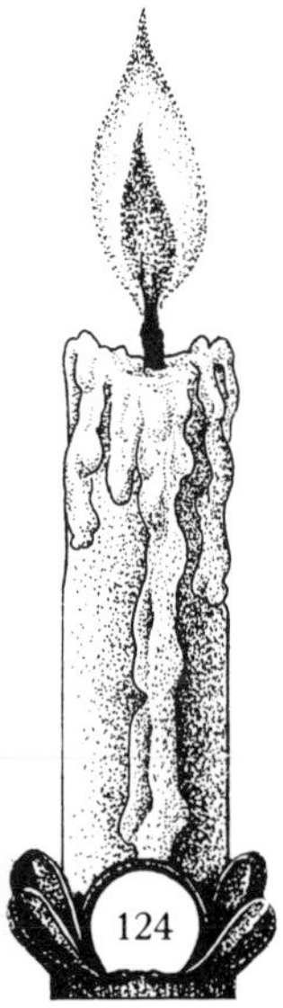

2 teaspoons mixed spice
4 oz (115 g) almonds, flaked
3/8 cup (55 g) glacé cherries, halved
3/4 cup (115 g) sultanas
1 teaspoon salt
3 large eggs
1 orange, rind and juice
1 glass brandy

Sift the flour into a large bowl and add the rest of the dry ingredients. Mix well. Beat the eggs with the brandy and the orange juice and then gradually mix this liquid into the other ingredients with a large wooden spoon. Add a little more brandy or orange juice if the mixture is too dry. Butter 2 quart (1 litre) pudding basins and fill them to within 1 in of the top. Put a double circle of buttered greaseproof paper inside the basin on top of the pudding and tie a larger circle of double aluminium foil round the outside of the basin. Make a pleat across the top of the foil to allow the pudding to rise. Steam the puddings over boiling water for 5-6 hours. Cool and change the foil for a fresh piece before storing them in a cool, dark place. Steam again for 3-4 hours on Christmas Day. Turn the pudding on to the serving dish, ladle some warmed brandy over the pudding and light it just as you carry it in to the table. Serve with brandy butter.

BRANDY BUTTER
1/2 cup (115 g) unsalted butter
1 cup (115 g) confectioners' sugar
1/4 cup (60 ml) brandy

Allow the butter to soften in a warm room and beat vigorously. Gradually add the confectioners' sugar and beat until pale and fluffy, adding the brandy a little at a time. Brandy butter can be made a week in advance if covered with aluminium foil and kept in a refrigerator.

8 MINCE PIES
For the pastry
1 1/2 cups (225 g) all-purpose flour
pinch of salt
5/8 cup (140 g) unsalted butter
4 tbs (30 g) confectioners' sugar
1 egg yolk
a few drops of lemon juice
For the filling
1 lb (450 g) jar mincemeat

Sift the flour and salt into a cold bowl. Mix confectioners' sugar with lemon juice and egg yolk. Add the butter cut into small pieces to the flour and rub in lightly until the mixture resembles breadcrumbs. With a fork, lightly mix the egg yolk mixture into the flour, adding a few drops of ice-cold water if necessary, to bind the pastry into a smooth, pliable dough. Wrap the pastry in plastic and chill for half an hour. Roll out on a floured board to about 1/8 in and cut in rounds with a 2 3/4 in cutter from just over half the pastry. Lay these in the 2 3/4 in tart pans and almost fill each one with mincemeat. Damp the edges of the pastry and cover pies with 2 1/4 in rounds cut from the remaining pastry and press gently round edges to seal. Cut a small cross in the tops with a sharp knife and bake in a hot oven, 425°F (220°C, Gas Mark 7) for 15-20 minutes. Dust with confectioners' sugar before serving. Mince pies can be served hot or cold.

9 PANETONE
Quantity sufficient for 2 loaves
3 cups (450 g) all-purpose flour
1 teaspoon salt
1/4 cup (55 g) granulated sugar
1 oz (30 g) fresh yeast
3/8-1/2 cup (90-125 ml) water
3/4 cup (115 g) sultanas
3/8 cup (55 g) citron peel or chopped mixed peel
1 lemon, rind and juice
3 eggs
1/2 cup (115 g) butter, softened
2 oz (55 g) flaked almonds
pinch nutmeg
For the topping
2 tbs (30 g) butter, melted

Sift the flour, salt and sugar into a large bowl. Dissolve the yeast in the warm water. Soak the sultanas and the peel in the juice of the lemon. Beat the eggs well and add them, together with the yeast mixture and the softened butter, to the flour. When the dough is manageable put on a floured board and knead in the drained fruit, the lemon rind, almonds and nutmeg. Add the lemon juice if the dough needs any more liquid. Continue kneading until the dough is smooth and elastic, then put it in a large greased plastic bag, cover with a cloth and allow to rise for between one and one and a half hours, until double in bulk. Divide the dough into two and put each piece in a lined and greased 6 in cake pan, to which you have tied a collar of greased foil to come 2 1/2-3 in above the top of the pan. Cover the pans with greased wrap and allow the panetone to rise well up in the pans. Brush the tops with melted butter and bake in a moderate oven 350°F (180°C, Gas Mark 4) for 40-50 minutes. Allow to cool in the pans until the sides shrink slightly, then gently remove and leave to cool on a wire rack.

10 BAVAROIS CLERMONT
4 tbs (30 g) powdered gelatine
3/8 cup (90 ml) water
6 egg yolks
7/8 cup (200 g) vanilla sugar
1 7/8 cups (425 ml) milk
3 tablespoons ice-cold milk
8 oz (225 g) chestnut purée
1 7/8 cups (425 ml) heavy cream
For the decoration
1 1/4 cups (280 ml) heavy cream
12 marrons glacés

Soak the gelatine in a small bowl with the water for a few moments, then set the bowl inside a saucepan of hot water over a low flame to melt the gelatine. Whisk the egg yolks with the sugar until pale and creamy. Heat milk until small bubbles form round the edge of the pan and pour slowly on to the egg yolks and sugar, stirring all the time. Put the mixture into the top of double boiler and stir continuously over hot, but not boiling, water until the custard thickens enough to coat the back of a wooden spoon. Stir in the melted gelatine, strain the custard into a bowl and mix thoroughly with the chestnut purée. Allow to cool. Mix the cream with the three tablespoons of ice-cold milk and whip until it forms soft peaks. Fold the cream thoroughly into the cold custard with a metal spoon and pour into a 1 1/2 quart (1 1/2 litre) oiled mould. When the Bavarois is set, loosen with a thin, flexible knife and dip the bottom for a moment into hot water. Turn the Bavarois out on to a moist plate, pushing gently to the centre. Pipe rosettes of whipped cream round the edge and decorate with whole marrons glacés.

11 CHRISTOLLEN
Quantities sufficient to make 2 loaves
4 1/2 cups (700 g) white bread flour
1 teaspoon salt
1/2 cup (115 g) granulated sugar
1 1/4 cups (300 ml) milk
1 oz (30 g) fresh yeast
3/4 cup (115 g) raisins
1/2 cup (85 g) glacé cherries
1/2 cup (85 g) candied peel, chopped
1 lemon, rind and juice
2 tablespoons rum
1/2 cup (115 g) unsalted butter, melted
3 eggs
6 oz (170 g) flaked almonds
For the topping
2 tbs (30 g) butter, melted
2 tbs confectioners' sugar, sifted
some glacé fruit and sliced, blanched almonds

Sift the flour, salt and sugar into a large bowl. Bring the milk to the boil and allow to cool. Dissolve the yeast in 3/8 cup (85 ml) of the lukewarm milk. Soak the raisins and the peel in the lemon juice and rum. Mix the yeast with the flour, adding the melted butter and the well-beaten eggs and enough of the milk to make a stiffish dough. Knead in the fruit, almonds and lemon peel and continue kneading until the dough is smooth and elastic. Put the dough in a large greased plastic bag, cover with a cloth and allow to rise for approximately one and a half hours, until double in bulk. Divide the dough into two pieces and return one piece to the plastic bag. Make the other into an oval shape and pat or roll out to approximately 12 in × 7 in. With the back of a long knife make two dents lengthways along the loaf and fold the sides towards the middle, using a little water to make sure that they stay in place. There should be a seam of approximately 1 1/4 in. Repeat this with the other half of the dough and place the loaves on a greased baking sheet. Cover with oiled wrap and allow to rise again for about 1 hour or until double in bulk. Brush with melted butter, and bake in a fairly hot oven 375°F (190°C, Gas Mark 5) for 40-50 minutes. If they are ready the loaves should sound hollow when tapped on the bottom. Cool on a wire rack. Sprinkle with confectioners' sugar and decorate with glacé fruit and blanched almonds.

SWEET-MEATS

A delicate, precious, Victorian table to encourage you to linger over the port, Stilton, nuts and sweetmeats. Antique lace cloths cover the table and mother-of-pearl-handled cutlery, and lustre bowls, filled with sweetmeats, softly reflect the candlelight. The centre wreath of varied evergreen, decorated with nuts and cones, supports dark green candles which give a soft subtle light.

1 Fudge, a year-round favourite but an absolute must at Christmas.

2 Chocolate rum truffles, richly made with cream and rum and rolled in powdered chocolate.

3 Pretty frosted fruits dipped in egg-white and castor sugar, piled high to make a spectacular centrepiece. Most successful are grapes, soft fruits such as strawberries or currants, or sharp Cape gooseberries.

4 Chocolate tangerines. You bite through the hard chocolate to the juicy fruit inside. These are also nice made with black or Muscat grapes.

5 Coconut ice, one of the easiest sweets to make and a special favourite with children.

6 Turkish Delight, exotic and delicately flavoured with orange flower or rose water, made with or without nuts, gives a pretty, fragrant and luxurious end to a meal.

7 Turron, a typical Spanish nougat made with ground almonds. Cut into diamond shapes and decorate with slivers of roasted almonds.

8 Torrone molle is an Italian nougat which requires no cooking. This confection of melted chocolate, nuts and crumbled almond macaroons is cooled in a refrigerator.

9 Peppermint creams are cool and refreshing after a heavy meal. Make them ice white or add some peppermint green colouring.

10 Toasted almonds or hazelnuts for those without a sweet tooth. Cook tossed in butter and season with salt and paprika.

7

8

9

10

Recipes for Sweetmeats

1 FUDGE
2 cups (450 g) vanilla sugar
¼ cup (55 g) unsalted butter
1¼ cups (275 ml) light cream

Put all the ingredients into a large pan (3 quarts). Heat gently, stirring until the sugar has melted. Bring to the boil and continue to boil rapidly, stirring at intervals for 10-15 minutes until the soft, ball stage has been reached. Take off the heat and beat with a wooden spoon until it thickens. Pour into buttered pan 6 in by 8 in and allow to cool. Mark into squares and cut when cold.

2 CHOCOLATE RUM TRUFFLES
12 oz (340 g) dark plain chocolate
2 tablespoons rum
⅝ cup (140 g) unsalted butter
1 tablespoon cream
cocoa powder for coating

Melt the chocolate with the rum in a bowl over a saucepan of hot water. Slowly work in the butter with a wooden spoon and finally the cream. Allow to cool until it thickens. Spoon on to greaseproof paper or parchment. When cold, shape into balls and roll lightly in the cocoa until coated. These are best eaten fresh.

3 COCONUT ICE
2 cups (450 g) vanilla sugar
⅝ cup (150 ml) light cream or milk
4 oz (115 g) dry shredded coconut
4 drops pink food colouring

Dissolve the sugar in the cream or milk over a low heat. Bring to the boil and boil until it starts to thicken (about 10 minutes). Do not allow it to change colour. Remove the pan from the heat and add the coconut. Blend well. Return to the heat and stir constantly until it thickens. Pour half the mixture into a buttered pan 6 in square. Colour the other half of the mixture and pour on top of the white layer. Leave until set and then cut into pieces 1 by 1½ in. Store for a short time only in an airtight tin as these sweets quickly go stale.

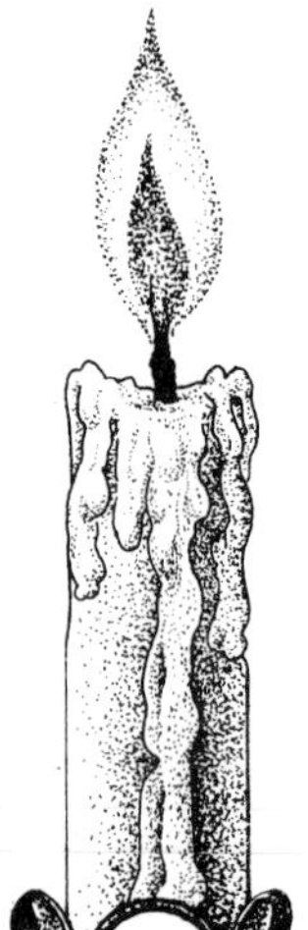

4 TURKISH DELIGHT
1¼ cups (275 ml) water
4 tbs (30 g) powdered gelatine
1¾ cups (400 g) granulated sugar
1 teaspoon rosewater or orange flower water
1 oz (30 g) pistachio nuts, blanched and split
4 drops red food colouring (optional)
Coating
½ cup (55 g) confectioners' sugar
3 tablespoons (30 g) cornstarch

Sprinkle the gelatine into the water in a saucepan. Warm gently, stirring until it has melted completely. Add the sugar and continue to stir over a low heat until it has dissolved. Boil gently for 20 minutes. Remove from the heat and add the rosewater or orange flower water, the food colouring and the split pistachio nuts. Stir. Pour into a buttered pan 6 in by 8 in. Allow to cool for at least 24 hours. Cut into squares and coat with the mixture of cornstarch and confectioners' sugar.

5 FROSTED FRUIT
2 egg whites
1 tablespoon water
½ cup (115 g) granulated sugar
grapes, strawberries, cherries, red or black currants, washed and dried

Whisk the egg whites and water with a fork until frothy but not stiff. Put the sugar in a shallow bowl. Dip individual fruits, or small bunches, into the egg white using a pastry brush to

make sure that they are thoroughly covered with liquid. Dip into the sugar and with a teaspoon pour the sugar over the fruit so that it is completely

coated. Shake off any excess and put the fruit on a wire rack to dry.

6 CHOCOLATE TANGERINES
8 oz (225 g) unsweetened chocolate
1-2 teaspoons Cointreau
tangerines

Melt the chocolate with the Cointreau in a double boiler over simmering water. Peel the tangerines and divide into segments. When the chocolate is melted remove it from the heat and using a toothpick dip the segments into the chocolate. Allow any excess chocolate to drip off and put the segments on a piece of baking parchment.

7 SPANISH TURRON
1 lb (450 g) almonds, blanched and skinned, or ground almonds
1½ cups (340 g) granulated sugar
2⅛ cups (500 ml) water
3 egg yolks beaten lightly
Decoration (optional)
toasted splinters of almonds

Line a shallow pan 6 in by 6 in with rice paper or baking parchment. Grind almonds to a paste in an electric blender or mince them finely. Dissolve the sugar in the water over a low heat, stirring constantly. Boil rapidly until it will form small hard balls when dropped on to a cold surface. Remove from the heat and add the ground almonds and beaten egg yolks. This should form a thick paste. Press it into the prepared pan, levelling the top. When cold, mark the top with a knife into diamonds. Place a splinter of almond in the centre of each diamond. Wrap in paper and store in an airtight container in the refrigerator.

8 TORRONE MOLLE
4 oz (115 g) unsweetened cooking chocolate
¼ cup (55 g) butter
½ cup (115 g) granulated sugar
4 oz (115 g) ground almonds
1 egg
1 egg yolk
3 oz (85 g) Amaretti or hard macaroons
4 oz (115 g) roasted hazelnuts

Melt the chocolate, butter and sugar together in a double boiler over simmering water. Remove from the heat and stir in the ground almonds and beaten egg and yolk. Crush the cookies and roasted hazelnuts in a mortar and stir gently into the mixture. Pour the torrone into a greased pan and put into the refrigerator to store. Do not keep torrone molle for more than two or three days.

9 SALTED ALMONDS
8 oz (225 g) almonds, blanched or with their skins on, or hazelnuts, pecans, walnuts or peanuts
1 tablespoon butter
salt to taste
pinch paprika (optional)

Melt the butter in a heavy frying pan. Toss the nuts over a medium heat until nicely brown. Sprinkle with salt and paprika if desired. Toss again and cool on a piece of absorbent kitchen paper.

10 PEPPERMINT CREAMS
2 egg whites
1 lb (450 g) confectioners' sugar
peppermint extract to taste

Put the egg whites into a bowl and beat them with a fork to form a froth. Sift the confectioners' sugar into the bowl until a thick paste is formed. Add the peppermint extract drop by drop and a few drops of food colouring if desired. Mix well. Work the paste out on a sheet of greaseproof paper until it is just under ⅜ in thick. Cut out into circles about 1 in in diameter. Leave to dry in a cool place overnight.

BOXING DAY & ST STEPHEN'S DAY

'Winter Sports – Coasting in the Country' drawn by Granville Perkins. Harpers Weekly, 1877.

Boxing Day derives its name from two possible sources. On the day after Christmas Day the alms boxes which were placed in churches over the festive period were opened and their contents distributed. Also on that day, apprentices and servants broke open the small earthenware boxes in which their masters and their masters' customers had deposited small sums. By the nineteenth century the practice of tipping people for services rendered during the year had expanded to include crossing sweepers, lamp lighters and even policemen. Today it is usual to recognize the work of postmen, dustmen and newspaper boys in the same way.

Although Boxing Day itself is generally regarded as having little religious significance it is the feast of St Stephen.

St Stephen's Day celebrates two saints of that name. One was the first Christian martyr, stoned to death for blasphemy soon after the crucifixion, the other a ninth-century missionary in Sweden, who was murdered by a heathen in a dark forest. The second St Stephen's name day originally was not in the Christmas season at all and indeed one theory has it that St Stephen did not exist but was invented to account for the many customs practised on the first martyr's day. Nevertheless St Stephen was made the patron saint of horses for his alleged special love of these beasts. It was said that he had five mounts, two red, two white and one dappled, which he rode in turn. When he died his body was tied to an unbroken colt, which did not pause until it arrived near the saint's home at Norrala. Sick animals, especially horses, were brought on pilgrimages to the church built over his grave. In England horses were ceremonially blooded and today there is commonly a Boxing

'The Snow Battle', an illustration from Harper's Weekly, circa 1872.

Throughout Christendom, 26 December is devoted to recovering from the excesses of the previous two days. Countries as far apart as the United States, Argentina and France manage this by the simple expedient of going back to work – Boxing Day is not a holiday for them. Elsewhere the accent is on informality, visiting, outdoor and indoor sports, entertainments, pantomime and parlour games.

Day Hunt Meet. Elsewhere horses were fed consecrated bread, salt or corn or blessed in church by the priest. Sweden, naturally, used to have a number of St Stephen's Day customs. Companies of 'Stephen's men' got up long before daybreak and raced from village to village waking the inhabitants with a folk song called 'Staffansvisa' and expecting to be treated to ale or spirits in return. Even earlier in the morning,

servants would mount horses and race to the nearest north-flowing water. The animals would be made to drink from the stream to ensure good health in the coming year.

A strange sacrificial ritual called 'hunting the wren' used to occur in many regions of Europe on Boxing Day. A wren was captured, killed and carried from house to house to collect money – often to finance a party later. The wren was regarded as the king of birds because, as legend has it, when the birds held a contest to see which could fly the highest, the eagle was just about to win when the wren, which had been nestling on the eagle's back, spread its wings and flew even higher. Hunting the wren was probably a survival of the ancient custom of sacrificing a divine animal. In Ireland the slain bird was carried on a holly bush, and even today Wren Boys carrying a beribboned bush go from house to house singing the Wren Song and collecting money.

Boxing Day is also the time for more formal performances. In Holland 'Second Christmas Day' often includes a play, a concert or dinner in a restaurant. In Hungary cinema and theatre-going feature in towns, and fortune-telling in villages. The circus, a direct descendant of the Roman games, is a common event of the day, and in Britain Boxing Day saw the opening of the pantomime season. Pantomime became inseparable from Christmas in the Victorian period, but its origins can be traced back to the great court masques and the mummers' plays. The first pantomime was performed in 1717. 'Harlequin Executed' brought together a serious classical fable with the commedia dell' arte story of Harlequin and Columbine, but classical themes were gradually discarded. The English pantomime became an elaborate fairytale fantasy for all the family, combining dancing and topical jokes and expensive transformation scenes featuring all the latest theatrical techniques. The tradition that calls for a masculine dame and a

'Our Reindeer Sleigh', an illustration from The Graphic, *1887, by Arthur Hopkins.*

female principal boy goes back to the topsy-turvy world of Misrule and the Roman Saturnalia. In the 1930s pantomime crossed to Jamaica, where local fictional characters such as Anancy the Spider Man and the Rolling Calf were incorporated.

Parlour games, another peculiarly British institution, also come to the fore in the relaxed atmosphere of Boxing Day. The origins of many parlour games may lie in ancient sacrificial rites. In Blind Man's Buff, a game known in most countries, the players probably wore masks, and the player who was 'it' was the sacrificer. More recently, the robust Victorians thought it the height of entertainment to lead the blindfolded player to trip over obstacles. When everyone is exhausted by the frolics, families relax telling old stories – ghostly, spine-chilling, tear-jerking or funny – all a part of Christmas celebrations.

Sports and outdoor games make a welcome and healthy change from overeating and overdrinking. In Australia there is surfing, swimming, tennis and cricket and each Boxing Day sees the start of the Sydney to Hobart yacht race. In Canada there is skating, skiing, tobogganing, ice hockey and curling. The Irish go in for hurling, horse racing and greyhound coursing, while in Britain there is a full programme of football fixtures and horse racing as well as traditional fox hunting and the Boxing Day Shoot. If Boxing Day has been well spent, everyone goes to bed fit and well, tired and happy, and ready for work again.

OUTDOOR GAMES

FLYING KITES

Kites used to be child's play, but now they are everybody's game. They come with two lines and one line, in serpent, delta, box and other exotic shapes at prices that range from stocking filler to very-best-friend. Cheap paper ones from China, India and Japan are so beautifully decorated that they look as good on the wall as they do in the air. Kites made from new plastic and nylon materials in brilliant colours are easy to care for and almost indestructible. There are simple and sophisticated designs to suit all wind conditions from almost flat calm to near gale force. Fanatics have a dozen kites, to be prepared for anything the climate may bring. Newcomers to the sport should go to a specialist shop and choose a kite to fit their age, skill and local weather. Some kites, such as the paper Indian fighting kites, will fly in almost windless conditions, but need skill. Take your kite to an open space away from buildings, trees and airports, stand with your back to the wind, let go gradually and the wind should take over. If the kite starts to dive about in ground turbulence, about fifty to a hundred feet up, do not pull it in or you'll simply make the trouble worse and the kite may crash. Give it a bit more line, and a chance to stabilize. After-care is simple. If the kite is at all damp (paper ones will not stand any moisture, of course) dry it well away from direct heat to prevent

'A Merry-Go-Round on the Ice' drawn by Robert Barnes, from The Graphic, 1890. (Below and previous page) The man who got lost in the snow.

mildew, then pack away. If you would prefer something a bit more down to earth, frisbees and boomerangs are making a comeback.

MAKE A SNOWMAN

If the weather turns seasonable, snowmen are irresistible. To make a good one, start off with a normal-sized snowball and roll it round the lawn or some other open, and not too sloping, place so that it grows larger as the snow sticks to it. Change direction often to get an even globe shape. When it is big enough, pat the snow firm and set it in position. Make a slightly smaller globe to form the upper part of the body and a third globe, smaller still, for the head. Ears, nose, arms and feet can all be moulded out of snow. Hat, muffler, pipe, pebble eyes and buttons and a mouth made from half a carrot are traditional.

A snowball fight provides more violent sports for all the family. The party divides into two and each side builds a protective snow wall. From behind this everyone hurls as many snowballs as they can make at the other side.

TOBOGGANING

This is an excellent sport for those energetic people who do not mind paying for the exhilarating flight down with a hard trek up. Families living in milder districts who do not want to spend a lot of money for perhaps one day's fun a year might buy a cheap moulded plastic toboggan that also runs over sand and floats in the sea. But for a better run, more power and control it is worth investing in a wooden toboggan with good runners. Choose a boulder-free slope of a steepness to suit your courage, lie flat on your stomach, kick off and steer by dragging one foot in the snow. This position reduces wind resistance and, in case of accident, makes it easy to roll to safety. Skilled, or foolhardy, practitioners might grease the runners for extra speed and try for a running start, bobsleigh fashion. More sedate riders sit upright and steer by lifting and twisting the front of the sledge. Toboggans need very little care. Just dry off, and cover the runners with grease or Vaseline to prevent rusting.

15

PARLOUR GAMES

CONSEQUENCES

Each player takes a long strip of paper and writes at the top of it one or more adjectives ('beautiful and witty', 'remarkably boring', or whatever appeals), folds the top of the paper down to cover the writing and passes the strip to the person on the right. On the received strip of paper, each player then puts down the name of a man, folds the paper down and passes it to the right. Following the same pattern of folding and passing between each section, the players go on to write down 'met' and then another one or two adjectives, a woman's name, where they met, what he gave her, what he said to her, what she said to him, what the consequence was and, finally, what the world said. When the strips of paper are complete each person reads out the one they hold.

Consequences can also be played with lines of poetry or pictures. For picture consequences, sections of a body are drawn in turn: head, trunk, legs and feet. Connecting lines are left showing when each strip is folded. Each player then unfolds the finished drawing to reveal a strange creature.

ANAGRAMS

Each player is given a name or word and from its letters forms another word or phrase which, at least, makes sense and uses all the letters, and at most, is witty and apt, e.g. William Shakespeare – We all make his praise. John Gay – Hang joy. Inkerman – Men in rank.

LISTS

Each player has a sheet of paper ruled into seven columns. In the left-hand column put several collective nouns, for example rivers, film stars, flowers, capitals. Select a six-letter word at random and put each letter at the top of the remaining columns. If the word selected is 'police', each player then writes down in the appropriate place the names of every river, film star, etc., he can think of whose names begin with P, then O, and so on. The winner is the one with the most names.

POETICAL DOMINOES

For the literary family. Select a number of poets and a brief quotation from each. Cut pieces of cardboard into domino-shaped pieces, draw a line down the centre and write in one half the name of a poet and in the other half a quotation from a different poet. (If three quotations are taken from Shakespeare, for example, Shakespeare's name must appear on three dominoes.) Shuffle and deal the 'cards'. One player lays a card in the middle of the table and reads out the quotation on it. If the player on his left has the author of the quotation he says so, reads the quotation on the other half of the card and lays it down on the table so that his author's name matches the quotation. If this second player does not have an author to match the quotation on the table he may use instead a quotation to match the author. When he has moved, or 'passed', the third player moves. The one who gets rid of his cards first wins.

MEMORY

Put a number of different items on a tray – about twenty to thirty if you can find them – let the players stare at them for thirty seconds then remove the tray and get everyone to write down as many as they can remember.

TO MAKE A CROSS

Of five pieces of paper cut into the following shapes, form a cross.

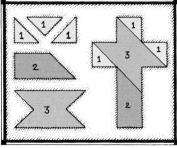

Answer. Cut three pieces in the shape of number 1 and one each like numbers 2 and 3 and place them together as shown above.

DEAD OR ALIVE?

These dogs are dead, perhaps you'll say;
Add four lines, and then they'll run away.
To bring these apparently dead dogs to life, fill in the dotted lines joining the front half of one dog to the back half of the other and then turn the page round.

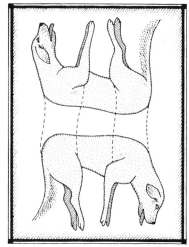

TWO SQUARES

How do you draw the figure below without ever removing the pencil from the paper, without crossing any line, or retracing any part?
Answer. Draw a line in the following sequence: 1 to 2 to 3 to 4 to 5 to 6 to 1 to 7 to 8 to 9 to 3 to 10 to 1.

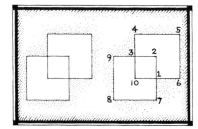

UPTURN A GLASS OF WATER

Fill a glass with water, cover the top with a piece of paper, put your hand over the paper and tip the glass upside-down sharply. Take your hand away and the paper will be held to the glass.

THE SCISSORS TRICK

Take a pair of scissors and a piece of string. Pass one loop through handle of the scissors, thread it through the rest of the loop and pull tight. The puzzle is how to remove the string from the scissors without letting go of the ends of the string. To do this, take hold of the end of the loop, pull at it until it is long enough to pass over the tips of the scissors. The string is then free.

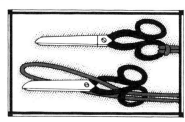

ALDERMAN GOBBLE'S DUCKS

A gentleman sent his servant with a present of nine ducks in a box upon which was written, 'To Alderman Gobble with IX ducks.' The servant stole three of the ducks and contrived it so that the number contained in the box corresponded with that written on the box. He did not erase any word or letter, so how did he do it?
Answer. The servant simply wrote the letter S before the two Roman numerals so the directions read: 'To Alderman Gobble with SIX ducks.'

DIVIDING THE GARDEN

A charitable person built a house in one corner of a square plot of land and let it to four persons. In the garden were four cherry trees and the garden had to be divided so that each person could have a tree and an equal portion of ground. How was it to be done?
Answer.

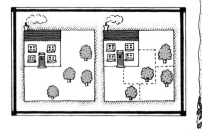

MAKE A 9

How can you add five lines to the six matches shown below and make nine? Answer. Draw in the lines as shown in the illustration below.

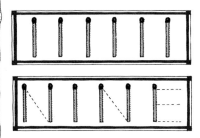

CAN YOU MOVE A HOUSE?

Arrange eleven matches to form a house. Ask a friend to turn the house round to face the other way by moving one matchstick only.

Answer. Simply alter the slant of the matchstick marked A.

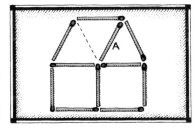

ATTRACTION AND REPULSION

Place a number of matches in the shape of a star on the surface of a bowl of water. Touch the water in the centre

of the star with a small piece of soap and the matches will make for the side of the bowl. Do the same with a piece of sugar and the matches will make for the sugar. The reason is that the soap dissolves, leaving a thin film which repels the matches, but sugar absorbs the water and attracts them.

TAKE ONE FROM 19 TO MAKE 20

From XIX (nineteen) take the I that stands between the two XX, and so leave XX (twenty).

SIX ROWS PUZZLE

Place 12 counters in six rows so that there are four counters in each row. Answer.

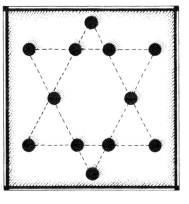

BLIND MAN'S BUFF

Choose one member of the party to be Blind Man and tie a handkerchief over his eyes. Turn him round three times and let him loose to catch whoever he can. When he has caught one of his friends and said who he is, he is freed and the captive becomes Blind Man in turn.

HUNT THE RING

Thread a ring or key on to a long piece of string, which is then knotted to form a circle. The company stands in a circle holding the string and slides the ring or key rapidly from hand to hand. One member of the party stands in the centre of the circle and has to guess who holds the ring at any given time. If he guesses right, the holder becomes the hunter.

THE MINISTER'S CAT

The best known of a number of alphabetical games. The first player might say, 'The minister's cat is an angry cat', then the other players in turn repeat the sentence each using a different adjective beginning with the letter A. They then move on to B and so on through the alphabet. Players who cannot think of a word beginning with the right letter, or who repeat one already used, drop out until only the winner is left.

RUMOURS

Also known as Gossip or Secrets. Everyone sits in a row and the first person whispers a secret – something silly like, 'The parson's got cold feet' – to his neighbour, who in turn passes it on, and so on right down the line. The last person repeats out loud what she has heard – probably something different from the original secret like, 'The dog's got nothing to eat'.

ELEMENTS

One member of the company throws a soft ball to another, at the same time naming one of the elements – earth, air, water or fire. If one of the first three elements is given, the person catching the ball has to name an animal living in the element within a count of ten. For example if water is called, the catcher might say 'whale'. Anyone speaking when 'fire' is called, or naming an animal wrongly, pays a forfeit. The catcher then throws the ball to another member of the group.

SIMON SAYS

Simon must be obeyed by all the party – provided his orders are prefaced with 'Simon says'. If he says, 'Simon says, "Bend a knee"', or 'Simon says, "Kiss your neighbour"', everyone must obey or pay a forfeit. But if he says, 'Blow your nose' or 'Shake your head' or anything without starting with 'Simon says', he must be ignored – and anyone obeying pays a forfeit.

THE LAWYER

The party sits in two rows facing each other with a space for the Lawyer to pass. The Lawyer asks one person a question, but it must be answered not by the person spoken to but by the one sitting opposite to him. The object is to get the person spoken to to answer or the one who should answer to stay silent. When that happens, the Lawyer changes places with the guilty party.

BUZ

Everyone sits in a circle. The first player says, 'One', the second, 'Two' and so on up to any number, except that where the number seven occurs, or any number into which seven can be divided, Buz must be said instead. Anyone calling, for example, 14, 27, 28, 47, 49, pays a forfeit. Seventy-one becomes Buz-one, seventy-seven, Buz-Buz.

SHADOW BUFF

If you have not got a plain white wall, hang a white sheet at one end of the room. Set a bright lamp on a table some distance from the wall and put out all other lights. One player sits quite near to and facing the wall and the other players take it in turns to pass behind the seated player but in front of the light, so that their shadows fall on to the wall. The seated player has to guess whose shadow he sees or pay a forfeit. Players can disguise themselves with false noses, etc.

CHARADES

The party divides into two and each group chooses a word which divides easily into two or three sections, for example, workmanship, earshot, homesick, season. One group performs with mime or dialogue each section of the word and finally the whole word for the other group to guess. The other group then acts out its own word. Make-up, costumes, disguises, etc., may be used.

CHEAT

Deal a pack of cards to any number of players. Players look at their cards, then the player on the left of the dealer opens by laying his lowest card (ace is lowest) face down on the table and calling out what it is. The next player puts down his card face downwards and calls the next number. For example, if the first player played two, the second must call three. The players don't have to put down the card with the number they call and any other player may challenge by calling 'Cheat'. If that happens the player must turn up his card and if it is not the same as the number he called he must pick up all the cards on the table. The first player to get rid of all his cards wins.

BROTHER JONATHAN

Draw a diagram similar to the one below, marking the larger spaces with smaller numbers and the smaller spaces with larger numbers. Players pitch a coin or something similar on to the board from a fixed distance away and score the number of marks on the square on which the coin lands – throws which land on lines do not count. The winner is the player who first reaches an agreed figure.

	7		20	18		14
	8	20		6		6
25	7		10		8	30
10			2			16
10		5		25		18

NAVETTE

Cut out a long bridge with a number of arches of different heights. Mark each arch with a number – highest for the lowest arches, lowest for the highest. Players roll marbles or small balls at the bridge, which is placed on a table, and score the number of points written over the arch through which their ball goes. The winner is the player with the highest score after bowling a fixed number of balls.

TO MAKE A PAPER BOAT

Fold an oblong piece of paper in half and fold corners A to meet at centre B. Fold corners C up either side. Bring

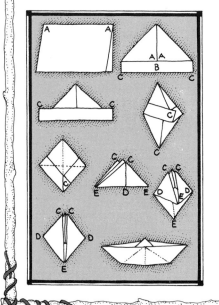

corners C together and fold in neatly. Fold corners C up along dotted lines. Pull points D open until corners E meet. Pull points C open to form boat.

MINIATURE BOOMERANG

Take a piece of cardboard and cut out a miniature boomerang about the size and shape of the diagram. Take a book in your left hand, place the boomerang on the edge so that one end sticks out over the edge about one inch. Tilt the book up slightly and flick away the projecting edge of the boomerang with a pencil so that it spins towards the far corner and comes back again.

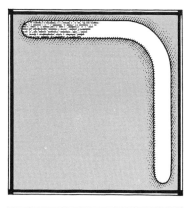

HIGHLANDER GLOVE PUPPET

Take an old glove and cut off the thumb and fingers to about the second knuckle. Make a pair of little socks

and shoes from a piece of cotton fabric, stuffing the shoe part with cotton wool. Colour the shoe black and stripe the socks tartan. Copy the picture of the highlander and stitch to the back of the glove. Fit the socks on your fingers and the highlander is ready to dance. Using this method you can design any number of figures.

TALKING HAND

Double your fist and draw a face on it. Make a sort of hood like a mitten with a hole in the side and sew a frill round it so that it looks like an old-fashioned woman's cap. Put the mitten over your fist so that the face shows

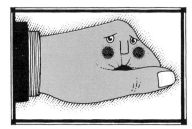

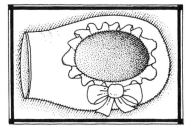

through the hole. Pin a shawl round the fist and you have an old lady whom you can make talk by moving your thumb up and down.

STAINED GLASS

Take a sheet of coloured tissue paper, fold it twice and, at the fold, cut half of some sort of heraldic shield shape, so that when the sheet is opened you have two shapes. Paste one on the centre of a window and the other over it, overlapping slightly. More interesting stained glass can be made by using two different coloured papers or cutting different shapes to fit inside each other. This also looks very attractive on a lantern.

PAPER TREE

Take a long roll of crêpe or tissue paper and make three deep cuts in the top. Grasp the centre point of the roll firmly and pull up into a tree.

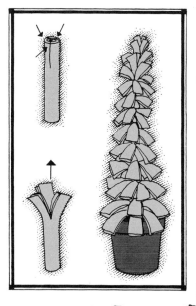

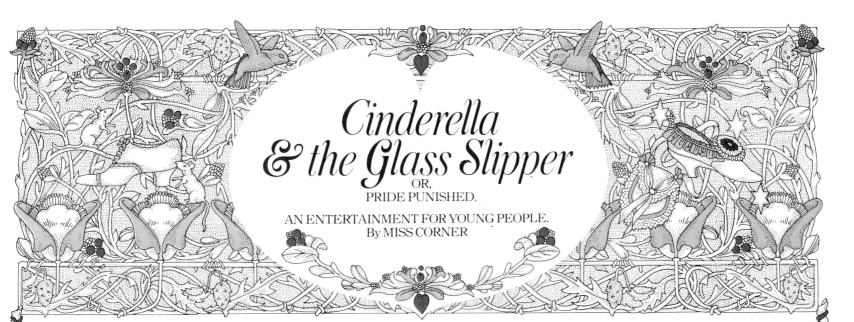

Cinderella & the Glass Slipper

OR,
PRIDE PUNISHED.

AN ENTERTAINMENT FOR YOUNG PEOPLE.
By MISS CORNER

GENERAL DIRECTIONS

In the getting up of these Plays, the arrangement of the scenes must of course depend in a great measure on the sort of room in which the performance takes place. Nothing could be better adapted to the purpose than two rooms opening into each other with folding doors, the stage being that into which the doors open, as they would form places for the exit of the different actors, who might retire behind the doors, instead of all going off the stage at the same point. These would also answer the purpose of a curtain, some person being stationed behind each to open and close them between the scenes. The prompter might also stand behind one of the doors. If, however, the play is to be acted in a single room, a curtain might be contrived to separate the stage from the part occupied by the audience; or rather, two curtains to close in the middle and draw to each side. They might be drawn on a string fastened by hooks from one side of the room to the other. Painted scenery would be a great advantage; but if this cannot be obtained, a few hints are given at the beginning of each scene as to the best mode of supplying the deficiency. The actors should learn their parts very perfectly, and rehearse the play at least three times before performing it.

CHARACTERS
THE PRINCE
MULEY . . . . .An Officer of the Court.
THE BARONESS
ULRICA   } . . . . .Daughters of the Baroness.
CHARLOTTE }
CINDERELLA . . . . .Step-daughter of the Baroness.
FAIRY . . . . .Cinderella's Godmother.

COSTUME
PRINCE White trousers, a coat, red or light blue, with a full skirt down to the knees, with a border of gold paper; a black velvet cap and white ostrich feather, and some glittering ornament in front; a scarf tied over one shoulder, and a lace collar turned down.
MULEY The ordinary dress would do, with a short cloak.
THE BARONESS A high turban on her head: a silk dress, and a thin shawl or lace cloak.
ULRICA and *CHARLOTTE* At first they should wear morning dresses, and change them for the ball, when they can dress according to fancy.

CINDERELLA A long loose gown of dark stuff or cotton with long sleeves. This must go over the ball dress, and be made to open in front and fastened round the waist with a band, that it may be easily thrown off. The ball dress should be white, ornamented with flowers and white satin ribbon, or silver ribbon, and she should have some glittering ornaments about her. White shoes, covered with silver ribbon, might be made to represent glass slippers.
FAIRY A cloak and hood, and a short wand.

SCENE THE FIRST
(Cinderella is discovered sitting on a low stool with her elbows on her knees, her head resting on her hands. She remains in this attitude silent for a short time, then raises her head and speaks.)

CINDERELLA   This is a wretched life: it can't be right
That I should have to scrub from morn till night,
And go in rags a beggar would disgrace,
Whilst my proud sisters dress in silk and lace.
They never have such dirty work to do:
And why should I not be a lady too?   (*She rises.*

Enter CHARLOTTE

CHARLOTTE   Pray, Cinderella, what are you about?
You know quite well that we are going out.
And you've not done down here. Do you suppose
That you can dress us with such hands as those?

CINDERELLA   I've almost done, Miss Charlotte.

CHARLOTTE   Don't tell me
You've almost done, when I can plainly see
The grate is still to clean – the hearth to scour,
Dishes to wash – you'll not be done this hour.

CINDERELLA   I'll come and dress you first.

Enter the BARONESS and ULRICA.

ULRICA   Where's Cinderella?
I'm waiting for her, sister: did you tell her?

CHARLOTTE	Yes, but her work is not half done, I find.
BARONESS	You idle little creature, I've a mind To box your ears; how dare you dawdle so? The fact is, you have been asleep – I know.
CINDERELLA	I've been at work since five o'clock this morning.
BARONESS	And so you ought, miss – now, don't stand there, yawning, But wash your hands directly, and make haste; My daughters have not any time to waste. [*Exit*
ULRICA	And mind, you must take pains to do your best, That we may both be very nicely drest, For this will be, I'm told, the grandest ball We've ever been invited to, at all. [*Exit*
CINDERELLA	And you will see the prince, too – Oh, dear me! How very, very happy you must be,
CHARLOTTE	Perhaps you'd like to go?
CINDERELLA	Indeed I should; Ah! dear Miss Charlotte, if you'd be so good As to lend me your pink gauze just for to-night, I might go in at least and see the sight.
CHARLOTTE	Don't talk such nonsense, child, for goodness sake! A pretty figure at a ball you'd make. [*Exit*

(*Cinderella alone; she washes her hands and puts on a clean apron; and while she is doing so talks to herself.*)

CINDERELLA	Plenty of work for me to-night – heigh oh! I hope it is not always to be so; However, I suppose that I must try To do my best, and bear it patiently. [*Exit*

Enter FAIRY

FAIRY	So, these two girls, if I have heard aright, Are going to the prince's ball to-night, While Cinderella's kept at home, I find, To wash the dishes – now, I have a mind That she shall go as well as they. Poor dear, They use her shamefully, that's very clear. [*Exit*

SCENE THE SECOND – A Dressing Room.

(*Charlotte and Ulrica appear dressed for the ball. Charlotte is standing putting on her gloves, and Ulrica is sitting before the glass, while Cinderella adjusts the flowers in her hair. When this is done she rises and comes forward.*)

ULRICA	(*to Charlotte*)	How do I look?
CHARLOTTE		Quite charming; but I think You would look better if your wreath was pink.
ULRICA		I don't think so at all; but that's your way, You always have some spiteful thing to say.
CHARLOTTE	(*aside*)	I like to vex her, she's so very vain.
ULRICA	(*aside*)	Charlotte is jealous of me, that is plain.

Enter the BARONESS – CINDERELLA sits down with a
melancholy air by the dressing-table

BARONESS		Come, children, are you ready?
CHARLOTTE		Yes, ma, quite.
BARONESS		Now, mind you try and do your best, to-night To get good husbands – Charlotte, do you hear? You poke your head most terribly, my dear.
CHARLOTTE		I mean to hold it high enough, you'll see, When I am married to some great grandee.
ULRICA	(*impatiently*)	Well, let us go – good night, mamma.
CHARLOTTE	(*they walk towards the door*)	Good bye.

BARONESS	Good night, my dears.
	    [*Exeunt* CHARLOTTE and ULRICA
	        They do look charmingly,
	And who knows but the prince himself might fall
	In love with one of them? 'tis not at all
	Unlikely. (*Turns to Cinderella*) Well, Miss, sitting at your ease,
	As if you'd nothing else to do – now please
	To get my supper; (*Cinderella rises slowly*) – let me see no airs!
	Then go and finish all your work down stairs. [*Exeunt.*

SCENE THE THIRD – The Kitchen
(*Cinderella is sitting by the fireplace, crying*)

Enter FAIRY

FAIRY	Why, Cinderella, what's the matter, dear?
CINDERELLA	(*starting up in joyful surprise*) Oh, Godmother, I'm so glad you're here.
FAIRY	But what have you been crying child, about? Is it because your sisters are gone out, And left you here at home?
CINDERELLA	'Tis wrong, I know; But yet I can't help wishing I could go.

FAIRY	Well, well, don't fret; we'll see what can be done! But first into the garden you must run And gather me a pumpkin – do you mind; And let it be the largest you can find. *[Exit CINDERELLA* The mother's gone to bed, and she shall sleep Until the morning sun begins to peep.

(Enter CINDERELLA, with a large pumpkin in her arms.

(This might be a great ball about three feet in circumference, made in eight portions of green and yellow calico, and stuffed with wool.)

CINDERELLA	This is the very largest I could bring.
FAIRY	Yes, that will do; it is the very thing I want. Now set it just outside the door, Then I must send you to get me something more. *(CINDERELLA takes the pumpkin out, and returns.* Down in the cellar there's a mouse-trap, dear, With six brown mice in it; go bring them here. *[Exit CINDERELLA*

(The FAIRY sits down, and in a few minutes CINDERELLA returns with the trap, which might be a bird cage.)

CINDERELLA	Here they are: see how they run about.
FAIRY	Aye, they will gallop famously, no doubt. Now go again, and if there is a rat Caught in the trap, why, you may bring me that.

(CINDERELLA goes, and returns immediately with another cage, which she puts down by the side of the FAIRY.)

FAIRY	That's right; but still, another thing we want, Or else our equipage will be but scant. Under the water-butt I think you'll see Four fine green lizards; bring them here to me.

(CINDERELLA goes again, and returns with four lizards (cut out of green paper), and gives them to the FAIRY. The FAIRY, after looking closely at the lizards, gives them back to CINDERELLA.)

FAIRY	Put all these creatures in the doorway, too; And then, see what your godmother can do.

(CINDERELLA carries out the lizards and the two cages, then places herself close to the FAIRY, who goes to the open door, and keeps waving her wand backwards and forwards.)

CINDERELLA	Ah! what is that? look, look! good gracious me! The pumpkin's turned into a coach! and see, The mice are horses! and look there, the rat A fine fat coachman – only think of that! The lizards, too, four footmen! oh, how grand They look in green and gold! – see, see! they stand Behind the coach
FAIRY	Well, poppet, will it do To take you to the ball?
CINDERELLA	How kind of you To do so much for me! but then, look here, I have no gown but this, Godmother, dear.
FAIRY	Poor child! well, take it off, and then we'll see What can be done.

(CINDERELLA throws off her old gown, and appears in a ball dress, and the FAIRY takes a wreath of flowers from under her cloak, and puts it on her head.)

CINDERELLA	Oh! goodness! look at me! I never saw so beautiful a dress: Why, I shall be as grand as a princess! But these old shoes?
FAIRY	*(takes the glass slippers out of her pocket)* Behold, my pretty lass A pair of shining slippers made of glass.
CINDERELLA	*(sorrowfully)* I cannot dance.
FAIRY	You need not be distressed. These fairy shoes will make you dance the best.

(CINDERELLA puts on the slippers, and looks at them admiringly.)

FAIRY	Now, listen well to what I'm going to say; Be very careful that you come away Before the clock strikes twelve, for then the charm Would cease, and you might come to some great harm, The coach become a pumpkin in a trice, The footmen lizards, and the horses mice. No trace of those fine clothes will then remain; You'll be poor Cinderella once again.
CINDERELLA	*(kissing her)* I'll come away in time, I promise you. *[Exit*
FAIRY	I shall be much mistaken if you do. *[Exit*

137

SCENE THE FOURTH – The Ball Room

(This being a Court Ball, the scene should be made as brilliant as possible with lights, festoons of flowers, and drapery. Some of the young ladies and gentlemen who form the audience might assist by going upon the stage to dance, as the company should appear as numerous as possible. It would be easy to provide a few coloured gauze scarfs, ribbons, and flowers, to decorate these extra performers for this scene. At the upper end of the room should be a sofa, on which the Prince is discovered seated between the two sisters, to whom he seems paying attention. A polka is being played, and one or two couples are dancing, while others are sitting here and there.)

Enter CINDERELLA

(The PRINCE sees her, and rises; the music ceases, and those who are dancing walk round the room in pairs.)

PRINCE	*(aside)* What a sweet creature! but who can she be; *(He approaches and takes her hand.* Lady, permit me; I am proud to see So fair a guest; although with shame I own Your name and rank are both to me unknown.
CINDERELLA	Prince, I am a stranger, and I came to see A court so famed for hospitality. Your kind reception charms me; yet I fear, You'll think me bold to come unbidden here.
PRINCE	Not so, indeed; it is a condescension That must command my very best attention.

(He leads her to the sofa, and seats her between her sisters, who appear delighted as she talks to each in turn, and gives them flowers from her bouquet. The PRINCE stands by, and seems to join in the conversation. While this is passing, two couples are walking round the room, and as they pass along the front they speak.)

GENTLEMAN	She's very handsome ——
LADY	Yes; and then her dress Is costly; she must be some great princess.

(That couple passes on, and another comes to the front.

LADY	There's no one here can learn from whence she came; Even the Prince himself don't know her name.
GENTLEMAN	Perhaps a foreign princess; but no doubt, His Highness will take care to find it out.

(They pass on; and a polka is played, and the PRINCE dances with CINDERELLA; two gentlemen offer their hands to the sisters, and the dance continues for a moderate time, when the music stops. The sisters then sit down, and their partners stand by them talking, and all the company must appear to be engaged with each other, while the PRINCE and CINDERELLA come to the front of the stage.)

PRINCE	But surely, lady, you will condescend To tell me who you are?
CINDERELLA	*(laughingly)* Nay, I intend To try your patience for one hour more; Then if you ask, I'll tell; but not before. *(Aside)* He cannot ask, for I shall then be gone: 'Tis past eleven – how the time runs on!
PRINCE	*(to the company, and giving his arm to CINDERELLA)* Then now to supper, friends, we lead the way.

PRINCE	*(doubtingly)* You mean to tell me ——
CINDERELLA	I mean what I say.

(He leads out CINDERELLA, and the rest follow in couples. A short time elapses, and the clock strikes twelve. This can be managed by striking twelve strokes on a glass tumbler. CINDERELLA enters hurriedly in her old dress, with the glass slippers in her hand. She goes to put them into her pocket, but in doing so drops one without perceiving it.)

CINDERELLA	Oh, dear! what shall I do? I've stayed too late; I wish that I could find the palace gate: I must run home on foot – I know the way; But if I'm seen, what will the servants say?
MULEY	Why, who are you? and what do you want here? The scullery's your proper place, my dear. *[Exit CINDERELLA*

Enter PRINCE

PRINCE	This is most strange: I missed her from my side All in a moment. Muley, have you tried To find the lady?
MULEY	Yes, your Highness: she Must certainly be gone, for we don't see Her carriage in the Court, and it was there Scarcely ten minutes since, they all declare.
PRINCE	How could it pass the gate without being seen?
MULEY	I do not know, my lord; four men in green There were, besides the coachman; and, I'm told, Their liveries were richly laced with gold. The chariot was splendid too, they say; 'Tis odd that no one saw it drive away.
PRINCE	I can't imagine which way she could pass, But behold! what's this? *(takes up the shoe)*, a slipper made of glass. 'Tis hers – that's fortunate – for I will find her By this small token she has left behind her.　　*[Exit*

SCENE THE FIFTH – The Dressing Room

CINDERELLA	Oh! what a happy, happy night I've spent; I scarcely can believe I really went. Who would suppose that, only two hours since, I was so gaily dancing with a prince. *(A loud knocking at the door.* *(She opens the door, and the two sisters enter.*

CINDERELLA	Oh dear! I am so tired – how late you've stayed. I should have gone to sleep, but was afraid That if I did I should not hear you knock. I do believe it is past three o'clock.
ULRICA	It is not two——
CHARLOTTE	We are not tired at all No more would you, if you'd been at the ball.
ULRICA	It would be strange indeed if we were tired, When we have been so very much admired.
CHARLOTTE	Yes – and there was a beautiful princess; I only wish you could have seen her dress: She came and sat by us – and was as free As if we'd been her equals.
CINDERELLA	(laughing aside) That was me.
ULRICA	She gave us flowers from her own bouquet.
CHARLOTTE	Mine was a rose,
ULRICA	And mine a sprig of May.
CHARLOTTE	And then the most obliging things she said; Which plainly showed she had at Court been bred.
CINDERELLA	'Tis well for you – I wish I had been there.
CHARLOTTE	It makes one laugh to hear you, I declare; Come, let us go to bed.
CINDERELLA	Shall you want me To help you to undress?
ULRICA	Yes; certainly. [Exeunt

SCENE THE SIXTH – A Room in the Palace
(The Prince alone, sitting by a table, with his elbow resting upon it. He has the glass slipper in his hand.)

PRINCE	I shall have neither rest nor peace of mind, Until that lovely creature I can find; For I am quite resolved that she alone Shall be my bride, and partner of my throne. *Enter MULEY* Well, Muley, what success?
MULEY	Your Highness, none; Yet all that you commanded, I have done; At every neighbouring Court I've made inquiries, But no princess can find.
PRINCE	Then my desire is, That there shall be a royal proclamation To all the single ladies of the nation, Declaring that my throne I mean to share With any one who can this slipper wear.
MULEY	But, sir, it might a dozen ladies fit.
PRINCE	No, no, good Muley, there's no fear of it; For there was not a single foot beside So small and beautiful. I'll have it tried, At any rate – and that without delay; So you may send the heralds out to-day. [Exit

MULEY	My royal master has gone mad – that's plain; This fair unknown has fairly turned his brain. [Exit

SCENE THE SEVENTH – The Dressing Room
(Cinderella sitting at work. The Baroness reading.)

BARONESS	(looking up from her book and speaking sharply) You are not sewing very fast, I'm sure
CINDERELLA	I am indeed. (Aside) I wonder who'd endure Such constant scolding.

Enter CHARLOTTE

CHARLOTTE	Oh, mamma, such news! I've hurried home that we no time may lose. It is about the Prince; it seems he found, After the Ball, a slipper on the ground; And now proclaims he'll marry any one, Whose foot is small enough to get it on.

Enter ULRICA (hastily)

ULRICA	I've heard it. – There's to be a public fête, When every girl, whate'er may be her state, Will be at liberty the shoe to try.
CHARLOTTE	I've a small foot, I'm sure, (puts out her foot)

ULRICA	(looks at her own foot) And so have I.
BARONESS	(rises) Now, children, I will tell you what to do: Try very hard to squeeze your feet into The smallest ladies' shoe you can obtain, The chance of being a queen is worth some pain. [Exit
CINDERELLA	(without looking up from her work) I wonder if the slipper would fit me?
CHARLOTTE	(laughing) Ha! ha! ha! ha! How proud the Prince would be Of such a bride; well, I shall be delighted To come to Court whenever I'm invited. (makes a very low curtsey) Perhaps, Ulrica, we shall have the honour, To be her train-bearers, and wait upon her.
ULRICA	(speaks in a tone of ill-humour) How can you talk such nonsense, Charlotte! You Encourage that girl's folly, that you do. [Exeunt CHARLOTTE and ULRICA (CINDERELLA throws down her work and comes forward.)

139

CINDERELLA	So, they may scoff, but if they only knew I was the owner of that little shoe. Their tone would change. I am resolved to go, Whether I can see my godmother or no. No one can get that slipper on but me, And here's the other (*takes it out of her pocket*). So the Prince can see I'm no imposter, though my dress is mean; Then, if he keeps his word, I shall be queen. [*Exit*		

SCENE THE EIGHTH – The same Room in the Palace as before
(*Ulrica, Charlotte, and Muley, are on stage. Charlotte is trying on the slipper*)

CHARLOTTE	I'll try the other foot.
MULEY	Nay, madam, nay, It would not do if you should try all day; You are the twentieth lady who has tried, And there are many waiting now outside.
CHARLOTTE	(*discontentedly*) Well, I must give it up, then I suppose. (*She takes her sister's arm, and they go off.*)
MULEY	(*laughing*) I think you'd better – ha! ha! ha! there goes Another would-be queen: 'Tis strange to see How people are misled by vanity.

Enter CINDERELLA

MULEY	Well girl, what now? This is no place for you
CINDERELLA	Sir, if you please to let me try the shoe, I think it would fit me.
MULEY	Why, child, you're mad; Or else impertinent, which is as bad.
CINDERELLA	I understood that any one might try ——
MULEY	Not kitchen-maids, my dear, decidedly.
CINDERELLA	Why, it could do no harm ——
MULEY	(*laughing*). Upon my word You are a saucy baggage – How absurd! I can't help laughing – well – there – sit down, A likely lass indeed to wear a crown.

Enter PRINCE
(*He looks fixedly at CINDERELLA, who sits down and puts on the slipper.*)

PRINCE	That face reminds me of my lady love.
MULEY	Why it goes on as easy as a glove.
PRINCE (*advancing eagerly*)	What do you say? – the slipper fits this maid?
MULEY	It does indeed, your Highness, I'm afraid; Yet more than twenty ladies have in vain Made the attempt ——
PRINCE	(*aside*) Then it is very plain That fate intends this damsel for my bride
MULEY	(*aside*) It is a thousand pities that she tried.

Enter ULRICA and CHARLOTTE
(*They are astonished at seeing CINDERELLA*).

ULRICA	Why, how is this? how dare you be so bold As to come here?
CINDERELLA	Nay, sister: do not scold; I thought it was no harm to come and see If the glass slipper would not do for me.
ULRICA	(*in a passion*) For you, indeed; a dirty kitchen maid! Go home and mind your work, you saucy jade.
PRINCE	(*approaching Cinderella*) Pray, madam, tell me who and what you are.
CINDERELLA	Prince, I was once a little evening star, That with a borrowed lustre faintly shone In these bright halls awhile and then was gone.
PRINCE	I'm still bewildered, how in this poor dress, Am I to recognize my fair princess?
CHARLOTTE	Your Royal Highness, 'tis an imposition; This is a girl of very low condition, She is our servant, though her foot is small; And never in her life was at a ball.
PRINCE	(*to Cinderella*) I'd give all I am worth to prove it true That this glass slipper does belong to you.
CINDERELLA	Here is the proof. (*Shows the other shoe.*
MULEY	(*aside*) The fellow slipper; truly She is a witch, or my name is not Muley.

Enter FAIRY

CINDERELLA	Ah; my kind, good old godmother is here; Now, then, indeed, I have no more to fear.
FAIRY	Pray stand aside, good folks, and let me see If I can solve this mighty mystery. Come hither, Cinderella; pr'ythee throw Aside those rags, my pretty child, and show That you are no imposter; but may prove Quite worthy of this noble Prince's love.

(*CINDERELLA throws off her old gown, and appears in the ball dress, having already put on the other glass slipper.*)

PRINCE	It is herself indeed!
MULEY	(*aside*) What shall I do? I called her wench, and saucy baggage, too.

(*The PRINCE takes the hand of CINDERELLA, and they stand in the centre; the FAIRY on one side of them, a little in advance; the two sisters on the other side, at a little distance, hanging down their heads in confusion; MULEY near the PRINCE'S elbow, rather behind.*)

FAIRY	Prince, I'm a fairy, and I hither came To raise the humble, and the proud to shame; In Cinderella you've a charming bride. Her goodness and her patience have been tried. You will be happy both – But (*pointing to the sisters*), ladies, you Will meet the punishment that is your due. Scorned and neglected, it shall be your fate To envy Cinderella's happier state.

(*The two sisters hide their faces with their handkerchiefs, and the scene closes.*)

CHRISTMAS EVE IN THE BLUE CHAMBER
Jerome K. Jerome

I DON'T WANT to make you fellows nervous,' began my uncle in a peculiarly impressive, not to say blood-curdling, tone of voice, 'and if you would rather that I did not mention it, I won't; but, as a matter of fact, this very house, in which we are now sitting is haunted.'

'You don't say that!' exclaimed Mr. Coombes.

'What's the use of your saying I don't say it when I have just said it?' retorted my uncle somewhat annoyed. 'You talk so foolishly. I tell you the house is haunted. Regularly on Christmas Eve the Blue Chamber' (they call the room next to the nursery the 'Blue Chamber' at my uncle's) 'is haunted by the ghost of a sinful man – a man who once killed a Christmas carol singer with a lump of coal.'

'How did he do it?' asked Mr Coombes, eagerly. 'Was it difficult?'

'I do not know how he did it,' replied my uncle; 'he did not explain the process. The singer had taken up a position just inside the front gate, and was singing a ballad. It is presumed that, when he opened his mount for B flat, the lump of coal was thrown by the sinful man from one of the windows, and that it went down the singer's throat and choked him.'

'You want to be a good shot, but it is certainly worth trying,' murmured Mr. Coombes thoughtfully.

'But that was not his only crime, alas!' added my uncle. 'Prior to that he had killed a solo cornet player.'

'No! Is that really a fact,' exclaimed Mr. Coombes.

'Of course it's a fact,' answered my uncle testily. 'At all events, as much a fact as you can expect to get in a case of this sort.

'The poor fellow, the cornet player, had been in the neighborhood barely a month. Old Mr. Bishop, who kept the 'Jolly Sand Boys' at the time, and from whom I had the story, said he had never known a more hard-working and energetic solo cornet player. He, the cornet player, only knew two tunes, but Mr. Bishop said that the man could not have played with more vigor, or for more hours a day, if he had known forty. The two tunes he did play were 'Annie Laurie' and 'Home Sweet Home'; and as regarded his performance of the former melody, Mr. Bishop said that a mere child could have told what it was meant for.

'This musician – this poor, friendless artist – used to come regularly and play in this street just opposite for two hours every evening. One evening he was seen, evidently in response to an invitation, going into this very house, *but was never seen coming out of it!*'

'Did the townsfolk try offering any reward for his recovery?' asked Mr. Coombes.

'Not a penny,' replied my uncle.

'Another summer,' continued my uncle, 'a German band visited here, intending – so they announced on their arrival – to stay till the autumn.

'On the second day after their arrival, the whole company, as fine and healthy a body of men as one would wish to see, were invited to dinner by this sinful man, and, after spending the whole of the next twenty-four hours in bed, left the town a broken and dyspeptic crew; the parish doctor, who had attended them giving it as his opinion that it was doubtful if they would, any of them, be fit to play an air again.'

'You – you don't know the recipe, do you?' asked Mr. Coombes.

'Unfortunately I do not,' replied my uncle; 'but the chief ingredient was said to have been railway dining-room hash.

'I forget the man's other crimes,' my uncle went on; 'I used to know them all at one time, but my memory is not what it was. I do not, however, believe I am doing his memory an injustice in believing that he was not entirely

A Hymn on the Nativity of My Saviour

I sing the birth was born to-night,
The Author both of life and light;
The angels so did sound it.
And like the ravished shepherds said,
Who saw the light, and were afraid,
Yet searched, and true they found it.

The Son of God, th'Eternal King,
That did us all salvation bring,
And freed the soul from danger;
He whom the whole world could not take,
The Word, which heaven and earth did make;
Was now laid in a manger.

The Father's wisdom willed it so,
The Son's obedience knew no No,
Both wills were one in stature;
And as that wisdom had decreed,
The Word was now made flesh indeed,
And took on Him our nature.

What comfort by Him do we win,
Who made Himself the price of sin,
To make us heirs of glory!
To see this Babe, all innocence;
A martyr born in our defence:
Can man forget this story?

BEN JONSON

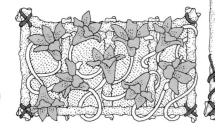

unconnected with the death, and subsequent burial, of a gentleman who used to play the harp with his toes; and that neither was he altogether unresponsible for the lonely grave of an unknown stranger who had once visited the neighborhood, an Italian peasant lad, a performer upon the barrel-organ.

'Every Christmas Eve,' said my uncle, cleaving with low impressive tones the strange awed silence that, like a shadow, seemed to have slowly stolen into and settled down upon the room, 'the ghost of this sinful man haunts the Blue Chamber, in this very house. There, from midnight until cock-crow, amid wild muffled shrieks and groans and mocking laughter and the ghostly sound of horrid blows, it does fierce phantom fight with the spirits of the solo cornet player and the murdered carol singer, assisted at intervals by the shades of the German band; while the ghost of the strangled harpist plays mad ghostly melodies with ghostly toes on the ghost of a broken harp.'

Uncle said the Blue Chamber was comparatively useless as a sleeping apartment on Christmas Eve.

'Hark!' said my uncle, raising a warning hand toward the ceiling, while we held our breath, and listened: 'Hark! I believe they are at it now – in the Blue Chamber!'

I rose up and said that *I* would sleep in the Blue Chamber.

'Never!' cried my uncle, springing up. 'You shall not put yourself in this deadly peril. Besides, the bed is not made.'

'Never mind the bed,' I replied, 'I have lived in furnished apartments for gentlemen, and have been accustomed to sleep on beds that have never been made from one year's end to the other. I am young, and have had a clear conscience now for a month. The spirits will not harm me. I may even do them some little good, and induce them to be quiet and go away. Besides, I should like to see the show.'

They tried to dissuade me from what they termed my foolhardy enterprise, but I remained firm and claimed my privilege. I was 'the guest.' 'The guest' always sleeps in the haunted chamber on Christmas Eve; it is his right.

They said that if I put it on that footing they had, of course, no answer, and they lighted a candle for me and followed me upstairs in a body.

Whether elevated by the feeling that I was doing a noble action or animated by a mere general consciousness of rectitude is not for me to say, but I went upstairs that night with remarkable buoyancy. It was as much as I could do to stop at the landing when I came to it; I felt I wanted to go on up to the roof. But, with the help of the banisters, I restrained my ambition, wished them all good-night and went in and shut the door.

Things began to go wrong with me from the very first. The candle tumbled out of the candlestick before my hand was off the lock. It kept on tumbling out again; I never saw such a slippery candle. I gave up attempting to use the candlestick at last and carried the candle about in my hand, and even then it would not keep upright. So I got wild and threw it out the window, and undressed and went to bed in the dark.

I did not go to sleep; I did not feel sleepy at all; I lay on my back looking up at the ceiling and thinking of things. I wish I could remember some of the ideas that came to me as I lay there, because they were so amusing.

I had been lying like this for half an hour or so, and had forgotten all about the ghost, when, on casually casting my eyes round the room, I noticed for the first time a singularly contented-looking phantom sitting in the easy-chair by the fire smoking the ghost of a long clay pipe.

I fancied for the moment, as most people would under similar circumstances, that I must be dreaming. I sat up and rubbed my eyes. No! It was a ghost, clear enough. I could see the back of the chair through his body. He looked over toward me, took the shadowy pipe from his lips and nodded.

The most surprising part of the whole thing to me was that I did not feel in the least alarmed. If anything I was rather pleased to see him. It was company.

I said: 'Good evening. It's been a cold day!'

He said he had not noticed it himself, but dared say I was right.

We remained silent for a few seconds, and then, wishing to put it pleasantly, I said: 'I believe I have the honor of addressing the ghost of the gentleman who had the accident with the carol singer?'

He smiled and said it was very good of me to remember it. One singer was not much to boast of, but still every little helped.

I was somewhat staggered at his answer. I had expected a groan of remorse. The ghost appeared, on the contrary, to be rather conceited over the business. I thought that as he had taken my reference to the singer so quietly perhaps he would not be offended if I questioned him about the organ grinder. I felt curious about that poor boy.

'Is it true,' I asked, 'that you had a hand in the death of that Italian peasant lad who came to the town with a barrel-organ that played nothing but Scotch airs?'

He quite fired up. 'Had a hand in it!' he exclaimed indignantly. 'Who has dared to pretend that he assisted me? I murdered the youth myself. Nobody helped me. Alone I did it. Show me the man who says I didn't.'

I calmed him. I assured him that I had never, in my own mind, doubted that he was the real and only assassin, and I went on and asked him what he had done with the body of the cornet player he had killed.

He said: 'To which one may you be alluding?'

'Oh, were there any more then?' I inquired.

He smiled and gave a little cough. He said he did not like to appear to be boasting, but that, counting trombones, there were seven.

'Dear me!' I replied, 'you must have had quite a busy time of it, one way and another.'

He said that perhaps he ought not to be the one to say so; but that really, speaking of ordinary middle-class society, he thought there were few ghosts who could look back upon a life of more sustained usefulness.

He puffed away in silence for a few seconds while I sat watching him. I had never seen a ghost smoking a pipe before, that I could remember, and it interested me.

I asked him what tobacco he used, and he replied: 'The ghost of cut cavendish as a rule.'

He explained that the ghost of all the tobacco that a man smoked in life belonged to him when he became dead. He said he himself had smoked a good deal of cut cavendish when he was alive, so that he was well supplied with the ghost of it now.

I thought I would join him in a pipe, and he said, 'Do, old man'; and I reached over and got out the necessary paraphernalia from my coat pocket and lit up.

We grew quite chummy after that, and he told me all his crimes. He said he had lived next door once to a young lady who was learning to play the guitar, while a gentleman who practiced on the bass-viol lived opposite. And he, with fiendish cunning, had introduced these two unsuspecting young people to one another, and had persuaded them to elope with each other against their parents' wishes, and take their musical instruments with them; and they had done so, and before the honeymoon was over, *she* had broken his head with the bass-viol, and he had tried to cram the guitar down her throat, and had injured her for life.

My friend said he used to lure muffin-men into the passage and then stuff them with their own wares till they burst. He said he had quieted eighteen that way.

Young men and women who recited long and dreary poems at evening parties, and callow youths who walked about the streets late at night, playing concertinas, he used to get together and poison in batches of ten, so as to save expenses; and park orators and temperance lecturers he used to shut up six in a small room with a glass of water and a collection-box apiece, and let them talk each other to death.

It did one good to listen to him.

I asked him when he expected the other ghosts – the ghosts of the singer and the cornet player, and the German band that Uncle John had mentioned. He smiled, and said they would never come again, any of them.

I said, 'Why, isn't it true, then, that they meet you here every Christmas Eve for a row?'

He replied that it was true. Every Christmas Eve, for twenty-five years, had he and they fought in that room; but they would never trouble him or anybody else again. One by one had he laid them out, spoiled and made them utterly useless for all haunting purposes. He had finished off the last German band ghost that very evening, just before I came upstairs, and had thrown what was left of it out through the slit between the window sashes. He said it would never be worth calling a ghost again.

'I suppose you will still come yourself, as usual?' I said. 'They would be sorry to miss you, I know.'

'Oh, I don't know,' he replied; 'there's nothing much to come for now; unless,' he added kindly, '*you* are going to be here. I'll come if you will sleep here next Christmas Eve.'

'I have taken a liking to you,' he continued; 'you don't fly off, screeching, when you see a party, and your hair doesn't stand on end. You've no idea,' he said, 'how sick I am of seeing people's hair standing on end.'

He said it irritated him.

Just then a slight noise reached us from the yard below, and he started and turned deathly black.

'You are ill,' I cried, springing toward him; 'tell me the best thing to do for you. Shall I drink some brandy, and give you the ghost of it?'

He remained silent, listening intently for a moment, and then he gave a sigh of relief, and the shade came back to his cheek.

'It's all right,' he murmured; 'I was afraid it was the cock.'

'Oh, it's too early for that,' I said. 'Why, it's only the middle of the night.'

'Oh, that doesn't make any difference to those cursed chickens,' he replied bitterly. 'They would just as soon crow in the middle of the night as at any other time – sooner, if they thought it would spoil a chap's evening out. I believe they do it on purpose.'

He said a friend of his, the ghost of a man who had killed a tax collector, used to haunt a house in Long Acre, where they kept fowls in the cellar, and every time a policeman went by and flashed his searchlight down the grating, the old cock there would fancy it was the sun, and start crowing like mad, when, of course, the poor ghost had to dissolve, and it would, in consequence, get back home sometimes as early as one o'clock in the morning, furious because it had only been out for an hour.

I agreed that it seemed very unfair.

'Oh, it's an absurd arrangement altogether,' he continued, quite angrily. 'I can't imagine what our chief could have been thinking of when he made it. As I have said to him, over and over again, "Have a fixed time, and let everybody stick to it – say four o'clock in summer, and six in winter. Then one would know what one was about."'

'How do you manage when there isn't any clock handy?' I inquired.

He was on the point of replying, when again he started and listened. This time I distinctly heard Mr. Bowles' cock, next door, crow twice.

'There you are,' he said, rising and reaching for his hat; 'that's the sort of thing we have to put up with. What *is* the time?'

I looked at my watch, and found it was half-past three.

'I thought as much,' he muttered. 'I'll wring that blessed bird's neck if I get hold of it.' And he prepared to go.

'If you can wait half a minute,' I said, getting out of bed, 'I'll go a bit of the way with you.'

'It's very good of you,' he replied, pausing, 'but it seems unkind to drag you out.'

'Not at all,' I replied; 'I shall like a walk.' And I partially dressed myself, and took my umbrella; and he put his arm through mine, and we went out together, the best of friends.

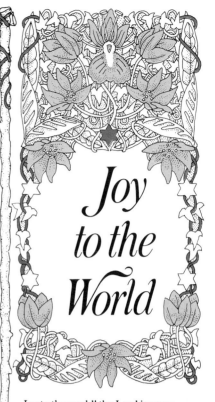

Joy to the World

Joy to the world! the Lord is come;
Let earth receive her King;
Let every heart prepare Him room,
And heaven and nature sing,
And heaven and nature sing,
And heaven, and heaven and nature sing.

Joy to the earth! the Saviour reigns;
Let men their songs employ;
While fields and floods, rocks, hills and plains
Repeat the sounding joy,
Repeat the sounding joy,
Repeat, repeat the sounding joy.

He rules the world with truth and grace,
And makes the nations prove
The glories of His righteousness,
And wonders of His love,
And wonders of His love,
And wonders, and wonders of His love.

ISAAC WATTS

HAPPY
NEW YEAR

NEW YEAR

EARLY ALL the practices connected with the New Year are based on the principles of 'start as you mean to go on' and 'a good beginning makes a good ending'. If you are clean, healthy, well fed, with money in your pocket and free of debts and devils when the New Year opens, you will remain so for the rest of the year. The turn of the year is also a most auspicious time for divining the future, particularly with regard to marriage partners, the weather and the fertility of crops and animals. One symbol of the New Year is Janus, the Roman god who presided over January. His name derives from the word meaning 'door' and he is always pictured with two faces, one looking backwards the other forwards, representing the link between past and future. Nowadays a more familiar symbol is the figure of Old Father Time bearing a newborn babe. The New Year baby is a symbol from ancient Greece when a baby was paraded at the ceremony of the annual rebirth of Dionysus.

In ancient times different peoples began the New Year on different dates according to a variety of agricultural and astronomical calculations. The old Celtic New Year began on 1 November. Europe generally settled for 25 March, a date near the Vernal Equinox. England did not officially adopt 1 January, the old Roman New Year's Day, until 1752, when the Gregorian calendar was accepted. The Treasury's attitude was even more diehard. For tax purposes they continued to begin their New Year on 25 March, which became 6 April under the new calendar – and they still do. While many

Old Father Time, holding a sickle, pushes the world through space.

of the old Roman New Year or Kalends customs shifted from January to Christmas, the Celtic New Year traditions attached themselves to the modern New Year. 1 January is the Feast of the Circumcision and 31 December is St Sylvester's Day, but almost all New Year customs and beliefs are wholly pagan.

Before the New Year can be welcomed in, the old year's evil and bad luck must be banished so that everyone can start with a clean slate. It used to be customary to load all misfortunes on to some sort of scapegoat which was then disposed of with its burden. In parts of Scotland all wickedness was transferred to a cat or dog and the beast was driven from the house. Sometimes the scapegoat was a dummy, like the Hungarian Jack Straw. This effigy was carried round the village and everyone seeing it thought of all their bad deeds which were burnt with it.

Of course, no one wanted to start the New Year with last year's evil spirits in tow so they too had to be driven away. The simplest way was to create a fearful din, which is why noise is produced with such fervour today as the old year departs and the new one is ushered in. Parts of Switzerland still celebrate Old Sylvester's Day by the Julian calendar on 13 January with good and bad Sylvesterklauses wearing fantastic costumes and enormous hats going from house to house in a symbolic representation of good driving out evil. In the Scottish Highlands the leader of a group of men used to wrap himself in a cow's hide and run off round the village pursued by the rest of the company striking at his hide. This group would go three times round each house banging on the walls and demanding to be let in. Once inside they were all offered refreshment and the leader used to give the head of the house a 'beast-stripe' – a strip of skin from a sheep, deer or goat wrapped round the tip of a stick. The householder set fire to it and each member of the household breathed in the fumes as a talisman against the demons and witches. The beast-stripe was called the

HERALDS OF THE NEW YEAR

The turn of the year is a time for omens and witches, presents and superstitions, for turning away from the old year and facing the new, and all these aspects of the season have their attendant characters in human form.

1, 2 & 3 Sylvesterklauses, monstrously hatted or masked, dance through the streets of the Appenzell mountain village of Urnäsch in Switzerland on the evening of Old Sylvester Day – New Year's Eve according to the Julian calendar – in symbolic representation of good and evil spirits. In return, villagers give them gifts and wine.

4 The first person to cross the threshold on New Year's Day indicates the sort of fortune the household may expect in the coming twelve months. This Scottish First-Footer – a young, healthy, dark-haired man carrying a lump of coal to symbolize the destruction of evil influences – portends good luck.

5 The New Year Babe, a popular image of the incoming year, leading in a host of fertility and harvest figures. In ancient Greece a baby cradled in a winnowing basket was paraded to represent the annual rebirth of Dionysus, god of fruitfulness.

6 Grandfather Frost, looking remarkably like Father Christmas, was substituted for the traditional Russian gift-bringers Babouschka and Kolyada after the Revolution. He visits on the non-religious holiday of New Year.

7 Janus, the Roman god of doorways and new beginnings, presided over the month of January and was usually pictured with two heads, one looking backwards and one forwards to symbolize the past and the future.

8 The ancient and pagan figure of Old Father Time, complete with sickle and the sands of time running out, traditionally represents the dying year. Here he is seen with the New Year Babe whose reign is just beginning.

'hogmanay', the term is also applied to the pieces of oatcake children beg of neighbours. The word probably derives from the French 'aguillanneuf' ('hoguinane' in Norman form).

Cleanliness of body and home was also important at the start of a fresh year and may have represented a form of purification. Even today people bustle about sweeping, polishing and mending, and spring cleaning probably developed more as a preparation for the old New Year than because of the season. In Scotland houses and byres were purified with water and burning juniper branches. Every member of the household drank from a pitcher of 'magic water', which was then sprinkled by the head of the house and his assistants on the beds and the other people there. All doors and windows were sealed and burning juniper boughs were carried through the house creating suffocating smoke and causing everyone to cough, sneeze and spit out all their latent germs and diseases. The animals had to undergo the same treatment.

When everyone was ready in body and spirit for the New Year the old one still had to be disposed of and the commonest way was to burn it ceremonially. Vast bonfires and tar barrels still blaze in parts of Scotland. In some districts of Holland Christmas trees are collected for huge bonfires. Some countries burnt effigies of the old year, like the Scottish 'auld wife' and others ritually buried the dead twelve months.

The old year banished, it was essential to begin the New Year correctly. Some people did a little token labour on the New Year's Day public holiday to ensure against unemployment in the coming months. New clothes were worn in the same spirit of turning over a new leaf, but were also thought to fool any demons still remaining. There were many ceremonies connected with fertility. It was the custom in parts of England to rise early and wassail the fruit trees with songs and libations and in other regions of Europe it was the practice to beat the trees to make them grow. In Scottish households the first to rise carried Drinking-Sowens (the liquid from boiled oatmeal) laced with whisky, or Het Pint, the hot Hogmanay drink of spiced ale, to everyone else still in bed. Animals were fed an extra sheaf of corn and formally blessed and each farm worker was given as 'handsel' (a New Year's gift) a sheaf for his cow and oatcakes for the family.

Present-giving used to be common at the New Year, mainly as a form of tokenism. Romans gave each other small gifts for luck on 1 January, and in England tenants and peasants were expected to give small samples of the fruits of their labour to the lords of the manor, who in turn were expected to send something rather more valuable to the monarch. In many countries men

and boys would go from house to house waking people up to wish them a happy New Year in hope of being rewarded with something to eat.

Scotland today is much noted for its Hogmanay parties. Traditionally it is a communal celebration and people used to gather in the streets, the churchyard and by the mercat, or market, cross. There was a spirit of general goodwill with drink flowing freely and considerable licence allowed. Today crowds wearing funny hats and carrying whistles, bells and streamers still spill out into the streets and, as the midnight bells ring out, fall silent before breaking out into deafening noise.

At home, housewives stock up with shortbread, black bun (a pastry case filled with a rich, spicy nut and dried fruit mixture), treacle bannocks, oatcakes and cheese and, of course, whisky and wine. Just before midnight the front door or the windows are opened to let out the old year and let in the new. The sound of church bells and car horns mingle at midnight with gongs and whistles and banged tin trays. Everyone crosses arms, holds hands in a circle and sings Robert Burns's *Auld Lang Syne*. Then the First Footer is awaited, the symbol of luck for the coming year.

Sober folk may choose to contemplate the coming twelve months in church at Watch Night services, but throughout the world people generally welcome in the New Year in a fashion similar to Scotland's. In England, in the past, New Year's Eve was more connected with pious resolutions and church bells, but now balloons and funny hats, streamers and *Auld Lang Syne*, drinking, dancing and making a noise are prominent on the New Year scene – particularly now that New Year's Day is a public holiday. Similar exuberance can be found in America, where, until the first years of this century, everyone

'London Society meeting A Jolly Time', a caricature of contemporary personalities.

held open house and laid on magnificent feasts for anyone who cared to drop in.

The Dutch often celebrate the New Year at home, finishing a cold meal at the stroke of midnight, when everything erupts in noise and light, bonfires, fireworks and ships' sirens playing a prominent part in welcoming the New Year. Everyone exchanges kisses and greetings. Germans enjoy parties of family and friends – a wider circle than at Christmas – at home or in restaurants and bars. At midnight everyone raises their glasses – champagne filled, with luck – in a toast to the New Year. Then they pour out into the streets to watch the great firework displays. Hungarians celebrating in restaurants or other public places hope to be touched for good luck by sooty chimney sweeps. Most Danes enjoy a party. There are masks and games, streamers and champagne, dancing and, as midnight approaches, elaborate practical jokes to be played on neighbours. In Italy the noise of breaking crockery is added to the rest of the din as old household goods are thrown out into the street to make way for new ones. New Year's Eve in France was traditionally the time for exchanging gifts and is a more festive occasion than Christmas. There, the midnight chimes are followed by another Réveillon, or midnight feast. Russian children anticipate a visit from Grandfather Frost, the post-Revolution giftbringer. In many countries the fun goes on into New Year's Day with carnivals and parades, such as the spectacular Mummers' Parade in Philadelphia.

Many of the customs and practices which seem just part of the fun today have pagan implications. The buffoonery and funny hats and streamers recall the topsy-turvy world of Saturnalia and the January Kalends as well as the medieval Lord of Misrule. The practice of holding hands in a circle to sing *Auld Lang Syne* goes back to the pagan meetings round a stone circle. The very sentiment of *Auld Lang Syne* – not written originally as a New Year song – is in tune with the ancient belief that at the New Year ancestors return to the family hearth.

New Year's Day is a public holiday in 125 countries and most people are happy to spend it recovering from the excesses of the previous night. Some families manage a great gathering round a laden table – this is the tradition in Scotland, where a festive haggis may appear – and for many, sport is the main occupation of the day. Nowadays New Year's Day, rather than Twelfth Night, marks the end of the Christmas season, and the return to ordinary life.

The New Year is a festival of renewal – of friendships reaffirmed, hurts forgiven, love recalled, hopes restored, and fortunes revived, when everyone can start again free from old cares.

TOASTING THE NEW YEAR

The ancient links between midwinter and drinking are festive and symbolic, Christian and pagan. Householders liberally dispensed seasonal cheer to waits and star singers, friends and neighbours. Steaming bowls passed from lip to lip to signify friendship and goodwill and to commune with the spirit of nature within the brew. Yule logs were blessed with wine in the name of the Father, the Son and the Holy Ghost, or in yet another unspoken appeal for a good harvest. Even animals found beer or spirits in their festive feed. Not to be outdone, priests blessed wine and beer for Christmas and strong church ale was sold in churchyards. Temperance was not a part of the festivities.

Drinking out the old year and drinking in the new is a popular custom with everyone. As midnight strikes across the world, glasses are filled and raised in a toast to the New Year, and to the health and happiness of family and friends.

Ale has a long connection with the Christmas season and feasting. The old English wassail bowl (from the Anglo-Saxon 'wes hal', meaning 'be whole') was traditionally filled with a blend of hot spiced ale and roasted apples called lamb's-wool. Drinking from the household's wassail bowl was part of the general conviviality of the season as well as a symbol of friendship. The custom of drinking people's health probably came to be called toasting after the pieces of toast floating in the lamb's-wool. Carol singers carried cups with them to fill at the wassail bowls of the various houses they visited. In Yorkshire, a hot sugared and spiced mixture of beer and milk called Ale Posset was drunk ceremonially last thing on Christmas Eve. Each member of the family took a sip and ate a piece of apple pie. Devon residents adapted their festive tastes to their local product and while the Yule log blazed, drank Egg-Hot, a blend of cider, eggs and spices. In Scotland a libation of beer or wine was poured over the Yule log in the continental tradition. On Hogmanay the Het Pint of spiced ale, eggs and whisky was carried through the streets for everyone to sip. Fruit trees as well as people were wassailed, either as an offering to the tree spirits or to encourage fertility. On the Eve of Epiphany, Devon farmers used to drink a cider toast to the most fruitful tree, then guns were fired. This ceremony took place on Christmas Eve in Sussex to the accompaniment of a trumpet.

Beer plays an important part in Scandinavian celebrations. Among his other roles, Odin was the god of intoxicating drinks and the Yule Beer was sacrificed to him and to Freya and Njård, gods of fertility. The belief in the Yule Beer's magical qualities continued into the Christian era and in the Middle Ages the blessing and drinking of this beer was made mandatory for every household. Later, clergymen tried to eradicate the custom of drinking beer in honour of the Holy Spirit, but Norwegian farmers continued to dedicate the Christmas beer or 'julesøl' until the last century. Home brewing continues in Norway and Finland, where they make a mild form of beer called 'kalja'.

Hot drinks are a great comfort in the cold dark days of midwinter, though today mulled wines and hot punches have replaced spiced ale. The hot Christmas drink in Scandinavia is 'glögg' a spiced mixture of red wine and spirits which is popular at home and liberally dispensed by businesses to their customers. 'Glühwein' performs a similar service for German and Austrian communities. In America, the eggnog, a blend of cream, sugar, eggs, grated nutmeg and brandy

Old Father Time enjoying 'The Wassail Bowl', from an engraving by J. Hollis.

Wassail Song

Oh, here we come a-wassailing
Among the leaves so green,
And here we come a-wandering
So fair to be seen.

*Love and joy come to you,
And to you your wassail too,
And God bless you and send you
A Happy New Year,
And God send you a Happy New Year.*

We are not daily beggars
That beg from door to door,
But we are neighbours' children
Whom you have seen before.

Chorus

Good Master and good Mistress,
As you sit by the fire,
Pray think of us poor children
A-wand'ring in the mire.

Chorus

God bless the Master of this house,
Likewise the Mistress too;
And all the little children
That round the table go.

Chorus

or whisky, has spread from the Southern states to be the favourite national Christmas drink. Eggnog is descended from the English sack posset, which was made from ale or a Spanish wine called sack. The Americans adapted the recipe to rum, bourbon and even cider. Warmer climates call for cooler draughts and iced wine cups and punches accompany Australian beach picnics and South African pool-side meals.

As well as mixed drinks that are traditional to the season, everyone drinks their national beverage. The Scots and the Irish continue to consume whisky; the Poles, their vodka; Scandinavians, schnapps or aqvavit. The best wines accompany the goose, the carp or the turkey to the table. But on New Year's Eve local preferences are forgotten and champagne corks pop across the world.

COCKTAILS, PUNCHES & MULLS

The New Year toast is traditionally champagne, but mulled ales and wines, cool party punches, and cocktails all play a part in the festivities.

The old New Year toasting the new.

1 *Planters' Punch.* A long, cool mix of rum and fresh lime juice.
2 *Whisky sour.* Bourbon or rye whisky with lemon juice and ice.
3 *Gin Fizz.* Gin, lemon and soda.
4 *Daiquiri.* Cocktail of light rum with fresh lemon or lime juice.
5 *Manhattan.* A sophisticated blend of whisky and sweet vermouth.
6 *Mulled cider.* A spicy, warming alternative to mulled wines.
7 *Glühwein* is the traditional, hot spiced wine served in Austria.
8 *Glögg* is the Swedish mulled wine with almonds and raisins.
9 *White wine cup* is made with sparkling white wine and sliced oranges.
10 *Eggnog,* the traditional American Christmas drink.
11 *Wassail,* old English mulled ale.
12 *Fish House Punch,* an eighteenth-century American punch with peaches.
13 *Sparkling Champagne cup.*

151

Mixing Cocktails, Punches & Mulls

1 JAMAICAN PLANTER'S PUNCH
1 dessertspoon sugar
1 dessertspoon fresh lime juice
3 tablespoons cold water
4 tablespoons rum

Put all ingredients into a large glass with plenty of crushed ice and stir well. Add slices of pineapple, orange and lemon and top with a sprig of mint and a maraschino cherry.

2 WHISKY SOUR
Pour over ice a tablespoon of lemon juice, two fluid ounces rye whisky or Bourbon, a dash of Angostura Bitters and a teaspoon of castor sugar. Stir well, strain into a glass and top with a slice of orange and a cherry. Scotch whisky can be substituted.

GIN FIZZ
Pour over ice a tablespoon of lemon juice, two fluid ounces of gin and a teaspoon of castor sugar, shake, strain into medium-sized glasses and top with soda water. Brandy can be used instead of gin.

4 DAIQUIRI
Into a cocktail shaker put crushed ice, two fluid ounces light rum, one tablespoon fresh lemon or lime juice, one teaspoon castor sugar, shake well and strain into cocktail glass.

5 MANHATTAN
Pour over ice three parts rye whisky (Scotch whisky will do), one part sweet vermouth and a dash of Angostura Bitters. Stir well and strain.

6 MULLED CIDER
40 fl oz (1 litre) cider, preferably still
2 small eating apples
6 cloves
1 stick cinnamon
2 teaspoons ground ginger
2 oz (55 g) soft brown sugar
5 fl oz (150 ml) water
1 small orange

Core apples and cut skin round centre. Stick 2 cloves in each apple and bake for twenty minutes in a moderate oven.

Heat cider gently, do not boil. Heat all other ingredients except the orange in a separate saucepan until sugar has dissolved, then simmer gently for 5 minutes. Put apples and sliced orange in punch bowl, strain in spiced water and pour in heated cider.

7 GLÜHWEIN
20 fl oz (600 ml) red wine
3 oz (85 g) brown sugar
2 sticks cinnamon
1 lemon stuck with 6 cloves
1 wine glass brandy

Simmer all the ingredients, except brandy, until sugar has dissolved (about five minutes). Take off heat, stir in brandy, strain and serve.

8 GLÖGG
1 bottle red wine
2-4 fl oz (50-100 ml) schnapps (or vodka or similar)
1 whole ginger root
2 pieces of stick cinnamon
½ teaspoon cardamom seeds
6-8 cloves
6 tablespoons seedless raisins
3 tablespoons blanched almonds

Pour wine and schnapps into saucepan and add spices. Allow to stand and draw. Put raisins and almonds into small mugs or glasses. Heat wine mixture almost to boiling and pour it over the nuts and raisins and serve piping hot.

9 WHITE WINE CUP
1 bottle white wine
4 fl oz (115 ml) vodka
1 bottle champagne or dry sparkling white wine
rind of one orange pared and finely shredded
one orange, sliced

Soak orange rind in vodka for 2 hours then strain into bowl chilled by standing in another filled with ice. Pour chilled white wine and add champagne just before serving. Put ice cubes and a slice of orange into each glass before pouring in wine cup.

10 OLD FASHIONED EGGNOG
12 eggs, separated
6 oz (170 g) castor sugar
40 fl oz (1 litre) milk
20 fl oz (600 ml) Bourbon
10 fl oz (300 ml) Jamaica rum
40 fl oz (1 litre) chilled double cream
nutmeg

Beat egg yolks slightly, adding sugar a little at a time. Beat with a balloon whisk until smooth and creamy. Add milk, Bourbon, and rum. Blend mixture well and leave to stand for at least two hours. Beat egg whites and cream separately till they stand in soft peaks. Fold egg whites and whipped cream first together and then into yolk mixture, gently but thoroughly. Serve chilled with freshly grated nutmeg on top.

11 WASSAIL CUP
120 fl oz (3 litres) brown ale
1 lb (450 g) soft brown sugar
1 large cinnamon stick
1 level teaspoon grated nutmeg
½ level teaspoon ground ginger
2 lemons, thinly sliced
1 bottle medium dry sherry
2 lb (900 g) apples, roasted

Gently simmer 2 pints (1 litre) of the ale with sugar and cinnamon stick until sugar is dissolved. Add the sherry, the remaining ale, spices and lemon slices. Add roasted apples before serving.

12 FISH HOUSE PUNCH
Traditional eighteenth-century New Year punch and a speciality of the State Club, Philadelphia
1 lb (450 g) sugar
40 fl oz (1 litre) lemon juice
80 fl oz (2 litres) Jamaica rum
40 fl oz (1 litre) brandy
5 fl oz (150 ml) peach brandy
80 fl oz (2 litres) water (optional)
peaches

Dissolve sugar in strained lemon juice. Add rum and water, if used,

brandy and peach brandy. Mix ingredients well and leave mixture to mellow for a couple of hours. Pour over a block of ice in a large punch bowl and garnish with sliced peaches, fresh ones if possible.

13 FRENCH CHAMPAGNE CUP
3 bottles dry champagne
3 tablespoons Cognac
3 tablespoons Cointreau
2 oranges
4 oz (115 g) raisins
4 oz (115 g) sultanas

Leave the champagne to cool in the refrigerator. Slice the oranges into fine rings and place in a large glass bowl with the raisins and sultanas, washed and drained. Sprinkle with the brandy and Cointreau. Cover the bowl with foil and leave in the refrigerator for at least an hour. When you are ready to serve, pour the chilled champagne over the fruit and serve immediately.

DRY MARTINI
Traditionally, the proportions were one part dry vermouth to three parts gin, but most connoisseurs find this blend too sweet and reduce the quantity of vermouth as low as one part to seven or eight parts gin. Stir or shake with ice, strain into a small glass and serve with a twist of lemon peel or a small green olive. To make Vodka Martini, substitute vodka for gin.

BISHOPS' PUNCH
1 bottle sherry or port
2 oz (55 g) lump sugar
2 lemons
6 cloves
½ teaspoon mixed spice
10 fl oz (300 ml) water

Stick cloves into one lemon and roast in moderate oven for half an hour. Boil the water and spice together and heat the port or sherry in a separate pan. Pour the water and sherry or port into a bowl with the baked lemon. Rub sugar on rind of second lemon and add sugar and juice of lemon to wine mixture. Serve hot.

SIDECAR

Shake with ice one part lemon juice, one part Cointreau and two parts brandy. Strain into cocktail glass.

GREEN-EYED MONSTER

Stir with ice one part gin, one part sweet vermouth and one part green chartreuse. Strain into cocktail glass.

FRUIT CUP

20 fl oz (600 ml) fresh or canned
  orange juice
20 fl oz (600 ml) ginger ale
20 fl oz (600 ml) boiling water
4 oz (115 g) castor sugar
2 lemons
2 oranges finely sliced

Halve and squeeze the lemons. Put squeezed halves in bowl with sugar and boiling water. Stir to dissolve sugar and leave until cooled. Strain into jug, add lemon juice and orange juice and chill. Just before serving add ginger ale and orange slices.

HOT TODDY

10 fl oz (300 ml) brandy or rum
40 fl oz (1 litre) boiling water
6 eggs
4 tablespoons brown sugar
2 tablespoons lemon juice

Beat eggs and brown sugar together. Stir in brandy or rum and slowly add water. Mix well. Stir in lemon juice and serve in heated mugs.

CHAMPAGNE COCKTAIL

Put a sugar lump into a champagne glass and moisten it with Angostura Bitters. Add a teaspoon of brandy (optional) and fill glass with chilled champagne. Serve with a slice of orange.

MILK PUNCH

3 fl oz (85 ml) single cream
2 fl oz (55 ml) Bourbon
2 teaspoons castor sugar
⅛ teaspoon vanilla essence

Mix ingredients together then shake them vigorously with a few ice cubes, strain into glass and top with grated nutmeg.

CLARET CUP

1 bottle claret
1 bottle soda water
2 glasses Curaçao
1 dessertspoon castor sugar
several strips of lemon rind
several strips of cucumber rind

Chill in a large jug the claret, lemon and cucumber rind for at least one hour. Just before serving add Curaçao and soda water. Stir and sweeten to taste.

SOHO COCKTAIL

Shake with ice one part sweet vermouth, one part grapefruit juice and two parts chianti. Strain into a cocktail glass.

EIGHTEENTH-CENTURY MULLED WINE

1 bottle red wine
20 fl oz (600 ml) boiling water
1 wine glass orange Curaçao
1 wine glass brandy
12 lumps sugar
6 cloves
nutmeg

Bring sugar, cloves and wine almost to boiling point. Pour in boiling water and add Curaçao and brandy. Pour into glasses and grate nutmeg on top.

HET PINT

80 fl oz (2 litres) mild ale
1 teaspoon grated nutmeg
4 oz (115 g) sugar
3 eggs
10 fl oz (300 ml) whisky

Bring ale and nutmeg almost to boil in a thick-bottomed saucepan, stir in sugar and allow to dissolve. Beat eggs and add gradually to ale mixture, stirring all the time so that the mixture doesn't curdle. Add whisky and heat but do not boil. Pour mixture to and from heated tankards until clear.

PORT AND CLARET MULL

2 bottles claret
1 bottle ruby port
8 oz (225g) brown sugar
2 sticks cinnamon
pared rind of 2 lemons
12 cloves

Heat all ingredients together very slowly in saucepan to just below boiling. Simmer for five minutes, strain and serve.

MULLED ALE

40 fl oz (1 litre) ale
1 tablespoon castor sugar
pinch ground cloves
pinch ground nutmeg
pinch ground ginger
1 glass rum or brandy

Put all ingredients except the rum or brandy into a pan and bring almost to boiling point. Add brandy or rum, more sugar or flavouring if needed.

SCREWDRIVER

Shake with ice one part vodka to two parts orange juice. Strain and serve with ice and a slice of orange.

MULLED WINE

10 fl oz (300 ml) water
6 cloves
¼ oz (8 g) bruised cinnamon
¼ oz (8 g) nutmeg
½ lemon
30 fl oz (900 ml) port or claret
sugar

Gently heat water, spices and thinly peeled lemon rind. Bring almost to boil and simmer for 10 minutes. Strain into basin and add wine and sugar to taste. Return to pan and heat but do not boil. Serve at once.

Hangover Cures

The festive season is full of pitfalls for drinker and non-drinker alike. Systems used to coping with any number of whiskies or gin-and-tonics are startled into revolt by exotic cocktails and too much port. Near teetotallers get into the spirit with deceptively innocuous-looking mulled wines and fruit cups. Here are a few hints on how to cope with the wassail bowl.

BE PREPARED

Anticipate trouble and line the stomach before drinking. Tomato juice, milk, thick soup, even olive oil will all help.

AT THE PARTY

Don't mix drinks too much.
Beware of strange concoctions.
Eat something, even if it is only peanuts or cheese and biscuits.
If saying 'no thank you' gives offence, give offence. Your host will be even more offended if you get drunk.
If your legs start to wobble, slow down. Mix mineral water with the wine, or drink plain tonic.

AND SO TO BED

Never go to bed while your head is whirling. Exercise as much as you are able, drink lots of water and take deep slow breaths of fresh air.
Drink Alka-Seltzer or fizzy fruit salts or aspirin and a glass of hot water.

NEXT MORNING

Start with a refreshing bath or shower. Drink lots of water – fizzy mineral water is most effective and very refreshing with ice and a slice of lemon. Eat if you can. If not, drink tomato juice or shock your system with a Prairie Oyster: put into a glass two teaspoons of Worcester sauce, the whole yolk of an egg, a little red pepper and salt. Top with two teaspoons of malt vinegar. Get some fresh air.

HAIR OF THE DOG

Some people find that a nice cold glass of champagne has all the effervescent qualities of fruit salts, but a much more stimulating effect. Make a Buck's Fizz by mixing champagne half-and-half with fresh orange juice to get vitamin C at the same time. The medicinal-tasting Italian bitters, Fernet Branca, is widely recommended for hangovers. Brandy and soda has its fans, as does Bloody Mary: mix one part vodka to four parts tomato juice and stir in ice. Add a dash of Worcester sauce, a squeeze of lemon juice and a little pepper.

153

NEW YEAR BUFFET

The table for the New Year supper party should look interesting and inviting. Guests will feel flattered if you have taken trouble to make the evening a truly memorable start to the New Year. Table garlands of evergreen should be fixed securely to a strong linen or cotton cloth. Use foliage soft enough to allow guests to approach the table without damaging either themselves or their clothes. The central table decoration should be high to give a dramatic emphasis to the table and avoid confusion with the food. Arrange dishes logically so that guests can easily find all they need. Provide plenty of cutlery and china and choose food which is easy to manage, a change from heavy Christmas dishes and imaginatively arranged and displayed to tempt the appetite.

Ideal food for the buffet table is suggested opposite.

Top, left to right: a light, fresh flavoured fish terrine; diced cucumber and cream cheese, decorated with sliced cucumber and set with gelatine in a ring mould; Gâteau St. Honoré of choux pastry balls, filled with cream, surrounded with threads of spun caramellized sugar, candles added for a specially seasonal touch; a rich game terrine in a pastry case, pre-sliced so that guests can help themselves.

On the table, left to right: chilled refreshing watercress soup and sharp, iced cherry soup; glazed ham decorated with cherries (cut in thin slices before the party starts); savoury olives to eat with pâté or terrine; fresh tossed green salad (add French dressing at the last minute); game pie in a hot water pastry crust, complicated to make but much appreciated by guests; sliced oranges in caramel, decorated with purple grapes; a towering 'croquembouche' of iced, cream-filled choux pastry puffs, topped with a suitable decoration; pears stewed in Burgundy arranged in a raised bowl; water ice made from fresh fruit and piled high in the fruit itself.

Planning a Buffet

Entertaining friends, especially to a New Year buffet party, can be one of the high spots of the festive season. Plan your party well ahead and make careful preparations. The last minute party will usually leave guests feeling let down and the hosts in a state of nervous collapse. There are a few important points to bear in mind. Remember that many people give New Year parties so send your invitations out early or your guest list may be very depleted. Weather can be unpredictable at this time of year so don't cast your invitations too far afield unless you plan to ask people to stay overnight; ask people within easy reach. This is especially important considering the drink and drive laws operating in most countries. Don't start the party too early. It must be in full swing at midnight, so nine o'clock is a good time to begin. Make it clear on your invitation that you intend feeding your guests so that they don't arrive late and full.

Set out the buffet table in a different room from the main party and try to provide plenty of seating. Most people find it next to impossible to eat while balancing a plate and a glass. Allow plenty of room around the table for people to circulate easily so that more than one person at a time can serve themselves. Place food and equipment in a logical order so that guests know what they are supposed to eat, when and with which equipment. Always over-estimate your requirements on everything, plates, glasses, napkins and cutlery, even if you have to hire extra. When setting out the buffet table make your centre decoration high rather than wide so that it is out of the way of the food and provides an interesting focus for the table. The buffet table should look appetizing right through the meal, so without being too obvious, clear up the table as you go, remove dirty plates and abandoned glasses, refill empty dishes or replace them with others already prepared in the kitchen. While guests are eating it is a good idea to whisk quickly round the main party room to clear away used glasses and empty ashtrays so that the room is fresh and inviting to return to.

When you plan the menu for your buffet party, bear in mind that although most people love rich food, they will probably have had more

AULD LANG SYNE.—(BURNS.)

SHOULD auld ac-quaintance be for-got, and ne-ver brought to mind;

Should auld ac-quaintance be for-got, And days of Lang Syne.

For Auld Lang Syne, my dear, For Auld Lang

Syne ,We'll tak' a cup o' kind-ness Yet, For Auld Lang Syne.

than enough over Christmas, so provide plenty of light, refreshing alternatives. Select dishes that you know well and have cooked before: this isn't a time for experimenting with exotic new recipes which could prove to be a disaster. Choose food which is easy to manage, not thick slices of meat which are difficult to cut or sloppy food which could spill. Season all dishes well so that guests don't have to hunt around the table for the salt and pepper, although both should be provided. Limit the number of alternatives for each course to two, or possibly three, depending on the number of guests you are inviting, but have more than one dish of each so that several people can help themselves at once.

When setting out the table, arrange the food in a logical order starting with several piles of plates, napkins, cutlery and the first course. The main course and salads should be in the centre of the table, the dessert at the far end. Put some of the dishes on stands to give more room and make the table look interesting. Provide appropriate cutlery with the main course and dessert and supply plenty of serving spoons. If you are serving a ham or other large joint of meat, such as venison or a sucking pig, cut several slices in advance and have a competent carver at hand to cut more as required. Remember that if you wish to serve cold meat it should be allowed to cool before it is carved. It should also be sliced very fine so that people can manage it easily.

Wine, glasses and jugs of iced water should be put on a separate table, but if this is not possible place them at the far end of the buffet table away from the start of the meal so that people move along the table. Order wine and glasses in advance and on a sale-or-return basis. Buy good wine, poor drinks will soon make your guests feel ill. Allow one bottle per person and hire a third more glasses than guests. If you are serving white wine and space in the refrigerator is limited, keep it out of doors in buckets of ice. Provide some non-alcoholic drinks such as homemade lemonade or fresh orange juice with slices of orange — these are especially welcome and refreshing later in the evening. If you are serving a hot punch put all the ingredients into a pan but don't heat until the last minute. Coffee can be made in advance and kept in a thermos flask to be decanted into a heated coffee pot when required. Have champagne chilled and glasses ready for the midnight toast and calculate quantities to give every guest a good glassful.

Arrange for entertainment to continue afterwards. Dancing, a collection of horoscopes to read out, some beautifully arranged dishes of sweetmeats or perhaps some small but unusual New Year good luck gifts, will all ensure that your party ends on a suitably exciting and uplifting note.

Food for a Buffet

STARTERS

It is wise to try to keep this part of the meal simple and to plan food that you can prepare ahead. Keep the food light and don't overload your guests at this stage or they will not be able to do justice to what follows. A selection of three or four fish and meat pâtés, terrines, savoury mousses or a fine galantine, served with brown bread, toast or crusty French bread is always popular with guests. Try a rough country game terrine or a more delicately flavoured fish version, served en croûte in a pastry case for a change. Light fish mousses of smoked haddock, trout, salmon or mackerel, or kipper, hare or fine chicken liver pâté are all delicious. Provide bowls of olives and gherkins to eat with them.

Soups are more difficult to serve but are very appetizing, especially chilled ones like cold watercress soup topped with cream and chopped fresh watercress, or a light, piquant iced cherry soup. Ring moulds of cream cheese and chopped cucumber, or minced ham with cream and sherry set in gelatine also look attractive on a supper table and are easy to manage.

Everyone enjoys a well chosen and displayed bowl or basket of crudités. Cover them with a damp cloth until the very last moment to preserve their crispness. Use any seasonal vegetables. The following are especially good: fine sticks of carrot, strips of red or green peppers, sliced fennel, celery, florets of cauliflower, button mushrooms and small mild spring onions. Serve the crudités with a selection of dips such as sour cream beaten with Roquefort cheese, anchovies melted over a low heat and mixed with double cream or mashed avocado and home-made mayonnaise with yoghurt and a dash of Tabasco.

MAIN COURSE

The first decision to take is whether to serve a hot or cold main course. Naturally it is simpler to serve cold food but there are several dishes which can be pre-cooked and then warmed up just before the party.

Quiches are easy to serve and eat and can be made with an interesting variety of fillings; smoked salmon, smoked mackerel, spinach, leeks, asparagus, and prawns with diced bacon are all delicious.

Chopped chicken with sliced mushrooms in a white sauce with wine makes a good savoury filling for vol-au-vents and might also use up some Christmas leftovers.

Another useful party recipe for using leftovers is turkey croquettes. Minced turkey is mixed with chopped onion and breadcrumbs, bonded with egg and rolled into balls which are covered in breadcrumbs and deep fried. Serve on sticks with cocktail sausages and chicken livers baked rolled up in bacon.

Cold dishes might include cold sliced turkey or chicken in a light curry sauce with fresh green grapes or cold chicken in a tarragon and cream sauce. A large ham sliced thinly and served with creamy mustard sauce looks impressive as does a large, beautifully arranged plate of mixed cold meats, beef, tongue, ham, poultry, or galantine of chicken, served with Mostarda di Cremona, a delicious Italian preserve of fruits in syrup and mustard oil. A raised game, chicken or turkey pie with an attractively decorated lid will impress your guests, although it is time consuming to prepare.

If you want to take the trouble to cook something hot and really impressive, roast sucking pig on a bed of rosemary, or a saddle of venison are both stupendous. You could also try a fillet of beef baked in a pastry case, spreading the beef with pâté for extra flavour. Boned chicken is also good cooked en croûte. Try stuffing the boned chicken with chopped mushrooms before cooking.

You can serve jacket potatoes with your cold dishes and a good selection of salads. Any of the following are interesting and unusual. Broad beans with tiny onions and cubes of bacon; chicory with sliced oranges and walnuts; celery, red cabbage and walnuts in yoghurt dressing; red kidney beans with chopped green peppers and chopped onion with strong French dressing; endive frisées with walnuts, croutons and a walnut oil dressing or a mixed green salad of as many different green leaves as you can find. Potato salad can be served hot or cold – cold with sour cream, chopped chives or a little onion, or sliced or diced hot with a French dressing, chopped onion and bacon and black olives.

SWEETS

Pretty water ices piled up in the appropriate fruits – tangerines, pineapple or melon for example – make a refreshing change after heavy Christmas food, or try a seasonal cranberry sorbet, or chestnut ice decorated with cream and marrons glacés.

Peaches or pears baked in red wine are easy to make and look spectacular piled high on a stand.

Unusual fruit salads with the emphasis on colour look more attractive than the usual mixed bowl. Try slices of oranges with a caramel sauce and purple grapes, a green fruit salad of melon, grapes and kiwi fruit, or a bowl of purple-black grapes, bilberries, fresh figs and black cherries. You can work out other colour schemes with either seasonal or frozen fruits. Serve with a generous jug of thick cream.

For something a little richer try individual pots of chocolate mousse with brandy or Cointreau, glasses of Athol brose – a smooth mixture of cream, whisky and honey topped with walnuts, ginger syllabub with preserved ginger and a fresh green fruit salad, a sharp lemon mousse served with slices of lemon or cranberry fool with small meringues and cream.

Guests feel flattered to be served something a little unusual. An iced strawberry or chocolate soufflé looks much more difficult to make than it really is, a tart filled with rose flavoured cream and piled with crystallized rose petals is exciting, and fromage à la crème – whipped cream, cream cheese and whisked egg whites – can look lovely with a sparkling crust of castor sugar, served with purple grapes or fresh figs. A marvellously shaped port wine jelly served with little macaroons and clotted cream will also look pretty and inviting.

If you want to try your hand at something even more spectacular there are several recipes based on little choux pastry buns filled with whipped or vanilla flavoured cream. For 'profiterolles' these buns are piled up and covered with hot chocolate sauce, for Gâteaux St Honoré they are dipped in caramel, piled on a pastry case and surrounded by spun caramel sugar. The most glamorous of all is the French 'croquembouche' where the buns are given a coating, or a touch, of pretty icing, carefully balanced in a towering pile and topped with a star or some other suitable decoration.

For simpler tastes you can make fresh fruit flans with the fruit placed in pretty patterns and glazed, or serve lots of good fresh fruit in an ice bowl made by placing a mixing bowl inside one slightly larger, filling the space with water and freezing.

SAVOURIES

There are always guests who don't have a sweet tooth and would appreciate something savoury to end the meal. Provide a nicely arranged basket or plate with a selection of salty, cheesy, or plain water biscuits. Crisp sticks of celery or fennel, or even apples give a good fresh crunch with the cheese, and a bowl of mixed nuts to crack is always popular, if rather messy. A fine Stilton will please most guests, alternatively you could provide a selection of other cheeses. An interesting cheese board should include a hard cheese such as Cheddar or Cheshire, a good blue cheese, one of the excellent French soft textured cheeses such as Camembert or Brie, a mild cream cheese and maybe even a goat cheese. Make sure all cheeses are in peak condition and if you have had to keep them in a refrigerator allow plenty of time for them to reach room temperature. If you want to try something rather more adventurous you could make a Camembert ice cream or a tangy Roquefort mousse.

DISGUISE & FANCY DRESS

From the Roman celebrations of Saturnalia and Kalends, to the tradition of star singers and mumming, Victorian pantomime and parlour games, dressing up has played an essential part in midwinter festivities. Costumes can be elaborate or impromptu affairs.

A Victorian pantomime.

1 The giant is a two-man disguise with a child sitting high on an adult's shoulders covered by a suitable cloak.
2 The dwarf disguise needs two people to achieve the shrinking effect. It is most convincing when performed on a table.
3 A cardboard tree costume, complete with clinging ivy is given a seasonal touch with sprigs and crown of holly.
4 Skeletons are easily made to look sinister with clinging black clothes and a fluorescent outline of bones.
5 The three-legged man can provide endless amusement for children and adults alike. Practise manipulating the false third leg.
6 An elephantine version of the pantomime horse. Two adults with strong backs are needed if rides are given.

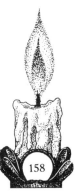

158

1

2

3

4

5

6

How to Disguise Yourself

Dressing up at Christmas and New Year is a centuries-old tradition. Costumes should not be elaborate, expensive affairs that you are afraid of spoiling, unless destined for a formal fancy dress party or competition. For normal family fun, charades and home entertainment, it is quite easy for ordinary people to disguise themselves as elephants, ducks, skeletons or witches with the most basic of props and a lot of imagination. All of the following ideas are easy to reproduce and provide effective disguise especially if make-up is also worn.

1 THE GIANT
Place a small child on the shoulders of an adult (fig 1) and throw a long cloak around the shoulders so that the person is completely hidden. Embel-

fig 1

lish with a hat, moustache and very long cane. To make a giant lady put a very long skirt round the adult's neck, wrap a cloak or shawl round the child's shoulders. You can add long pigtails, cap or bonnet and basket.

2 THE DWARF
A small child wearing a false moustache and beard rests his hands in a

fig 2

pair of boots on a table (fig 2). A taller person stands behind with his arms reaching over the child's shoulders. The only essential prop is a loose cloak to allow the arms of the taller person to appear as if they were the arms of the child. The child's upper arms are then clothed in a waistcoat or pullover in such a way as to suggest the body of a dwarf.

3 THE TREE
This is not an easy costume to move around or sit down in but it's effective for home entertainment. Make a long tube of slightly crumpled thick brown paper or, better still, use corrugated paper. Cut the top and bottom in ragged edges to suggest a hollow tree and roots. Paint with a good bark pattern and staple on some strands of ivy. Wear the paper tube over a matching polo-neck sweater and tights, preferably in green or brown. Cover your head with a balaclava helmet to which you have attached some twigs.

4 THE SKELETON
The more black clothes you can collect together the more effective this costume will be. It could be a combination of black tights, leotard, polo-neck

sweater, gloves and balaclava or black stocking pulled over the face, but the entire body must be covered. The face covering must be easy to breathe through. The skeleton is painted directly on to the material, so use old clothes. If you don't have suitable items available in black you can dye any old unwanted clothes black instead as long as you have enough to cover you completely. You can paint the skeleton on in white, but far more effective, especially at night, would be luminous paint. You may need two coats of paint to get a really clear skeleton.

5 THE THREE-LEGGED MAN
Dress as usual but wear an extra large overcoat. Stuff one sleeve of the coat with newspaper to make a false arm and attach a glove filled with cotton

fig 3

wool to the lining. Screw a length of broomstick to a wooden shoe tree in a third shoe and bind newspaper around the broomstick with Sellotape to make the shape of a leg. Tie on a discarded trouser leg. Your own arm manipulates the third leg from inside the coat. (fig 3) Practice until you can synchronize the movements.

6 THE WITCH
This disguise requires a tall black hat with straggly wool or string hair attached to it and some frightening make-up (fig 4). The witch will also need a large black sheet or curtain and a knotty stick. The hat is made by fitting

fig 4

a cone of black paper to the head and drawing a line round where it sits securely. Cut the card about 3cm below this line and cut up to line at several points and fold back into tabs. These are stuck to the underneath of a circle of black card with a circle cut out of the centre to fit the cone (fig 5).

fig 5

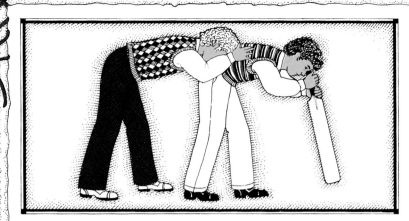

fig 6

7 THE ELEPHANT

This requires two people wearing galoshes or boots to bend forward, one behind the other, as if to form a pantomime horse (fig 6). The first carries a rolled grey rug to represent the elephant's trunk. A large dark grey blanket is spread over the two. Paper eyes are stuck or sewn on and ears of rags or felt added. Tusks are made from twisted white paper and pinned inside the blanket. A small tail of grey felt stitched round a length of rope can be attached.

8 SHAGGY ANIMALS

Make almost any sort of shaggy animal by drawing an animal face on stiff card. Add whiskers, teeth, ears or tusks and fix by elastic to the child's head. Cut holes to look through and allow a good breathing space if the mask is to cover the face. The child then goes on all fours, (fig 7) wearing wellington boots on the front 'paws'. An appropriately shaggy rug is then flung over the child's back and grunts and growls complete the disguise.

9 DANDY

To achieve the best effect this disguise should be worn by a man with a high receding forehead. A face is painted on the forehead and a false moustache

fig 8

added. The side hair is then brushed up and a large white cravat wound round to give a long elegant neck. Arrange the knot so that it hides a small hole cut to see through (fig 8). Carry a top hat and cane.

10 A ROMAN

One of the easiest of disguises. All you need are some thonged sandals, a T-shirt and a sheet. The sheet is draped over the body following the numbering shown in fig 9. One end of the sheet hangs down the body, the other is

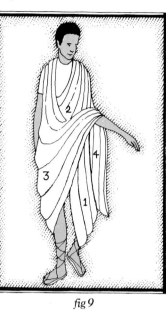

fig 9

taken over the shoulders and round the back and under the arm, then across the front, round behind the neck, then loosely across the front of the body to hang over the other arm. Add a laurel wreath to turn the Roman into a hero.

11 A DUCK

Strap a board to a child's back (fig 10). Pad the body out with old sheets, rags or towels to make a duck shape and tie the whole lot together with a large

sheet, knotted at the tail end. Make the head from a ball of rags tied in a cloth with two pieces of orange card for the bill. Stitch this to the body and add a feather duster or some feathers from the Christmas bird for the tail to disguise the knot. Stick orange card webbed feet on top of the child's own. Obviously this costume is best for family fun, not a long fancy dress party, as the child will find the back board cumbersome after a while.

MAKE-UP

Effective fancy dress relies heavily on make-up and disguise. False beards, fierce, beetling eyebrows, strange hair styles or bald heads and dramatic make-up all help to create an illusion. Masks can also come in useful for more bizarre effects. Make-up can be done with normal cosmetics or special face paints which are easy to remove and completely safe for children. Moustaches, beards and eyebrows can be painted on but look more convincing if you buy or make fabric based ones to stick on. Brushed rug wool, scraps of fur, or unravelled rough string can be used either glued to or woven into a muslin backing. String, long plaits of knitting wool, ringlets of

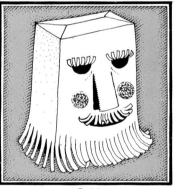

fig 11

wood parings or discarded wigs can be used to create hairstyles. Bald head shapes are easy to find in theatrical shops but can be made from the crown of an old hat or a fine swimcap. Spray paint flesh colour and stick tufts of 'hair' round the edges. The easiest way to make a mask is with a paper bag with gussets (fig 11). Paint on a face cutting holes for eyes, mouth and nose flap. Embellish with fringed paper.

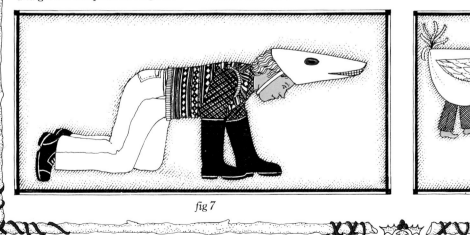

fig 7

fig 10

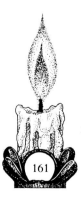

THE MEZZOTINT
M.R. James

 OME TIME ago I believe I had the pleasure of telling you the story of an adventure which happened to a friend of mine by the name of Dennistoun, during his pursuit of objects of art for the museum at Cambridge.

He did not publish his experiences very widely upon his return to England; but they could not fail to become known to a good many of his friends, and among others to the gentleman who at that time presided over an art museum at another University. It was to be expected that the story should make a considerable impression on the mind of a man whose vocation lay in lines similar to Dennistoun's, and that he should be eager to catch at any explanation of the matter which tended to make it seem improbable that he should ever be called upon to deal with so agitating an emergency. It was, indeed, somewhat consoling to him to reflect that he was not expected to acquire ancient MSS. for his institution; that was the business of the Shelburnian Library. The authorities of that might, if they pleased, ransack obscure corners of the Continent for such matters. He was glad to be obliged at the moment to confine his attentions to enlarging the already unsurpassed collection of English topographical drawings and engravings possessed by his museum. Yet, as it turned out, even a department so homely and familiar as this may have its dark corners, and to one of these Mr. Williams was unexpectedly introduced.

Those who have taken even the most limited interest in the acquisition of topographical pictures are aware that there is one London dealer whose aid is indispensable to their researches. Mr. J. W. Britnell publishes at short intervals very admirable catalogues of a large and constantly changing stock of engravings, plans, and old sketches of mansions, churches, and towns in England and Wales. These catalogues were, of course, the ABC of his subject to Mr. Williams: but as his museum already contained an enormous accumulation of topographical pictures, he was a regular, rather than a copious, buyer; and he rather looked to Mr. Britnell to fill up gaps in the rank and file of his collection than to supply him with rarities.

Now, in February of last year there appeared upon Mr. Williams's desk at the museum a catalogue from Mr. Britnell's emporium, and accompanying it was a typewritten communication from the dealer himself.

This letter ran as follows:

DEAR SIR,

We beg to call your attention to No. 978 in our accompanying catalogue, which we shall be glad to send on approval.

Yours faithfully, J. W. BRITNELL.

To turn to No. 978 in the accompanying catalogue was with Mr. Williams (as he observed to himself) the work of a moment, and in the place indicated he found the following entry:

978. – *Unknown.* Interesting mezzotint: View of a manor-house, early part of the century. 15 by 10 inches; black frame. £2.2s.

It was not specially exciting, and the price seemed high. However, as Mr. Britnell, who knew his business and his customer, seemed to set store by it, Mr. Williams wrote a postcard asking for the article to be sent on approval, along with some other engravings and sketches which appeared in the same catalogue. And so he passed without much excitement of anticipation to the ordinary labours of the day.

A parcel of any kind always arrives a day later than you expect it, and that of Mr. Britnell proved, as I believe the right phrase goes, no exception to the rule. It was delivered at the museum by the afternoon post of Saturday, after Mr. Williams had left his work, and it was accordingly brought round to his rooms in college by the attendant, in order that he might not have to wait over Sunday before looking through it and returning such of the contents as he did not propose to keep. And here he found it when he came in to tea, with a friend.

The only item with which I am concerned was the rather large, black-framed mezzotint of which I have already quoted the short description given in Mr. Britnell's catalogue. Some more details of it will have to be given, though I cannot hope to put before you the look of the picture as clearly as it is present to my own eye. Very nearly the exact duplicate of it may be seen in a good many old inn parlours, or in the passages of undisturbed country mansions at the present moment. It was a rather indifferent mezzotint, and an indifferent mezzotint is, perhaps, the worst form of engraving known. It presented a full-face view of a not very large manor-house of the last century, with three rows of plain sashed windows with rusticated masonry about them, a parapet with balls or vases at the angles, and a small portico in the centre. On either side were trees, and in front a considerable expanse of lawn. The legend 'A.W.F. sculpsit' was engraved on the narrow margin; and there was no further inscription. The whole thing gave the impression that it was the work of an amateur. What in the world Mr. Britnell could mean by affixing the price of £2 2s to such an object was more than Mr. Williams could imagine. He turned it over with a good deal of contempt; upon the back was a paper label, the left-hand half of which had been torn off. All that remained were the ends of two lines of writing: the first had the letters *--ngley Hall*; the second, *--ssex.*

It would, perhaps, be just worth while to identify the place represented, which he could easily do with the help of a gazetteer, and then he would send it back to Mr. Britnell, with some remarks reflecting upon the judgement of that gentleman.

He lighted the candles, for it was now dark, made the tea, and supplied the friend with whom he had been playing golf (for I believe the authorities of the University I write of indulged in that pursuit by way of relaxation); and tea was taken to the accompaniment of a discussion which golfing persons can imagine for themselves, but which the conscientious writer has no right to inflict upon any non-golfing persons.

The conclusion arrived at was that certain strokes might have been better, and that in certain emergencies neither player had experienced that amount of luck which a human being has a right to expect. It was now that the friend – let us call him Professor Binks – took up the framed engraving, and said:

'What's this place, Williams?'

'Just what I am going to try to find out,' said Williams, going to the shelf for a gazetteer. 'Look at the back. Somethingley Hall, either in Sussex or Essex. Half the name's gone, you see. You don't happen to know it, I suppose?'

'It's from that man Britnell, I suppose, isn't it?' said Binks. 'Is it for the museum?'

'Well, I think I should buy it if the price was five shillings,' said Williams; 'but for some unearthly reason he wants two guineas for it. I can't conceive why. It's a wretched engraving, and there aren't even any figures to give it life.'

'It's not worth two guineas, I should think,' said Binks; 'but I don't think it's so badly done. The moonlight seems rather good to me; and I should have thought there *were* figures, or at least a figure, just on the edge in front.'

'Let's look,' said Williams. 'Well, it's true the light is rather cleverly given. Where's your figure? Oh yes! Just the head, in the very front of the picture.'

And indeed there was – hardly more than a black blot on the extreme edge of the engraving – the head of a man or woman, a good deal muffled up, the back turned to the spectator, and looking towards the house.

Williams had not noticed it before.

'Still,' he said, 'though it's a cleverer thing than I thought, I can't spend two guineas of museum money on a picture of a place I don't know.'

Professor Binks had his work to do, and soon went; and very nearly up to Hall time Williams was engaged in a vain attempt to identify the subject of his picture. 'If the vowel before the *ng* had only been left, it would have been easy enough,' he thought; 'but as it is, the name may be anything from Guestingley to Langley, and there are many more names ending like this than I thought; and this rotten book has no index of terminations.'

Hall in Mr. Williams's college was at seven. It need not be dwelt upon; the less so as he met there colleagues who had been playing golf during the afternoon, and words with which we have no concern were freely bandied across the table – merely golfing words, I would hasten to explain.

I suppose an hour or more to have been spent in what is called common-room after dinner. Later in the evening some few retired to Williams's rooms, and I have little doubt that whist was played and tobacco smoked. During a lull in these operations Williams picked up the mezzotint from the table without looking at it, and handed it to a person mildly interested in art, telling him where it had come from, and the other particulars which we already know.

The gentleman took it carelessly, looked at it, then said, in a tone of some interest:

'It's really a very good piece of work, Williams; it has quite a feeling of the romantic period. The light is admirably managed, it seems to me, and the figure, though it's rather too grotesque, is somehow very impressive.'

'Yes, isn't it?' said Williams, who was just then busy giving whisky-and-soda to others of the company, and was unable to come across the room to look at the view again.

It was by this time rather late in the evening, and the visitors were on the move. After they went Williams was obliged to write a letter or two and clear up some odd bits of work. At last, some time past midnight, he was disposed to turn in, and he put out his lamp after lighting his bedroom candle. The picture lay face upwards on the table where the last man who looked at it had put it, and it caught his eye as he turned the lamp down. What he saw made him very nearly drop the candle on the floor, and he declares now that if he had been left in the dark at that moment he would have had a fit. But, as that did not happen, he was able to put down the light on the table and take a good look at the picture. It was indubitable – rankly impossible, no doubt, but absolutely certain. In the middle of the lawn in front of the unknown house there was a figure where no figure had been at five o'clock that afternoon. It was crawling on all-fours towards the house, and it was muffled in a strange black garment with a white cross on the back.

I do not know what is the ideal course to pursue in a situation of this kind. I can only tell you what Mr. Williams did. He took the picture by one corner and carried it across the passage to a second set of rooms which he possessed. There he locked it up in a drawer, sported the doors of both sets of rooms, and retired to bed; but first he wrote out and signed an account of the extraordinary change which the picture had undergone since it had come into his possession.

Sleep visited him rather late; but it was consoling to reflect that the behaviour of the picture did not depend upon his own unsupported testimony. Evidently the man who had looked at it the night before had seen something of the same kind as he had, otherwise he might have been tempted to think that something gravely wrong was happening either to his eyes or his mind. This possibility being fortunately precluded, two matters awaited him on the morrow. He must take stock of the picture very carefully, and call in a witness for the purpose, and he must make a determined effort to ascertain what house it was that was represented. He would therefore ask his neighbour Nisbet to breakfast with him, and he would subsequently spend a morning over the gazetteer.

Nisbet was disengaged, and arrived about 9.30. His host was not quite dressed, I am sorry to say, even at this late hour. During breakfast nothing was said about the mezzotint by Williams, save that he had a picture on which he wished for Nisbet's opinion. But those who are familiar with University life can picture for themselves the wide and delightful range of subjects over which the conversation of two Fellows of Canterbury College is likely to extend during a Sunday morning breakfast. Hardly a topic was left unchallenged, from golf to lawn-tennis. Yet I am bound to say that Williams was rather distraught; for his interest naturally centred in that very strange picture which was now reposing, face downwards, in the drawer in the room opposite.

The morning pipe was at last lighted, and the moment had arrived for which he looked. With very considerable – almost tremulous – excitement, he ran across, unlocked the drawer, and, extracting the picture – still face downwards – ran back, and put it into Nisbet's hands.

'Now,' he said, 'Nisbet, I want you to tell me exactly what you see in that picture. Describe it, if you don't mind, rather minutely. I'll tell you why afterwards.'

'Well,' said Nisbet, 'I have here a view of a country-house – English, I presume – by moonlight.'

'Moonlight? You're sure of that?'

'Certainly. The moon appears to be on the wane, if you wish for details, and there are clouds in the sky.'

'All right. Go on. I'll swear,' added Williams in an aside, 'there was no moon when I saw it first.'

'Well, there's not much more to be said,' Nisbet continued. 'The house has one – two – three rows of windows, five in each row, except at the bottom, where there's a porch instead of the middle one, and —'

'But what about figures?' said Williams, with marked interest.

'There aren't any,' said Nisbet; 'but —'

'What! No figure on the grass in front?'

'Not a thing.'

'You'll swear to that?'

'Certainly I will. But there's just one other thing.'

'What?'

'Why, one of the windows on the ground-floor – left of the door – is open.'

'Is it really? My goodness! he must have got in,' said Williams, with great excitement; and he hurried to the back of the sofa on which Nisbet was sitting, and, catching the picture from him, verified the matter for himself.

It was quite true. There was no figure, and there was the open window. Williams, after a

163

moment of speechless surprise, went to the writing-table and scribbled for a short time. Then he brought two papers to Nisbet, and asked him first to sign one – it was his own description of the picture, which you have just heard – and then to read the other, which was Williams's statement written the night before.

'What can it all mean?' said Nisbet.

'Exactly,' said Williams. 'Well, one thing I must do – or three things, now I think of it. I must find out from Garwood' – this was his last night's visitor – 'what he saw, and then I must get the thing photographed before it goes further, and then I must find out what the place is.'

'I can do the photographing myself,' said Nisbet, 'and I will. But you know, it looks very much as if we were assisting at the working out of a tragedy somewhere. The question is, Has it happened already, or is it going to come off? You must find out what the place is. Yes,' he said, looking at the picture again, 'I expect you're right: he has got in. And if I don't mistake there'll be the devil to pay in one of the rooms upstairs.'

'I'll tell you what,' said Williams: 'I'll take the picture across to old Green' (this was the senior Fellow of the College, who had been Bursar for many years). 'It's quite likely he'll know it. We have property in Essex and Sussex, and he must have been over the two counties a lot in his time.'

'Quite likely he will,' said Nisbet; 'but just let me take my photograph first. But look here, I rather think Green isn't up to-day. He wasn't in Hall last night, and I think I heard him say he was going down for the Sunday.'

'That's true too,' said Williams; 'I know he's gone to Brighton. Well, if you'll photograph it now, I'll go across to Garwood and get his statement, and you keep an eye on it while I'm gone. I'm beginning to think two guineas is not a very exorbitant price for it now.'

In a short time he had returned, and brought Mr. Garwood with him. Garwood's statement was to the effect that the figure, when he had seen it, was clear of the edge of the picture, but had not got far across the lawn. He remembered a white mark on the back of its drapery, but could not have been sure it was a cross. A document to this effect was then drawn up and signed, and Nisbet proceeded to photograph the picture.

'Now what do you mean to do?' he said. 'Are you going to sit and watch it all day?'

'Well, no, I think not,' said Williams. 'I rather imagine we're meant to see the whole thing. You see, between the time I saw it last night and this morning there was time for lots of things to happen, but the creature only got into the house. It could easily have got through its business in the time and gone to its own place again; but the fact of the window being open, I think, must mean that it's in there now. So I feel quite easy about

leaving it. And, besides, I have a kind of idea that it wouldn't change much, if at all, in the daytime. We might go out for a walk this afternoon, and come in to tea, or whenever it gets dark. I shall leave it out on the table here, and sport the door. My skip can get in, but no one else.'

The three agreed that this would be a good plan; and, further, that if they spent the afternoon together they would be less likely to talk about the business to other people; for any rumour of such a transaction as was going on would bring the whole of the Phasmatological Society about their ears.

We may give them a respite until five o'clock.

At or near that hour the three were entering Williams's staircase. They were at first slightly annoyed to see that the door of his rooms was unsported; but in a moment it was remembered that on Sunday the skips came for orders an hour or so earlier than on week-days. However, a surprise was awaiting them. The first thing they saw was the picture leaning up against a pile of books on the table, as it had been left, and the next thing was Williams's skip, seated on a chair opposite, gazing at it with undisguised horror. How was this? Mr. Filcher (the name is not my own invention) was a servant of considerable standing, and set the standard of etiquette to all his own college and to several neighbouring ones, and nothing could be more alien to his practice than to be found sitting on his master's chair, or appearing to take any particular notice of his master's furniture or pictures. Indeed, he seemed to feel this himself. He started violently when the three men came into the room, and got up with a marked effort. Then he said:

'I ask your pardon, sir, for taking such a freedom as to set down.'

'Not at all, Robert,' interposed Mr. Williams. 'I was meaning to ask you some time what you thought of that picture.'

'Well, sir, of course I don't set up my opinion again yours, but it ain't the pictur I should 'ang where my little girl could see it, sir.'

'Wouldn't you, Robert? Why not?'

'No, sir. Why, the pore child, I recollect once she see a Door Bible, with pictures not 'alf what that is, and we 'ad to set up with her three or four nights afterwards, if you'll believe me; and if she was to ketch a sight of this skellinton here, or whatever it is, carrying off the pore baby, she would be in a taking. You know 'ow it is with children; 'ow nervish they git with a little thing and all. But what I should say, it don't seem a right pictur to be laying about, sir, not where anyone that's liable to be startled could come on it. Should you be wanting anything this evening, sir? Thank you, sir.'

With these words the excellent man went to continue the round of his masters, and you may

be sure the gentlemen whom he left lost no time in gathering round the engraving. There was the house, as before, under the waning moon and the drifting clouds. The window that had been open was shut, and the figure was once more on the lawn: but not this time crawling cautiously on hands and knees. Now it was erect and stepping swiftly, with long strides, towards the front of the picture. The moon was behind it, and the black drapery hung down over its face so that only hints of that could be seen, and what was visible made the spectators profoundly thankful that they could see no more than a white dome-like forehead and a few straggling hairs. The head was bent down, and the arms were tightly clasped over an object which could be dimly seen and identified as a child, whether dead or living it was not possible to say. The legs of the appearance alone could be plainly discerned, and they were horribly thin.

From five to seven the three companions sat and watched the picture by turns. But it never changed. They agreed at last that it would be safe to leave it, and that they would return after Hall and await further developments.

When they assembled again, at the earliest possible moment, the engraving was there, but the figure was gone, and the house was quiet under the moonbeams. There was nothing for it but to spend the evening over gazetteers and guide-books. Williams was the lucky one at last, and perhaps he deserved it. At 11.30 p.m. he read from Murray's *Guide to Essex* the following lines:

16½ miles, *Anningley*. The church has been an interesting building of Norman date, but was extensively classicized in the last century. It contains the tombs of the family of Francis, whose mansion, Anningley Hall, a solid Queen Anne house, stands immediately beyond the churchyard in a park of about 80 acres. The family is now extinct, the last heir having disappeared mysteriously in infancy in the year 1802. The father, Mr. Arthur Francis, was locally known as a talented amateur engraver in mezzotint. After his son's disappearance he lived in complete retirement at the Hall, and was found dead in his studio on the third anniversary of the disaster, having just completed an engraving of the house, impressions of which are of considerable rarity.'

This looked like business, and, indeed, Mr. Green on his return at once identified the house as Anningley Hall.

'Is there any kind of explanation of the figure, Green?' was the question which Williams naturally asked.

'I don't know, I'm sure, Williams. What used to be said in the place when I first knew it, which was before I came up here, was just this: old

Francis was always very much down on these poaching fellows, and whenever he got a chance he used to get a man whom he suspected of it turned off the estate, and by degrees he got rid of them all but one. Squires could do a lot of things then that they daren't think of now. Well, this man that was left was what you find pretty often in the country – the last remains of a very old family. I believe they were Lords of the Manor at one time. I recollect just the same thing in my own parish.'

'What, like the man in *Tess of the D'Urbervilles?*' Williams put in.

'Yes, I dare say; it's not a book I could ever read myself. But this fellow could show a row of tombs in the church there that belonged to his ancestors, and all that went to sour him a bit; but Francis, they said, could never get at him – he always kept just on the right side of the law – until one night the keepers found him at it in a wood right at the end of the estate. I could show you the place now; it marches with some land that used to belong to an uncle of mine. And you can imagine there was a row; and this man Gawdy (that was the name, to be sure – Gawdy; I thought I should get it – Gawdy), he was unlucky enough, poor chap! to shoot a keeper. Well, that was what Francis wanted, and grand juries – you know what they would have been then – and poor Gawdy was strung up in double-quick time; and I've been shown the place he was buried in, on the north side of the church – you know the way in that part of the world: anyone that's been hanged or made away with themselves, they bury them that side. And the idea was that some friend of Gawdy's – not a relation, because he had none, poor devil! he was the last of his line: kind of *spes ultima gentis* – must have planned to get hold of Francis's boy and put an end to *his* line, too. I don't know – it's rather an out-of-the-way thing for an Essex poacher to think of – but, you know, I should say now it looks more as if old Gawdy had managed the job himself. Booh! I hate to think of it! have some whisky, Williams!'

The facts were communicated by Williams to Dennistoun, and by him to a mixed company, of which I was one, and the Sadducean Professor of Ophiology another. I am sorry to say that the latter, when asked what he thought of it, only remarked: 'Oh, those Bridgeford people will say anything' – a sentiment which met with the reception it deserved.

I have only to add that the picture is now in the Ashleian Museum; that it has been treated with a view to discovering whether sympathetic ink has been used in it, but without effect; that Mr. Britnell knew nothing of it save that he was sure it was uncommon; and that, though carefully watched, it has never been known to change again.

LUCK & SUPERSTITIONS

Almost everything that happens at the New Year affects the fortunes of the coming twelve months so you cannot be too careful how you spend your time. If you are good-humoured or quarrelsome, that will be your mood for the rest of the year. If you want to be rich and well fed, make sure that you have money in your pockets, that you eat lavishly and your cupboards are well stocked. A brief spell of labour will guard against ruin or, in the case of housework, ensure domestic fortune. Complete all business transactions as anything unfinished will stay with you through the New Year. Anything borrowed and not returned will mean dependence on others. Nothing that normally forms part of the household should leave it – be it a person or a sack of rubbish – or there will be a loss to the family in the coming year. It is particularly unlucky to let a fire die or take a light out of the house.

The first person to cross the threshold after midnight indicates the sort of luck the household can expect in the coming year. Care is still taken in Scotland to ensure that the First Footer is auspicious. Requirements vary, but generally the preferred First Footer is a man, dark-haired (a fair-haired man might have been a Viking invader), healthy, good natured and prosperous with a foot 'that water runs under' – flat feet, poor eyesight and other physical defects are ill omens. The bad luck brought by an ill-fated First Footer may be averted by throwing salt on the fire before he (or, worse, she) enters, speaking first, making the sign of the cross or putting a red

The First Footer is welcomed into a Scottish home just after midnight on New Year's Eve.

ember into a pan of water as soon as he or she leaves. But it is easier to make sure the First Footer is someone with the right qualifications. The First Footer should bring a symbolic gift or 'handsel' – to arrive empty-handed is unlucky. Fuel, usually a piece of coal, is a common gift. Salt for hospitality or bread for life have also been carried. In rural areas a sheaf of corn is popular; in fishing communities, a red herring. Whisky is always welcome. The First Footer wishes the family a happy New Year, kisses all the women and shares a drink with the party. Though the custom is now best known as part of the Hogmanay celebrations it used to be common in other parts of Europe.

The first sight on New Year's Day was also held to be an omen for the coming year. In northern England to see a man with his arms loaded was lucky. Elsewhere beggars and grave diggers brought misfortune. Bavarians thought it bad luck to encounter a cat before meeting another person, but the Scots were delighted to look from the windows and see an animal facing their way – though if it faced in the other direction it was bad luck.

Germans anxious to peer into the future used to drop molten lead into cold water and deduce from the shapes what the fates held in store for them – a ship might mean a journey, a heart a marriage. In England the shapes indicated the occupation of a girl's future husband. In Scotland a slice of Hogmanay cheese or a piece of rind with a hole cut in it was lucky, and useful for dreaming on. Likewise, anyone putting nine holly leaves tied in nine knots in a handkerchief under the pillow would dream of a future spouse. Eating black-eyed peas brought good fortune in the southern states of America. The Swiss ate whipped cream, dropping some on the floor to signify abundance. Several nations believed that the shape of the ashes of the previous night's fire could be 'read' first thing on New Year's Day. If a foot was discerned with the toes pointing to the door then someone was going to leave the family circle. Toes pointing away from the door meant an addition to the household. In Scotland, a brightly burning fire on the morning of New Year's Day portended prosperity in the coming year, a dull one indicated trouble.

Unfortunately few people now believe in these superstitions and the customs connected with them have fallen into disuse. But everyone still wants to turn over a new leaf with the start of a New Year – and how better to start than rich, well fed and happy.

EPIPHANY

PIPHANY is one of the oldest and most important festivals in the Christian church. Its name derives from the Greek word for manifestation, as the feast on 6 January commemorates first of all the manifestation of Christ to the Gentiles at the Adoration of the Magi. It also marks Christ's baptism by John the Baptist and the first miracle, the transformation of water into wine at the wedding feast at Cana. Before 25 December was selected as the date of the Nativity many sections of the Church believed that 6 January was His physical as well as His spiritual birthday, others that He was not born divine but attained divinity on His baptism. Since the acceptance of 25 December, Epiphany in the Eastern church has been primarily noted for the baptism; in the Western Church, for the visit of the Magi.

It is unclear how the Magi came to be known as the Three Kings. The number of Magi varied in the past anywhere from two to twelve, but the Western Church finally settled for three, presumably to equal the number of gifts. They probably came from Persia and were disciples of Zoroaster. Gradually they were assigned names and characteristics. Young Caspar brought frankincense for divinity, old Melchior bore gold for kingship and black Balthazar carried myrrh for humanity and the bitterness of the Crucifixion.

Their arrival at the stable in Bethlehem was celebrated on Twelfth Night with a party. It was a popular festival, the final fling at the end of the Christmas season. The Twelfth Night cake, baked in honour of the Kings, contained a bean and a pea, and whoever found them played king

and queen for the evening, ordering games and demanding forfeits just like the Lord of Misrule and the king who presided over the Saturnalian revels. Sometimes other charms were mixed into the cake – bells for a wedding, perhaps, or a thimble for an old maid. In ancient times the bean itself was a sacred vegetable. In England the tradition of the cake goes back as far as the medieval court of Edward II. Now it has merged with the Christmas cake: many of the old Epiphany customs have moved back to New Year and Christmas.

The Wise Men, an engraving after Gustav Doré.

The Twelfth Night party was even more popular in France. The finder of the bean or a porcelain figure played king for the night and the ceremony used to be surrounded by other rituals and practices. In Berry the Gâteau des Rois was divided among the number of guests plus one, the extra piece being called *la part du bon Dieu* and given to the first person to claim it – usually a visiting band of children who came and sang a song. Sometimes the appointed king dressed in full robes and was accompanied by a fool. In Lorraine the first slice of cake was for *le bon Dieu*, the second for the Blessed Virgin, and these two portions were given to the first poor person to ask. The Gâteau des Rois is still one of the high spots of the season in French homes. Epiphany cakes and kings were also found in Holland and Germany.

The Three Kings, bearing gold, frankincense and myrrh, were natural candidates for the roles of gift-bringers. Spanish children leave out empty shoes and straw for the camels and hope that the Kings passing by on their annual visit to Bethlehem will take the straw and fill the shoes with sweets and presents. 6 January is a public holiday featuring parades heralding the arrival of the Three Kings and firework displays. The Three Kings extended their activities to those South American countries that came under Spanish influence and Epiphany is still the chief time for Mexican and Puerto Rican children to receive presents. Syrian children receive their presents at the same time from the Wise Men's smallest camel, which refused to give up the arduous journey to Bethlehem. The camel was rewarded by Jesus for his determination by the gift of immortality and renewed strength.

'Burning the Christmas Greens' an engraving from Harper's Weekly, Christmas 1876.

In Italy presents are brought not by the Three Kings – though their arrival is celebrated – but by Befana, whose name is a corruption of Epiphany. According to legend, this old woman was busy cleaning her house when the Wise Men passed by. When she learned where they were going she asked them to wait until she had finished her work so that she could go with them, but they would not wait. Later she set out to follow them, lost their track and has been searching ever since for Jesus. Riding a broomstick, Befana goes down chimneys and leaves gifts in stockings for all children in the hope that one might be the Holy Child. Naughty children are supposed to receive a lump of coal, but these days it is usually made of marzipan. Russian children used to be visited at Epiphany by a similar character called Babouschka, or 'grandmother'. Legend has it that she misdirected the Three Magi and in atonement must wander the earth in a hopeless search for Jesus. Recently she has been replaced by Grandfather Frost.

A number of other national customs are – or used to be – connected with Epiphany and the end of the festive season. Epiphany used to be very important in Germany. Relics alleged to be those of the Three Magi were brought to Cologne in 1164 and the great cathedral was built to house their shrine. In the old days on the eve of 6 January, houses and stables were smoked out by burning consecrated branches, and 'C+M+B' – the initials of the Three Kings – together with the year were written in consecrated chalk over the door. In some regions parties of Star Singers, often dressed as the Magi – went from door to door singing, in exchange for gifts of food. Similar customs were found in Poland, Czechoslovakia, Switzerland and Sweden, where Star Boys also used to write 'C+M+B' over front doors at Epiphany.

In Hungary the Three Kings were played by small children in folk costumes. They had set out at Christmas to re-enact the journey and finally arrived at the stable on Twelfth Night.

Twelfth Night is called Thirteenth Night in Iceland and is celebrated with dancing round bonfires – the participants often dressed as elves. Icelandic cattle gain the power of speech at Epiphany rather than on Christmas Eve. In Ireland 6 January is called Women's Christmas or Little Christmas. On the eve the Christmas candles are lit for the last time and after the meal on Women's Christmas Day there is the custom of the Thanksgiving Drink. In memory of the wedding feast at Cana it is believed that water turns to wine between sunset on 5 January and daybreak the following day. In Denmark three candles are sometimes lit as a token substitute for the tree which by now is in the garden hung with fat and nuts for the birds. The Yugoslavian Kolach cake is finally eaten after all three candles have been lit. In Greek communities 6 January is Greek Cross Day and is celebrated with the Blessing of the Waters in commemoration of the turning of water into wine, and of Christ's Baptism.

Under the Julian Calendar January 5 is Old Christmas Eve. Old Christmas is particularly noted for the legend of the Glastonbury Thorn, a tree which grew from Joseph of Aramathea's staff and which always bloomed at Christmas. When England adopted the Gregorian calendar in 1752 there was great curiosity to see which Christmas – Old or New – the tree would blossom on. The diehards were encouraged to ignore the new calendar when the tree chose the old date. Those English fruit trees which had not been wassailed at Christmas or the New Year received encouragement on the Eve of Epiphany.

These days Epiphany is mainly marked as being the end of the festive season and the time to take down all decorations. Greenery is burned, buried or saved until next year, according to local custom, and cribs are dismantled. As well as signifying the end of Christmas, Epiphany used to see the start of the South American carnival season, which continued until Shrove Tuesday, but now these carnivals are limited to the three days just before Lent.

In England the day after Epiphany is called St Distaff's Day and was traditionally the time for women to return to their spinning, though the men managed to delay their return to work until Plough Monday, the first Monday after Epiphany. Finally 2 February, Candlemas, saw the Feast of the Purification of the Virgin and the Presentation of Christ in the Temple. Candles were blessed in church and the final farewells were said to Christmas with the kindling of the Christmas brand from the Yule log. Sometimes a bowl of snowdrops was put in place of the Christmas evergreens to signify that Candlemas was not just the end of Christmas but the start of spring.

CLEARING UP

In olden days, the prudent house-holder could not be too careful when getting rid of decorations. Although the Christmas greenery was intrinsically lucky, one mistake in its disposal could bring bad luck on the family for the rest of the year. House decorations had to stay up until Epiphany, those in the church until Candlemas. The mistletoe bough, a remedy against poison and a guarantee of fertility, was kept until the new one was cut the following year. Holly had to be burned or buried, left to shirvel or fed to the cows, according to local custom. Sometimes a sprig was kept for good luck. It was considered most inauspicious to drop a piece of holly while removing it from the house. Charcoal from the Yule log was carefully preserved. It was believed to prevent lightning from striking the house and guarded people and animals from various diseases. Fed to the cows or dug into the earth, it encouraged fertility. Spring-sown seeds benefited if charcoal was ploughed into the field.

Although few people nowadays would go to these lengths when they take down their decorations, it is still a good idea to pack up carefully after the Christmas celebrations have drawn to a close.

THE CHRISTMAS TREE
If your Christmas tree was for 'one season only', you will probably find a pile of needles underneath. These can be swept up and dug into the garden, where they will benefit other plants. Small twigs and branches can be used for kindling wood and the trunk can be sawn into sections to provide aromatic logs. If you bought a rooted tree, planning to keep it for another year, you will probably have bedded it into a suitable tub already. If so, carry the tub into the garden, water well and place in a sheltered spot until the tree has had time to acclimatize. If you wish to replant the tree, dig a hole deep enough to allow the roots plenty of room and loosen the roots if they have become cramped in the tub. Fork some peat into the earth and make sure the tree is firmly bedded in and well watered.

CHRISTMAS TREE LIGHTS
Check the lights are in good working order before you put them away. Tighten the bulbs and wrap the flex carefully around a strong piece of card. Put the lights in a box with a layer of sponge or cotton wool on either side to protect the bulbs.

TREE DECORATIONS
To ensure these survive safely from year to year, wrap each one separately in soft kitchen paper and pack them in a strong cardboard box.

WRAPPING PAPER
Now that so many people rely on Sellotape to hold their packages together, wrapping paper is often damaged beyond reuse. However, there are often parts which survive. Cut these out, iron on the wrong side with a warm iron and wrap around a cardboard tube. These small pieces will come in useful next year to wrap tree presents or little packages and will save cutting into a large, expensive sheet.

WREATH FRAME
If you have bought or made an effective wreath frame, unpick the dead foliage and wipe the frame clean. Dry thoroughly with kitchen paper, rub with a little oil and wrap in newspaper.

CHRISTMAS CARDS
People often jot changes of address on their Christmas cards, so when you take your cards down, check them through for any messages or notes. If you do not want to keep the cards, look in the newspaper for charities who might be able to use them, or take the cards to a local nursery school for the children to use in their artwork. Another nice idea is to keep the more original or colourful cards and make a collage. This unusual decoration will serve as a reminder of happy Christmases of the past.

Twelfth Night
LOUIS MACNEICE

Snow-happy hicks of a boy's world –
O crunch of bull's eyes in the mouth,
O crunch of frost beneath the foot –
If time would only remain furled
In white, and thaw were not for certain
And snow would but stay put, stay put!

When the pillar-box wore a white bonnet –
O harmony of roof and hedge,
O parity of sight and thought –
And each flake had your number on it
And lives were round for not a number
But equalled nought, but equalled nought!

But now the sphinx must change her shape –
O track that reappears through slush,
O broken riddle, burst grenade –
And lives must be pulled out like tape
To measure something not themselves,
Things not given but made, but made.

For now the time of gifts is gone –
O boys that grow, O snows that melt,
O bathos that the years must fill –
Here is dull earth to build upon
Undecorated; we have reached
Twelfth Night or what you will . . . you will.

Christmas Bills

(With the humblest possible apology to the shade of Edgar Allan Poe.)

JOSEPH HATTON

I

SEE dear Pater with the bills –
                  Christmas bills!
What unhappy omination their presence
                  now fulfils!
How they wrinkle, wrinkle, wrinkle
                  Pater's frowning brow!
While figures oversprinkle
Paper that seems to twinkle
                  Three columns in a row.
Keeping time, time, time
In a sort of Runic rhyme
To the concatenacious thought that so
                  uncomfortably fills
Pater's mind from the bills, bills, bills,
    Bills, bills, bills –
From the winking and the blinking of the
                  bills.

II

Here are Monsieur Vintner's bills,
    Sherry bills!
How the Spanish golden liquor woeful
    melancholy kills!
In the murky air of night
What glories, what delight!
    From the molten golden stream
    Like a happy summer dream;
      And all the time
    What a fragrant sweet perfume
    Floats all about the room
      Above the table.
    Oh! how the bosom thrills!
But how it saddens with the bills –
    Christmas bills,
    Vintner's bills,
And all the other ills
That the time is bringing in
    With the bills, bills, bills, bills,
    Bills, bills, bills –
That the time is bringing in with the bills.

III

Here are Madame Fashion's bills,
    Brazen bills,
    Mill'ner's bills
Made up chiefly— silks, so much, and so
                  much more for frills,
    The startled eye of Pater
    How it looks from that to Mater;
      Too much horrified to speak,
      Pater only gives a squeak
                  Out of tune,
In a clamorous appealing to the mercy of his
                  spouse,
In a mad expostulation 'gainst the ruin of his
                  house.
    Mater's courage leaping higher
    With a desperate desire
    And a resolute endeavour
    Now, now to be or never,
Sufficient mistress of her purse
    To get rid of all such bills
                  In the future –
    Such "horrid nasty" bills,
    Such dreadful brazen bills,
    At the closing, the weird closing
                  Of the year!

IV

Come now the Doctor's bills –
    Welcome bills!
What a world of solemn thought their
                  monody distils
    In the mind!
At the melancholy menace of the time
    When throughout the livelong night
    We shivered with affright,
And marked each echoing chime
                  With a groan!

And the people – ah the people!
They that dwell up in the steeple
    All alone
Thought of tolling, tolling
In that muffled monotone,
Whilst Doctor Mills was rolling
    From the human heart a stone;
And those people in the steeple
    That are ghouls,
Yelled fierce and shrill and loud,
When Doctor Mills allowed
    His hungry patient rolls,
      Penny rolls,
      Smoking rolls,
      Crusty rolls,
    Rolls, rolls, rolls, rolls,
    Rolls.

Then a paean for Doctor Mills
And all his little bills
    That Pater's anger quells,
    Whilst Mater's bosom swells
      With a sort of grateful throbbing
      As she tells
The success of Doctor Mills.
At once we'll pay *his* bills
    Thinking nought of all his pills –
His black and bitter pills,
    And the draughts of colch: and squills
    That washed them down.
Vowing in the future
    No more to talk of ills
In connection with Old Christmas,
    Despite his little bills,
His expensive little bills,
    His many coloured bills, bills, bills,
                  Bills, bills, bills –
His Mater-christened "Very proper Bills."

THE STAR
Arthur C. Clarke

IT IS 3000 light-years to the Vatican. Once, I believed that space could have no power over faith, just as I believed that the heavens declared the glory of God's handiwork. Now I have seen that handiwork, and my faith is sorely troubled. I stare at the crucifix that hangs on the cabin wall above the Mark VI Computer, and for the first time in my life I wonder if it is no more than an empty symbol.

I have told no one yet, but the truth cannot be concealed. The data are there for anyone to read, recorded on the countless miles of magnetic tape and the thousands of photographs we are carrying back to Earth. Other scientists can interpret them as easily as I can – more easily, in all probability. I am not one who would condone that tampering with the truth which often gave my order a bad name in the olden days.

The crew are already sufficiently depressed: I wonder how they will take this ultimate irony. Few of them have any religious faith, yet they will not relish using this final weapon in their campaign against me – that private, good-natured but fundamentally serious war which lasted all the way from Earth. It amused them to have a Jesuit as chief astrophysicist: Dr. Chandler, for instance, could never get over it (why are medical men such notorious atheists?). Sometimes he would meet me on the observation deck, where the lights are always low so that the stars shine with undiminished glory. He would come up to me in the gloom and stand staring out of the great oval port, while the heavens crawled slowly round us as the ship turned end over end with the residual spin we had never bothered to correct.

'Well, Father,' he would say at last, 'it goes on for ever and for ever, and perhaps *Something* made it. But how you can believe that Something has a special interest in us and our miserable little world – that just beats me.' Then the argument would start, while the stars and nebulae would swing around us in silent, endless arcs beyond the flawlessly clear plastic of the observation port.

It was, I think, the apparent incongruity of my position that caused most amusement to the crew. In vain I would point to my three papers in the *Astrophysical Journal*, my five in the *Monthly Notices of the Royal Astronomical Society*. I would remind them that my order has long been famous for its scientific works. We may be few now, but ever since the eighteenth century we have made contributions to astronomy and geophysics out of all proportion to our numbers. Will my report on the Phoenix Nebula end our thousand years of history? It will end, I fear, much more than that.

I do not know who gave the nebula its name, which seems to me a very bad one. If it contains a prophecy, it is one which cannot be verified for several thousand million years. Even the word nebula is misleading: this is a far smaller object than those stupendous clouds of mist – the stuff of unborn stars – that are scattered throughout the length of the Milky Way. On the cosmic scale, indeed, the Phoenix Nebula is a tiny thing – a tenuous shell of gas surrounding a single star.

Or what is left of a star . . .

The Rubens engraving of Loyola seems to mock me as it hangs there above the spectrophotometer tracings. What would *you*, Father, have made of this knowledge that has come into my keeping, so far from the little world that was all

the universe you knew? Would your faith have risen to the challenge, as mine has failed to do?

You gaze into the distance, Father, but I have travelled a distance beyond any that you could have imagined when you founded our order a thousand years ago. No other survey ship has been so far from Earth: we are at the very frontiers of the explored universe. We set out to reach the Phoenix Nebula, we succeeded, and we are homeward bound with our burden of knowledge. I wish I could lift that burden from my shoulders, but I call to you in vain across the centuries and the light-years that lie between us.

On the book you are holding the words are plain to read. AD MAIOREM DEI GLORIAM, the message runs, but it is a message I can no longer believe. Would you still believe it, if you could see what we have found?

We knew, of course, what the Phoenix Nebula was. Every year, in our galaxy alone, more than a hundred stars explode, blazing for a few hours or days with thousands of times their normal brilliance before they sink back into death and obscurity. Such are the ordinary novae – the commonplace disasters of the universe. I have recorded the spectograms and light curves of dozens, since I started working at the Lunar Observatory.

But three or four times in every thousand years occurs something beside which even a nova pales into total insignificance.

When a star becomes a *supernova*, it may for a little while outshine all the massed suns of the galaxy. The Chinese astronomers watched this happen in A.D. 1054, not knowing what it was they saw. Five centuries later, in 1572, a supernova blazed in Cassiopeia so brilliantly that it was visible in the daylight sky. There have been three more in the thousand years that have passed since then.

Our mission was to visit the remnants of such a catastrophe, to reconstruct the events that led up to it and, if possible, to learn its cause. We came slowly in through the concentric shells of gas that had been blasted out six thousand years before, yet were expanding still. They were immensely hot, radiating still with a fierce violet light, but were far too tenuous to do us any damage. When the star had exploded, its outer layers had been driven upwards with such speed that they had escaped completely from its gravitational field. Now they formed a hollow shell large enough to engulf a thousand solar systems, and at its centre burned the tiny, fantastic object which the star had now become – a white dwarf, smaller than the Earth yet weighing a million times as much.

The glowing gas shells were all around us, banishing the normal night of interstellar space. We were flying into the centre of a cosmic bomb that had detonated millennia ago and whose incandescent fragments were still hurtling apart. The immense scale of the explosion, and the fact that the debris already covered a volume of space many billions of miles across, robbed the scene of any visible movement. It would take decades before the unaided eye could detect any motion in these tortured wisps and eddies of gas, yet the sense of turbulent expansion was overwhelming.

We had checked our primary drive hours before, and were drifting slowly towards the fierce little star ahead. Once it had been a sun like our own, but it had squandered in a few hours the energy that should have kept it shining for a million years. Now it was a shrunken miser, hoarding its resources as if trying to make amends for its prodigal youth.

No one seriously expected to find planets. If there had been any before the explosion, they would have been boiled into puffs of vapour, and their substance lost in the greater wreckage of the star itself. But we made the automatic search, as always when approaching an unknown sun, and presently we found a single small world circling the star at an immense distance. It must have been the Pluto of this vanished solar system, orbiting on the frontiers of the night. Too far from the central sun ever to have known life, its remoteness had saved it from the fate of all its lost companions.

The passing fires had seared its rocks and burnt away the mantle of frozen gas that must have covered it in the days before the disaster. We landed, and we found the Vault.

Its builders had made sure that we should. The monolithic marker that stood above the entrance was now a fused stump, but even the first long-range photographs told us that here was the work of intelligence. A little later we detected the continent-wide pattern of radioactivity that had been buried in the rock. Even if the pylon above the Vault had been destroyed, this would have remained, an immovable and all but eternal beacon calling to the stars. Our ship fell towards this gigantic bull's-eye like an arrow into its target.

The pylon must have been a mile high when it was built, but now it looked like a candle that had melted down into a puddle of wax. It took us a week to drill through the fused rock, since we did not have the proper tools for a task like this. We were astronomers, not archaeologists, but we could improvise. Our original purpose was forgotten: this lonely monument, reared at such labour at the greatest possible distance from the doomed sun, could have only one meaning. A civilization which knew it was about to die had made its last bid for immortality.

It will take us generations to examine all the treasures that were placed in the Vault. They had plenty of time to prepare, for their sun must have given its first warnings many years before the final detonation. Everything that they wished to preserve, all the fruits of their genius, they brought here to this distant world in the days before the end, hoping that some other race would find them and that they would not be utterly forgotten.

If only they had had a little more time! They could travel freely enough between the planets of their own sun, but they had not yet learned to cross the interstellar gulfs, and the nearest solar system was a hundred light-years away.

Even if they had not been so disturbingly human as their sculpture shows, we could not have helped admiring them and grieving for their fate. They left thousands of visual records and the machines for projecting them, together with elaborate pictorial instructions from which it will not be difficult to learn their written language. We have examined many of these records, and brought to life for the first time in six thousand years the warmth and beauty of a civilization which in many ways must have been superior to our own. Perhaps they only showed us the best, and one can hardly blame them. But their worlds were very lovely, and their cities were built with a grace that matches anything of ours. We have watched them at work and play, and listened to their musical speech sounding across the centuries. One scene is still before my eyes – a group of children on a beach of strange blue sand, playing in the waves as children play on Earth.

And sinking into the sea, still warm and friendly and life-giving, is the sun that will soon turn traitor and obliterate all this innocent happiness.

Perhaps if we had not been so far from home and so vulnerable to loneliness we should not have been so deeply moved. Many of us had seen the ruins of ancient civilizations on other worlds, but they had never affected us so profoundly. This tragedy was unique. It was one thing for a race to fail and die, as nations and cultures have done on Earth. But to be destroyed so completely in the full flower of its achievement, leaving no survivors – how could that be reconciled with the mercy of God?

My colleagues have asked me that, and I have given what answers I can. Perhaps you could have done better, Father Loyola, but I have found nothing in the *Exercitia Spiritualia* that helps me here. They were not an evil people: I do not know what gods they worshipped, if indeed they worshipped any. But I have looked back at them across the centuries, and have watched while the loveliness they used their last strength to preserve was brought forth again into the light of their shrunken sun.

I know the answers that my colleagues will give when they get back to Earth. They will say that the universe has no purpose and no plan, that since a hundred suns explode every year in our galaxy, at this very moment some race is dying in the depths of space. Whether that race has done good or evil during its lifetime will make no difference in the end: there is no divine justice, for there is no God.

Yet, of course, what we have seen proves nothing of the sort. Anyone who argues thus is being swayed by emotion, not logic. God has no need to justify His actions to man. He who built the universe can destroy it when He chooses. It is arrogance – it is perilously near blasphemy – for us to say what He may or may not do.

This I could have accepted, hard though it is to look upon whole worlds and peoples thrown into the furnace. But there comes a point when even the deepest faith must falter, and now, as I look at my calculations, I know I have reached that point at last.

We could not tell, before we reached the nebula, how long ago the explosion took place. Now, from the astronomical evidence and the record in the rocks of that one surviving planet, I have been able to date it very exactly. I know in what year the light of this colossal conflagration reached Earth. I know how brilliantly the supernova whose corpse now dwindles behind our speeding ship once shone in terrestial skies. I know how it must have blazed low in the East before sunrise, like a beacon in that Oriental dawn.

There can be no reasonable doubt: the ancient mystery is solved at last. Yet, oh God, there were so many stars you *could* have used. What was the need to give these people to the fire, that the symbol of their passing might shine above Bethlehem?

ACKNOWLEDGEMENTS

Harrow House Editions and the editors of this book would like to thank the following people for their valuable assistance:

David Drummond for his expert research and advice on the ephemera of Victorian Christmas, in particular for providing us with the pantomime on page 135, and the following poems: *Christmas Bills* by Joseph Hatton, *The Christmas Hamper* and *A Child's Christmas Day*.

Research: Mary Corcoran, Suzanne Hodgart, Franny Singer
General Assistance: Theresa Alexis, Ramona Darvas, Cathy Gill, Patricia Isted, Zoe Richmond-Watson
Special Assistance: David Constable and Candle Makers Supplies for design and information on making candles; Robert Day for design and information on wreaths, rings, garlands, Christmas trees and the traditional nativity crib; Michael Hunt for design and instructions for Christmas stockings; Millimetre Ltd. for design of cards; Valerie Robinson for table arrangements; Lucy Sisman for design of parcel wrapping; Joan Steeds for design and instructions for a wide range of craft materials included in the book; Patricia Weaver for instructions on Christmas crackers.

Harrow House Editions would also like to thank the following people for their permission to include the items listed below:

STORIES
A Christmas Memory by Truman Capote, Copyright 1956 Truman Capote. Reprinted from *A Christmas Memory* by Truman Capote by permission of Random House, Inc.
The Gift of the Magi by O Henry from *The Complete Works of O Henry* (volume 1), Doubleday and Company Inc.
The Mezzotint by M. R. James from *The Ghost Stories of M. R. James* published by Edward Arnold (Publishers) Ltd.
The Star by Arthur C. Clarke, reprinted by permission of the author and the author's agents, Scott Meredith Literary Agency Inc., 845 Third Avenue, New York, New York 10022

The Three Low Masses by Alphonse Daudet, from *Letters from my Windmill*, translated by Frederick Davies (Penguin Classics 1978), reprinted by permission of Penguin Books Ltd.

POEMS
Christmas by John Betjeman from *Collected Poems*, John Murray (Publishers) Ltd. and Houghton Mifflin Co.
Innocents' Song by Charles Causley from *Collected Poems*, Macmillan, London.
Shepherds, Shake Off Your Drowsy Sleep by Eleanor Farjeon from *The Oxford Book of Carols*, reprinted by permission of Oxford University Press.
The Christmas Tree by C. Day Lewis from *Collected Poems 1954*, by permission of the Executors of the Estate of C. Day Lewis and publishers Jonathan Cape Ltd. and Hogarth Press.
The Oxen by Thomas Hardy, by permission of Macmillan Administration (Basingstoke) Ltd.
Twelfth Night by Louis MacNeice from *The Collected Poems of Louis MacNeice*, reprinted by permission of Faber and Faber Ltd.

CAROLS
We would like to thank Oxford University Press for granting us permission to use the following English translations from *The Oxford Book of Carols*:
Es ist ein' Ros' by Ursula Vaughan Williams
In Dulci Jubilo by Percy Dearmer
Puer Nobis by Percy Dearmer

The following English translations are the copyright of Harrow House Editions:
O Du Fröhliche by Romana Unger-Hamilton
Noël Nouvelet by Cordelia Chitty
Il est né, le divin Enfant by Cordelia Chitty

The musical arrangements of all the carols in this book are by Derek Walters and are the copyright of Harrow House Editions.

The editors have made every effort to trace copyright owners. We apologise if any copyright has been unwittingly infringed.

Picture Credits
A, above; B, below; C, centre; R, right; L, left.

DAVID DRUMMOND COLLECTION
10; 20; 21; 27; 46; 48; 54; 60(L); 61; 63(R); 64; 85; 86(B); 96; 101; 102; 110; 111(C); 113(AR); 129(B); 130; 131; 136; 137; 138; 139; 150; 158.

MARY EVANS PICTURE LIBRARY
32; 59(L, R); 62 (L); 65; 66; 87; 91; 93; 95; 97; 103; 104; 111(R); 113(BR); 156; 167.

MANSELL COLLECTION
9; 11; 15; 16(AL, R); 17(B); 25; 59(C); 88; 111(L); 112(A); 165.

ANN RONAN PICTURE LIBRARY
17(A); 49(L); 60(R).

Illustration Credits
AC, above centre; B, below; BC, below centre; FR, far right; ID, inside decorations.

PHILIP HOOD
34/35; 38/39; 42/43; 46/47; 50 house; 52/53; 66/67; 70/71; 74/75; 76/77; 78/79; 114/115; 118/119; 122/123; 126/127; 146/147; 150/151; 154/155; 158/159; and all candles in margins.

CAROLINE McDONALD-PAUL
4; 5; 6; 7; 8; 9; 14; 15; 18; 28; 31; 44; 45; 53(FR); 55; 56; 58; 81; 82; 84; 85; 87; 108; 135; 141; 142; 143; 144; 145; 162; 166; 167; 171; and all borders.

RAY AND CORRINNE BURROWS
22/23 (fig 1–fig 13); 24 (fig 1–8); 26/27 (fig 1–9); 33 (fig 1–7); 36 (fig 8–15); 37 (fig 1–3); 40/41 (fig 1–11); 50 four diagrams; 51 diagram; 68/69 (fig 1–13); 72/73 (fig 1–4); 80 (fig 1–2); 89/90 (fig 1–4); 117 (fig 1–2); 128 (fig 1–2); 132/133 puzzle pictures; 134 puzzle pictures; 160/161 (fig 1–11).

GILLIAN SHANKS
19(ID); 23(FR); 27(ID); 61(FR); 63 (AC); 65(BC); 80(FR); 83; 107(ID); 110(ID); 149(FR); 169(ID); 170.

VANA HAGGERTY
89(B) crib; 90(BC); 90(FR).

ANDREW FARMER
end papers.

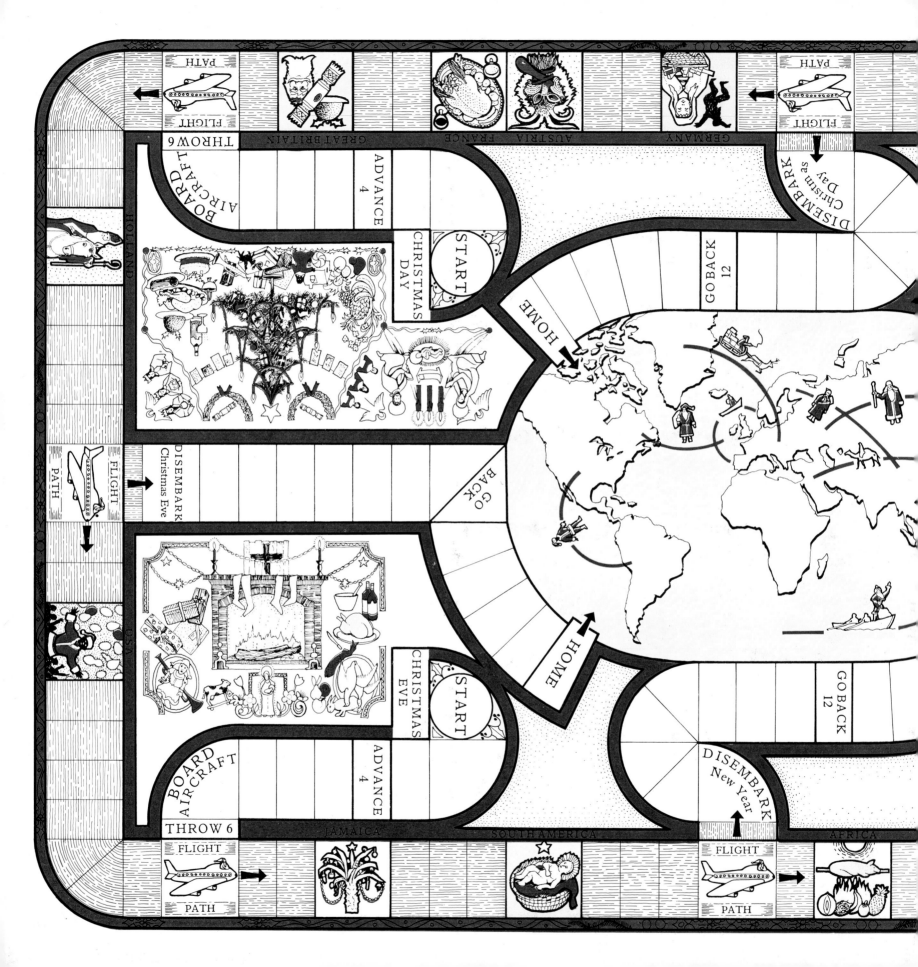